AF470528

Prescriptions

— of a —

Pox Doctor's Clerk

By the same author

fiction
Landscape with Dead Dons
The Conspiracy
Bad Dreams

non-fiction
Inside Robert Robinson
The Dog Chairman

as editor
The Everyman Book of Light Verse

Prescriptions *of a* Pox Doctor's Clerk

ROBERT ROBINSON

WEIDENFELD AND NICOLSON
LONDON

First published in Great Britain in 1990 by
George Weidenfeld & Nicolson,
91 Clapham High Street, London SW4 7TA

Some of these pieces first appeared in
The Times, *The Sunday Times* and *The Listener*.
The author is grateful for permission to reprint them.

British Library Cataloguing-in-Publication Data
Robinson, Robert, 1927–
Prescriptions of a pox doctor's clerk.
I. Title
828.91407

ISBN 0-297-81143-6

Printed and bound in Great Britain
at The Bath Press, Avon

≡ CONTENTS ≡

The very first time I heard that someone was 'dressed up like a pox doctor's clerk' the eccentric music of the words sounded to me like the horns of elfland faintly blowing. But when I made it generally known that this was new to me, I heard from people who had lived their lives in the sunshine of the phrase.

Mr P.V. Harris, writing from Southampton, said he was disturbed that I had come to it so late – 'especially,' he wrote, 'since you are perfectly familiar with the phrase "Admiral of the Scouse Boats".' (*qv*). Though even ignorance, Mr Harris went on, wouldn't excuse my mispronunciation – 'Its "pox doctor's *clurk*".'

Agnes Kinnersley, of Swiss Cottage, was in the vocative: 'Come *on*, Robinson,' she cried, 'you may not have heard of the phrase, but do try to get it right – the correct usage is "a *Chinese* pox doctor's clerk".' Miss Kinnersley says she believes it means a person who is not quite a gentleman, but has lovely manners.

I felt I should get someone to introduce me to a pox doctor's clerk, but was anyone in a position to do this? Mr E. de C. Tillet of Crowborough made it clear that far from being a person of low degree, a pox doctor's clerk is to be envied: 'Over the last sixty years,' Mr Tillet told me, 'whether afloat in great waters or messing about on the golf course, I have always heard the phrase used in the congratulatory mode. You sink your putt for a birdy and the cry goes up "He has the luck of a pox doctor's clerk!"'

It is not invariably seen in this light. Max Bernstein of Clapton Common pointed out that the rules of hierarchy in the East End during the Thirties were inflexible, and if sartorially you came on above your perceived station the comment 'He's dressed up like a pox doctor's clerk' was unforgivingly applied. Amanda Smith who worked at Tesco's in 1973 says the description was endemic among her colleagues, and goes so far as to suggest that Tesco's 'cohened' the phrase.

A correspondent from the West Midlands – Mr Ronald Sleigh, of Aldridge – was more peremptory. 'Any pox doctor's clerk of your acquaintance who seems not to realize that this is his given station in life should be told without ceremony that he needs stuffing with the broad end of a ragman's trumpet.' It was at this point I opened an envelope from Grange-over-Sands.

The letter was from a Mr Eric Loudermilk with whom I had from time to time been in correspondence. He had once asked me for counsel on the subject of the fury which invades him when he sees a man in a restaurant holding his knife like a dart – a subject touched on in the fictional tableau *Bagfox Hall* which appears elsewhere in this volume.

'I wonder,' Mr Loudermilk pleasantly began, 'whether you couldn't have carved out something of a career as a pox doctor's clerk yourself? The fine cursive hand you used when you replied to me on an earlier occasion, a certain spinsterishness in the way you express yourself which is occasionally at odds with an intrusive coarseness, and a brisk way in handing out prescriptions for absolutely everyone, might have made you an ornament to any pox doctor's consulting-rooms. Did you miss your way, as we say in Lancashire?'

I took the hint.

It's a Poor Belly that can't Warm its Own

ALL proverbs sound the same, as though there were a proverb factory in Crawley New Town mass-producing stuff like 'Memory is a falcon that cannot be held; loyalty is a sparrow's nest which cannot be repaired' (even at the fourth reading I still think Quality Control should have sent that one back). Or, for all lovers of the opaque, 'Climb like a cucumber, fall like an aubergine'.

Some students believe all Chinese proverbs were invented by Ernest Brahmah who wrote the Kai Lung stories before the First World War. For example 'It is the politest pig which loses its place at the trough' or 'The wise duck keeps its mouth shut when he smells frogs'. And its quite likely that Brahmah set up the works at Crawley to give the things a professional polish – 'It is a mark of insincerity of purpose to spend one's time searching for the sacred emperor in low-class tea-shops.'

The common factor is the long portentous stare at the obvious. The know-all tone combining with a total lack of obliqueness betrays the souvenir produced under licence and distributed worldwide. 'He who praises wishes to sell', 'Thatch your roof before the rain falls', 'In China we have only three religions but we have a hundred dishes we can make from rice'. At Crawley, the outworkers who invent the sentiments know that deprecation flatters national pride because it suggests character – 'After shaking hands with a Greek, count your fingers', 'Will any but an Irishman hang a wooden kettle over a fire?', 'A Hungarian is one who enters a revolving door behind you, but comes out in front', 'Malta would be a delightful place if every priest were a tree'.

All of the Crawley output is antiqued before delivery, the closest I ever came to hearing an up-to-date proverb was a Lloyds underwriter muttering 'Writing fire business at the moment is like bending down to pick up sixpence and putting your arse through a plate-glass window.' And once in a restaurant when I complained that the food was cold, the waitress replied solemnly 'Its a poor belly that can't warm its own.' But both may simply have been forgeries.

These are Crawley's abiding headache – 'You make few friends driving northwards on a southbound carriageway' found its way on to the market via Col. W.F.N. Watson and the *New Statesman*, and C.W.H. Roll had considerable currency with 'He whose head resembles a Dutch cheese does not rest it on the grocer's counter'. N.J. Rock's 'Do not wear ear-muffs in the land of the rattlesnake' was only withdrawn by Sotheby's in the nick of time.

Like those awful tunes you can't get out of your head, the fraudulent old saw seems to invent itself: 'When peewits fly low, then shall we have snow': 'A dowly sky means a fly in your eye': 'If seaweed fries easy, you're eating Chinesey'. But Crawley would be first to agree that its stock of proverbial weather lore is beginning to look a little shopworn – a line like 'If if rains on Easter day, there shall be good grass but very bad hay' calls for an up-date and Martin Bell provided –

> *If church spire be clear*
> *'Twill be damp round here.*
> *If it be not,*
> *'Twill be bloody hot.*
> *When thee can't see spire*
> *Church be on fire,*
> *And we'll hang parson, squire*
> *And the whole bleeding choir.*

Sometimes the China section – in fact, a lady who lives in Petworth and also paints trays – goes soaring over the top, as in 'A bird in the soup is better than an eagle's nest in the desert': one knows roughly what she was getting at, but the image of a bird sitting up and splashing your shirt-front is far stronger than any general principle the statement illuminates. That's the danger with the more vivid examples, the illustration is too bright and obscures the moral. Once you read 'He who takes a donkey up a minaret must bring it down again' you start hearing the conversation. 'Its more than my job's worth to let that donkey into this minaret.' 'I tell you my good man, I have permission of the Imam himself.' Bystander: 'What beats me is how you're going to get it down again.' Man in charge: 'No, no, that's not the point – how's he going to get it through the turnstile?'

Well, as they say of the oboe, its an ill wind that nobody blows good.

The Chums of MI5

GREAT confusion was caused by the claim that a man called Harry Wharton was a member of MI5, and that he had recruited Cecil King, the fat-headed newspaper magnate. King always denied he was ever a spy, but it seemed much more important to establish that Harry Wharton had left Greyfriars, where he was leader of the Famous Five, to join another subversive group with a suspiciously similar name.

The chap I spoke to on the phone said Oh yes, they had Harry Wharton, Harry Tate, Harry Worth and Harry Hotspur on the strength. Only the papers were wrong when they said Wharton had recruited Cecil King, in fact he had recruited George V. 'Unless', said the bloke, 'it was George V who recruited Harry Wharton.'

When he rang off, I thought that if any of the Chums of the Remove *were* going to end up in MI5 I'd have put my money on Bob Cherry – all that used-car salesman heartiness. He only ever said two things, one was 'Hullo, hullo, hullo' and the other was 'Ha, ha, ha'. The enemy would assume nobody would be daft enough to make a spy out of a man whose bonhomie was so transparently bogus, and a neat double bluff would have been pulled. Harry Wharton, on the other hand, being the equivalent of a faithful labrador, would surely have been recognized as a con-artist the minute he helped an old lady across the road.

But there's just a chance that Cecil King, if he *was* invited to be a spy (and some said that King was offered a Life Peerage but turned it down on the grounds that he wanted to be a Life Earl) may not have understood that his handler was making a joke when he announced himself as Harry Wharton. By all accounts King was a pompous man with no sense of humour and could well have told members of his club that Harry Wharton had promised to put the arm on Mr Quelch who would force Dr Locke to resign in favour of Lord Mountbatten, and King would be appointed Matron.

Most of the Greyfriars boys were too good to be true, and its easy to imagine them ending up in MI5 or Marbella. Wingate, captain of the school, masterminded the Brinks Mat robbery and now wears gold medallions in Brazil, Fisher T. Fish, the arbitrageur, is doing time for insider-dealing, while Horace Coker of the Fifth became Mayor of a town in the Midlands where he was done for adulterating the concrete in fly-overs. Dr Locke and Mr Quelch are still at large, selling degrees at five hundred pounds a go from the *Université de Greyfriars et de l'Univers*, while Gosling, the school porter, is in an open prison, having turned to bigamy.

The only honest ones were Hurree Jamset Ram Singh who now has a chain of newsagents' shops, and Vernon Smith who gave up smoking and went into a monastery where as Brother Herbert he runs a poker school after chapel, but only for matches. As we know, Wharton is in MI5 where to his chagrin B sends him out to buy jam tarts and insists on him repeating the password, 'Yarooh is Hooray spelt backwards.'

A Car Called Towser

ROVER cars have been taken over so often you'd think at least once the parent company would have been tempted to change the name to Towser. Rover still has the image of a well trained Sealyham, housebroken and very faithful, taking its master for a run – in earlier days the horn had a distinct woof-woof when sounded. The Rover I knew was driven by an uncle who looked grave when the AA man forgot to salute, and when he exceeded his spouse's own personal speed-limit – 28 mph – she would smilingly intone, 'Mistakes *will* occur, in even the best regulated circles.'

Badge-engineering ruined the true identities of cars, but unsolved mysteries remain: how could a car be named after a railway-station nobody ever got out at, Vauxhall? Even Earlsfield would have been preferable. And the maddest name of all, the Hillman Avenger. With a rubber dagger like that, what could you possibly avenge? I once sat with a man driving me up the M1 who said he was reclaiming the Jaguar for civilization, and my grandmother never quite disentangled the sauce from the motor-car – Lea Francis or Lee and Perrins, one or the other, and she spoke of the car of her dreams as an Armstrong-Tiddly.

Bugatti has always suggested a superior sort of insect repellent, while Ferrari and Lamborghini sound like places on the Mediterranean where the outfall pipe is too close to the shore. And how come Daimler Benz is also Mercedes Benz? Did Gottfried Daimler (*von und zu*) run away with Birgitta Benz, who later fell into the arms of a chancer called Carlos Maria Tortilla Chorizo Gaspacho Mercedes, the last man in Juan-les-Pins to wear two-tone shoes and mean it? Was some sort of *ménage à trois* patched up? Its a funny name, Mercedes, coming to its full wild flower in that splendid American actress, Mercedes McCambridge, whose name plays three wrong notes simultaneously.

There was a sheep in wolf's clothing called a Fuego, where the advertising gave the game away by going in for the fearful lisping line 'My name is Fuego'. This made you think of Bambi or Dopey. The Hispano-Suiza was a creature of myth, but these days it sounds like some sort of orange drink – a Hispano-Squeezer, not unlike that other old motor-car the Pina-Collider. And varieties of car were puzzling: what was a *sedanca-coupé*? Sounded like a petrol-engined version of a sofa. And a *coupé-de-ville*? I see Queen Mary in the back of one, telling the chauffeur through a speaking-tube to get his foot down.

But the older car names, Wolseley, Austin, Morris, not only didn't suggest speed, they didn't suggest movement at all. You could have slipped in a car called Dunroamin, in those days, and nobody would have noticed. Thunderbird was fine, but when it was diminished to T-Bird it sounded like a steak, and a T-Bird steak puts you in mind of vultures or ostriches.

Remember the Austin-Rolls? I can't have dreamt it – it came out in the early Fifties, when some barmpot had the bright idea of putting a Rolls-Royce engine into an Austin body. A spectacular own-goal, since of course it should have been the other way round. Owners of Austin Rollses (if there ever were any) would never have had time to drive the car, since they'd be continuously throwing open the bonnet to show off the engine. Compounding the idiocy of the original idea, it became known as 'the poor man's Rolls', not only a contradiction in terms, but a club you can't imagine anyone queuing up to join.

But would you want to join the *real* Rolls Royce club, these days? Over the years the cars have gone on looking like bungalows fitted with drawbridges, but now they are driven by ruffians wearing false beards and bear number-plates saying FU 2 or (if the owner is Chinese) 1 TON. Figure to yourself, then, my pleasure when I found myself following a Roller whose driver was a grey-haired party wearing a pullover, and whose number-plate read – such diffidence – 20MPH.

Was this a proclamation – no, no, the word won't do, you don't *proclaim* 20MPH – a modest proposal that here we had the ideal, the magic figure? Was the man indicating that it was his steady twenty miles an hour through life that had brought him to his present affluence? Or (and I was behind him in slow-moving traffic for some time, which allowed me to winnow the possibilities) was it perhaps more of a stern warning to the rest of us (more authoritative than the fatuous 'Keep Your Distance!') that peasants must on no account exceed a lowly number of miles an hour on pain of having their sparking-plugs confiscated?

Approaching the Ace of Spades roundabout, I was besieged by other possibilities – that he wanted everyone to know he'd bought his Rolls very cheaply because it had no engine, and he'd made a sort of wooden one worked by an elastic band whose absolute top limit was twenty miles per hour. As he turned off towards Surbiton, I finally decided he'd gone down to the showroom to buy the car and had been told by the salesman that because he wasn't chairman of a handmade-kitchen company, a cold-caller for an off-shore insurance group, or a supplier of fibre-glass containers for garden centres, his qualifications for owning a Rolls were woefully inadequate, but that they'd sell him one if he agreed to display the numberplate '20MPH' to make it perfectly clear he wasn't entitled to put on airs.

Taking Uxbridge

The papers said Ken Livingstone had 'flounced out' of somewhere, and the picture conjured up is of Ken in one of those multi-tiered dresses worn by Spanish dancers who are perpetually annoyed about something. His 'blood was boiling' and bystanders presumably heard a noise like a kettle when the automatic cut-out hasn't worked and the kitchen fills with steam. If he'd been 'hopping mad' into the bargain, onlookers would have been reminded of the one-legged man in the arse-kicking contest.

To 'storm out' is another matter, and involves crying 'Aaaargh' like they do in the *Dandy*, and bursting through a closed door with your arms held wide above your head so that you leave a spreadeagled gap in the woodwork. 'Incandescent with rage' is different again, and the person turns into a combination of table-lamp and electric-fire. If you're 'beside yourself' its as far as you can go in this mode, because it means there are two of you, one of whom is gibbering.

There's a grotesque charm to be had from the stone-age usages of Fleet Street if you ignore the label and listen to the actual words. One of the papers described Mr Tony Benn as 'the veteran rabble rouser' and the question arose whether this meant that though he is now a 'grizzled oldster' (itself a phrase of museum quality) he is still going on doing it, able to rouse a rabble should he come upon one, so long as he's given a moment to put his teeth in. Or does the phrase imply retirement, with Mr Benn in sheltered housing, recalling in the sunset of his years the rabbles he once roused, enthralling a company of superannuated footpads and toothless incendiarists?

Personally, I'm rather fond of 'walked free', which papers use of an individual they had thought unlikely to get off, on a charge they assume the readers think he's guilty of. Magistrates quash the proceedings, and he is said to have 'walked free' as one might speak of a man who had nicked the spoons, though nobody can prove it, and who raises two fingers to everyone on his way down to the pawnbrokers. The prejudice which lies behind the label is to be rejected on every possible ground, but I like the words, which seem to be descriptive of that style of locomotion the Irish call 'walking aisy' – a sort of drunken swagger.

The late Bernard McElwaine of the *Sunday Mirror*, was curator-in-chief of this curious Fleet Street volapuk, and my old friend Jack Waterman, once Captain Spyglass of the *Daily Bugle*, tells me that when he ran into Bernard, at that time also a racing correspondent, they would gravely greet each other on the course at Sandown or Lingfield with lines from long-gone sporting sheets: 'Men, not given to guesswork, piled on the dibs with such alacrity as to make settling-day a remote possibility.' Bernard had a handy line in translating such petrified tropes, and would say that a 'luxury flat' meant there was an inside lavatory, and that 'an attractive brunette' (they were always featuring in *News of the World* copy) simply meant the woman didn't have two heads.

I once had the pleasure of seeing my name in the *Daily Star*. The sub had the task of thumbnailing me, and came up with 'Bob the Boffin'. He may have meant 'ratfink', and was shy of being too precise, but ever since I've thought of Bob the Boffin as a small penguin hobbling round the Arctic Circle shouting 'Kee*rist*, its cold'. But I was a good long way from 'taking umbrage', a phrase from the lexicon of angry departure that stimulates conflicting images. Sometimes they are of a man who is plucking umbrage from the hedgerow and taking it for his sciatica, sometimes it is a sketch of the family butler: 'Taking Umbrage?' 'Good lord, yes. Couldn't do without him. The man's a treasure,' and you see a sleek fat figure in a morning coat packing the family's bags for the annual visit to Broadstairs.

Once this sort of obsession takes hold its easy to get Umbrage tangled up with Uxbridge and begin to wonder whether 'taking Uxbridge' isn't old-fashioned slang for someone leaving an hotel without paying.

Quick, Quick, Slow

THE man telephoned the dancing school and told them he wanted to learn to dance. There was a slight pause as though he'd said could he bring a friend to dinner as well. Then the lady said they didn't open till two o'clock.

'I can't tell you how much it will cost until I have a look at you,' she said in a worried tone, as though she expected someone was going to be vulgar.

'Like an antique shop,' the man was able to say, but the lady didn't understand. 'There are code words on the price tickets until they've got you inside the shop,' he explained.

The lady had still not replied, but then she said, '*Can* you dance?'

'Well, I think I can. I'm very good at it *on my own* –'

'You want to prove yourself.'

Then the lady said, 'Harris has got another think coming.' Then it went blurry. 'I'm sorry, someone came in.'

The man said, 'Are you all dancers there?'

'Yes, yes, yes,' the lady replied in a light tone. Then after a short pause she said more soberly, 'We have to be.'

'You don't have to swear you're able to dance as a condition of employment, do you? I can understand the actual instructors –'

'We all dance except the cashier,' said the lady.

'Doesn't she –'

'Where would you like to begin?'

The man said, 'I would like to begin at that little run they suddenly do as if the floor had gone into molehills and they were skipping over them. I haven't put it properly, they rise up and down as though they had one eccentric leg or say you were running along with a foot in the gutter –'

'We'd like you to come along,' said the lady.

'What's the running thing called?'

'It hasn't got a name,' said the lady.

'Will I need a key-chain?'

Then there was a silence.

'What for?' the lady intoned as if she had drawn away from the telephone and stepped into an echo-chamber.

'I thought it might turn out to be standard equipment. The gentlemen wear them when they are doing the little run and smiling at their partners.'

'Oh that's *exhibition* dancing,' said the lady, flooding back to the instrument in great relief, as though the crisis were over. 'That's exhibition dancing. You've been watching the television. Is that where you first got the idea?' she asked sympathetically.

'Yes,' said the man huskily.

'Never mind,' she said.

'My difficulty –' The man stopped because there was a roar from the other end of the line as though someone was rolling milk-churns through a lion-house. A voice cried, 'Harris, Harris, Harris,' and the lady must have put her hand over the mouthpiece because everything went muffled. Then she took her hand away and said, 'Did you want to decide now?'

'My difficulty –'

'You've obviously never danced before –'

'Oh yes I have, but I've never been able to talk and dance at the same time and I want to know if you have anyone who pays particular attention to that side of things.'

The lady seemed to be scratching something, say custard, that had once been in a molten state and had now hardened from its nebula into a small planet-like globule on the rim of the hand-set.

'It's all a state of mind,' said the lady, 'we can all overcome our little – All these little nervous. You come in shy and you go out – you go out – you –'

'I don't think so, that doesn't bother me,' said the man, 'it's more fitting the words into the steps. Casual chatting without forgetting the steps, if you get my drift.'

'You'll make all sorts of friends,' said the lady.

'Mmm,' said the man.

'Age need be no bar.'

'Oh no, well I wouldn't –'

'We trained a lady of seventy-two for her bronze.'

'Trap one!' shouted the man, ironic but friendly. The lady was silent.

'The talking,' resumed the man. 'Would a metronome be of any assistance? I could bring one.'

There was a small abrading noise from the other end as though a cricket had got into the mouthpiece and was rubbing his back legs together very slowly. Then the lady said, 'What do you want to talk about? You mustn't be too ambitious if you're a beginner. Now can I book you –'

There was a jarring thud at the lady's end of the telephone and she said, 'Files again! Sorry. Yes – what day?'

The man said cautiously, 'What day does Harris come?'

Ferret-proof

I SAW a pair of stout knickerbockers in a shop in Oxford, and the ticket pinned to them said they were guaranteed by the Country Gentleman's Association, or some such name, and underneath that it said 'Ferret-proof'. I wondered how the point was established. I concluded it must be carried out, under conditions of scientific rigour and strict control, at ferret-proofing grounds, probably just south of Bicester. A handpicked member of *Burke's Landed Gentry* is buttoned into the knickerbockers – 'Whenever you're ready, m'lord' – 'Very well, Thomas, let the little beggars out.' And a sackful of ferrets tumble over each other, giving their characteristic high mewing cry – sure sign they have sighted a pair of knickerbockers – and once more, hope undiminished by experience, they attempt for the umpteenth time the impossible penetration, and for the umpteenth time the buckles frustrate them. 'I think that puts it beyond dispute, eh, Thomas?' And the coveted certificate is (like those seals of efficiency handed out to Swiss watches) reluctantly conceded.

The Three Jolly Gallstones

SOME people go loopy when they stay in hotels. They write of the experience as though a weekend in Loamshire were the equivalent of having died and gone to heaven. Do hoteliers slip visitors a special mickey finn while they're signing the book at Reception? How else account for the mad messages the clients send out to *The Good Hotel Guide*? 'We felt like privileged guests throughout the weekend', 'It was like staying with considerate, generous and discriminating friends'. One hotelkeeper was described as 'sharing his beautiful home with the general public', as though the writer was getting up a petition to instal a collecting-box at the entrance for those who wished to contribute a few ha'pence towards their board and lodging.

The battiness of the bourgeoisie who use hotels is matched by the people who run the places. 'Mrs Wallace makes a point of being present to keep dinner-party conversation going (meals are eaten communally). One recent visitor enjoyed a midnight search for ghosts in the local churchyard which Mrs Wallace had organized. "Why had no one else the imagination to give us such a night out?"' If crawling about the graveyard doesn't make your flesh creep, there are other entries which may. 'Our warm and generous hosts introduce guests to each other in the lounge, then sit down to dinner with them, one at each end of the table.' I couldn't sleep the night I read that bit. Of course, this sort of comment in *The Good Hotel Guide* may well be a coded warning, and thus of real service. We learn of one hotel where 'everyone is on first-name terms', and to be certain about the precise location of this place would alone be worth the price of the book. There is another hotel where 'we were treated as special friends in Joyce and Brian's house'. Who, I wonder, is so short of friends? And what value is there in such overnight friendship, when you are billed for it in the end? I might perhaps put up with being treated as a publican's chum, but only if *le guillaume* was withheld.

One hotel has a room whose walls are covered in rolls of shirting, and the pictures are strung from men's braces. Clearly the Beachcomber

Memorial Suite, and the editor of the guide notes what he calls 'the extrovert enthusiasm of the owner' which may or may not mean he serves breakfast on roller-skates. The schnauzer dog, a feature of the premises, is compared to a regimental goat: how ashamed other hoteliers must be when customers query the absence of such an amenity. 'No regimental *goat*, landlord?' 'Sorry, sir, we've just had him fricasseed, you'll be seeing him at supper.'

Sometimes those communicating to *The Good Hotel Guide* betray a certain defensiveness. 'If you want to stay in a civilized comfortable quiet country-house hotel, this will suit you very well,' says one enthusiast, 'but if your ideal is an airport hotel and your preferred restaurant a motorway cafe, it won't.' Here we have an entirely false antithesis, since there is no one who does not like quiet country hotels, though there may be those who might not like this one. What the correspondent really seems to be doing is fending off a blow that has yet to fall – the possibility that those who *don't* agree with him may question his judgement.

There's a similar sort of absolutism when it comes to the food. At the dinner hour, somewhere in England, on any night of the year, a middle-aged married couple is encountering roast duck, quails' eggs, pig's cheek, lamb's pluck, sausage toad that is – the phrase never varies – 'the best we have ever eaten'. Can there be so many unique experiences, so often? Who but writers to hotel guides encounter such extremes; and do I detect a note in these encomia, as of people who have at last been offered in the form of food, drink, and deference, the tribute they perceive as rightfully their own? Oh, for a touch of the comparative, to sweeten such self-regard.

And complacency on the guest's part encourages the same in his host. A puff for one place runs 'We want our guests to feel they are staying in a country home rather than a hotel, and to enjoy being in a beautiful house which has known centuries of gracious living ...' This kind of tushery aims at stifling dissent; any criticism of the cold bedrooms will betray a woeful ignorance of gracious living. But if you're feeble-minded enough to believe you're not staying in a hotel when you are, then you may already be living in a beautiful country home, surrounded by men in white coats.

The glaring sunshine of endorsement makes the occasional oasis of disaffection a great relief – 'Reception dour – almost unfriendly. Room disappointing ... Flowers consisted of some artificial poppies and weed grass pushed into a vase ... Plain toast and one croissant – no rolls ... Not much to look at in the way of a garden, needs a lot of work...' Or more pithily, 'My room was cramped, low-ceilinged and overpriced'. The custard level falls, and what was a glittering caravanserai is just a bed for the night at the Three Jolly Gallstones.

Which isn't what the readers of *The Good Hotel Guide* are looking for. Romance is what they want, a feeling that they are taking part in one of those chandelier movies where you can't tell where the decor ends and the actors begin. I felt very strongly one night as I walked over the Aubusson to the grand staircase, making my way past the glowing torchères towards my stately damask-hung bedroom, that I ought to be bumping into Ginger Rogers any minute now.

Well, it could have been sooner than I was expecting, for as I put my hand on the lion's-head brass handle of the bolection-moulded bedroom door a tall senatorial American cried out in alarm, 'My wife's in there!' I said, apologetically, 'She would have thought her Prince had turned into a frog,' and reaching my own room, realized I wasn't Fred Astaire, I'd been given the Edward Everett Horton part. Though on reflection I felt there'd been a certain ambiguity in the American's tone, not so much scaring off a predator, as offering a friendly warning.

Sometimes *The Good Hotel Guide* seems half to open a stranger's door for you, and you read 'Bedrooms prettily done, bed good and firm. Blissfully quiet.' The hidden private side of someone's daily routine is partially revealed, and you find yourself thinking about the 'Carol Jackson' who signs this entry, and wondering if you'd been in the room next door would you have heard her soft breathing in that blissful quiet, and was it right that you should know she likes her beds so firm? Another signatory in a recent edition is 'Joanne Kinsey Calori' and the reader nods, knowing that whatever the nature of the hotel fantasy, Kinsey and calories are in there somewhere.

The Yoghurt Vats of Albania

IT came as no surprise to me to learn that five thousand million pots of yoghurt are consumed between Michaelmas and Lammastide, since the appetite for yoghurt is uncontainable, and you see crowds outside Sainsbury's hardly able to wait for the lorries to unload the stuff, fresh from the yoghurt vats of Albania.

Cows play some part in its manufacture, they tell me – probably the hooves, which give it that gluey texture. But little did Otto the Corpulent's second chef realize what an uncontrollable force he was releasing as he magi-mixed the first consignment, that quiet Sunday in faraway Transylvania.

Of course, the secret ingredient was invisible – it was *goodness*. When Otto the Corpulent gave up drinking the blood of virgins and took to yoghurt, he became Otto the Slender, Otto the Extraordinarily Pleasant. Only very lovely people eat yoghurt, their purity is guaranteed the instant their lips touch the carton. But speaking for the impure backlash, I say yoghurt tastes of cream that's off, and I say the hell with it.

Above the Snow Line in SW1

THERE was a terrible crash from the back end of the drill-hall. A heavy man had fallen over.

The instructor didn't hear, he was busy demonstrating something, clumping about the dais on his skis.

'Well go on, get me up,' roared the heavy man at the back of the hall who was flat on his back with his feet apparently buttoned to the floor by the skis. A youth in a coloured sweater levered him into a crouching position.

The instructor saw him and said, 'All the better if you fall over a bit, it shows you're really relaxed.'

There were beads of sweat on the heavy man's face. He was sitting on his haunches like an elderly party half way through getting out of a bath. Then he urged himself forward and managed to rise slowly upright.

'That's all very well,' he said. 'I only came in for the magic-lantern and the next I know I'm arseovertip on the floor.'

'We have the films afterwards,' said the instructor. 'Now what I want you to do is stretch out your arms and swing from side to side like this without moving your hips. *And –*'

The instructor stood up and swivelled his haunches gracefully. The heavy man started going left and right like an old-fashioned coachman hindered by four or five greatcoats.

'Hey – did you see me?' he muttered to his wife who was swinging away at his side.

'I heard the pillars come down,' the wife said, 'and I looked round and there was Samson.'

'Ho, ho,' said the man.

In the course of the swinging exercise two ladies hit each other mortal blows on the side of the head, but apart from that the only other noise was a kind of continuous gasp.

'We'll do the knees-bend exercise,' the instructor said. His pupils were ranged in lines down the hall in front of him, and he stood on the dais with a piano at one side, a piano-stool a little in the rear, and a blackboard to the left. Everyone went crash, crash to get the skis into the right position, and the heavy man stood knock-kneed, sagging a bit, as though waiting for surgical intervention.

'Forward,' shouted the instructor, and they all went forward a couple of paces, the heavy man stamping his feet, perhaps thinking that if he stamped hard enough he'd break the legs and qualify for a new pair.

'I didn't half rick my neck,' he whispered to his wife.

'Cheer up, *mon brave*, they haven't lost a man in these latitudes yet,' said his wife.

The instructor got everyone to do a sort of tap-dance with the skis. You raised your knee so that the ski was six inches or so off the floor, then flicked the front of the ski against the floor by flexing your ankle rapidly. Tap, tap, tap went the instructor delicately, crash, crash, crash went the class as if they were shaking mud off their wellies.

'No, no,' shouted the instructor. 'I don't want to see *this*.' And he imitated the flailing movement they'd all been doing. 'I want to see –' But before he could change down into the proper gear the back end of his ski dashed against the piano stool and slid under the lid, and he stood for a moment like a stork doing a double-take. The youth in the coloured jersey ran forward to render aid, but the instructor said sharply, 'All right, all right, let's get on.'

Then the instructor said 'Skis together. I want you all to lie back on the floor and when I say "Up" I want you to spring forward and get to your feet. All right?'

The man at the back got into the prone position.

'Ready?' said the instructor. '*Up.*'

There was a concerted scuffle through the room and lots of heavy breathing as if a couple of dozen burglars were robbing the same house at the same time. Then a certain amount of groaning broke out, and one cry of despair from the man at the back. The rest of the class had managed to scramble to their feet, but he lay prone and twisted like one of Blake's mystical engravings.

'And down,' said the instructor.

The man at the back relaxed.

'And up.'

This time the man at the back dragged himself on to one elbow.

'And down.'

But the man got the other elbow up and reclined on both until the exercise was finished. Then he said to the lad in the coloured sweater, 'Get the chocks out, son.' The youth pushed him upright again.

The door at the end of the hall swung open and two men, black from top to toe, save that their eyes gleamed white, entered. They wore caps as black as themselves and carried long brushes over their shoulders. The instructor was doing the tap-tap routine with the back end of the ski and the class was going crash, crash, crash.

'Where's the boilers?' roared one of the black men.

'Excuse me, sir,' said the other black man, 'we're after the chimbleys. We were rung for the flues.'

'Not here,' the instructor said. 'Flues. Flues. I'm conducting a ski-school.'

'That's all right, sir,' said the second man. They both appeared to stand momentarily at an angle of forty-five degrees to the door, then they withdrew.

'Now I want you to try a stem turn,' the instructor continued. 'Say I'm standing like this and the hill's above me and the valley's below I make a triangle with my skis then I throw my weight on the left-hand ski if I'm making a right-hand turn and I drop my left-hand arm and shoulder and let the edge of the ski drive into the snow and I turn.'

'Only he's not standing the same way we are,' the man at the back muttered. 'Is the hill the piano and the blackboard the valley or the piano the blackboard I mean the piano the valley and the blackboard –'

'Now an exercise for the legs. I want you to kick the ski upwards until it's resting on its rear end,' said the instructor. '*And –*'

The skis came up like good soldiers, all except one which flew straight as an arrow through the air and got the instructor in the chest.

'Whoops,' said the man at the back, hopping on one foot.

604

I'D been thinking about the trolleybuses that grazed the tarmacadam
pastures of my childhood, harmless red herbivores which would make
the patient whiffling noise of their species, and gather up the citizens
of the suburb as uncomplainingly as elephants used to give rides to children at the Zoo. And I was trying to put a number – I nearly said
a name, something like 'Douglas' would have been suitable – to the
one which stopped (as it were, to water) just past the level-crossing
and opposite the school. And then in this anthropomorphic reverie, the
number came back to me – it was a 604, and it took you to Malden
and Kingston and Hampton Court.

All the trolleybuses looked like tall and amiable ruminants, they staggered along as though on large flat feet, and I thought of them going
home, not to a depot, but to some natural geological burrow, say a
vast airy cave tucked away under Box Hill, where they slumbered between
shifts.

Well, one afternoon I was strolling through Covent Garden, and I
turned into the London Transport Museum, and what I saw made me
laugh aloud so that people looked round. There it was, a 604, roosting
shyly under the high roof of the place, and a printed card against the
wall saying the vehicle dated from the late Thirties, and that the route
had been served by five of them. That's why I laughed. It was an actuarial
impossibility that the contribution of my own behind to the wear and
tear so stoutly resisted by the dim blue upholstery of this very bus could
be excluded!

I jumped on to the conductor's platform and wondered how many
of my own footsteps I trod across – aged seven, as we took our sandwiches
and the Box Brownie to Hampton Court, sitting ahead of my parents
in an empty seat on the top deck, right at the front, and pretending
to drive; or ten years later, on my way to Bentalls to hunt down a pair
of suede shoes on thick crepe soles, without which life had suddenly
become unendurable.

I went upstairs – 'outside only' – and sat down. A vehicle that had to be *helped* to go in the right direction by means of a long bamboo pole which poked the spastic trolleys into reverse when it was time to turn round, was doomed to extinction. It ate grass, and polluted nothing, but diesel-breathing dragons lay in wait at Shannon Corner and Worple Road, and the trolley-buses were consumed, and disappeared from the earth.

The route doddered quietly past the sports grounds and the avenues, and at request-stops the bus would pause and sigh. That is what I was doing now, sitting alone in the empty upstairs. What I'd never noticed about the route when I travelled by it was the other dimension it passed through. I didn't realize it was moving through time as well, and that every time you got off there was one request-stop fewer.

An Unsatisfactory Christmas Dinner
in West Africa

'WHAT we want then,' McIntish clapped his lips together, 'after the richness of the *pâté*,' he worked his tongue against his palate, 'is something to dry the mouth up.' McIntish had thought of groundnut soup with a sprinkling of raw onion, but on the actual day the drying process set in before the second course had reached the table.

Someone made a joke about marriage and Colonel Bowkett – the Lagos Idiot – said abruptly, 'I was married once.' The three young subalterns were only just out from England, and fresh from the OCTU they thought of Mess life as a kind of obstacle-course full of conundrums about etiquette that they were never going to be able to answer. 'But she ran away. She left me for another man.' The silence deepened terribly and one of the subalterns found that the piece of bread he was chewing had got bigger. 'Oh, it's not as bad as you're all thinking,' said the Lagos Idiot, 'he was a regular officer.'

McIntish had planned the meal and done the decorations – artificial snow, some balloons, and a couple of dozen coloured pin-up pictures cut out of a magazine – and he sat at the table grimly watching the movement of the knives and forks, determined not to let anyone off a mouthful. It was the first meal he'd eaten in the Mess for a twelvemonth, having sworn not to enter it as long as his enemy Foster remained in the colony. But Foster was returning to England on the day following, and McIntish made a concession to Christmas.

'Ice-' – and Foster's big square missis, who both talked and moved slower than a tin of treacle, paused as she raised her glass of lemon-squash – 'cold,' she said finally. She sat next to the DDT and O, who was the Lagos Idiot's immediate superior and a sort of emperor as far as everyone else was concerned. Foster was there, a pale fat man who walked as if he had a green banana stuck up his backside. In the background, lightly tethered, was the Lagos Idiot's parrot.

Everyone had been drinking fairly freely, except the subalterns, who couldn't afford to, and Mrs Foster, who loved lemonade. Dogo and Audu (the Fosters' boy) came in with the main course and Mrs Foster said – as though she had been recorded at $7\frac{1}{2}$ and was being played back at $3\frac{3}{4}$ – 'Have you been for that sheet?'

'Sheet!' cried the parrot.

Audu, who was simple-minded, looked at his mistress in amazement, then nodded.

'We thought it had been stolen,' Foster's wife confided to the DDT and O, with glacier-like slowness, 'but it was probably just held up at the laundry.'

The main dish was an enormous pie made under McIntish's instructions as a change from the traditional turkey. It was a pigeon-pie and the pigeons had been shot by McIntish himself using a .22 rifle, a weapon he beguiled himself with in the afternoons after he had absorbed his ration of the *Argosy*.

'I was commanding a fort at your age,' said the Lagos Idiot to one of the subalterns.

'Sheet!' yelled the parrot.

Audu and Dogo came in again with roast yams.

'Delicious,' said Mrs Foster, managing to string the word out as though it was somebody's collected works. 'Do you like yams?' she asked the DDT and O.

'We transport them in bulk,' he said.

'Who's going to be father?' asked Foster.

'What?' said the DDT and O.

'Will you carve the thing, sir?'

The DDT and O was the sort of high-ranking officer who had difficulty knotting his tie. The Lagos Idiot cut the pie and McIntish watched him narrowly.

Mrs Foster said to Audu, 'Where is the sheet now?'

Audu said, 'In the bush, madam.'

The pie was handed about and McIntish ate his share, his eyes moving sharply from mouth to mouth.

'Bags of flavour, sir,' said one of the subalterns.

'You call me *George*, in the Mess,' said McIntish.

The Lagos Idiot chewed abstractedly, his attention engaged by the pin-up pictures pasted round the walls. 'They're extremely handsome. Very taking. They're very taking, sir,' he said to the DDT and O, who made a noise in reply that sounded like 'Mmmm.'

'Pigeon,' muttered Foster. 'Where did you bag this little lot?'

McIntish said, 'At the Command Supply Depot. They tend to group on the roofs.'

'I knew it!' cried Foster, 'these aren't pigeons, they're bloody doves.'

'I really don't know what you're doing with a sheet in the bush,' said Mrs Foster, turning time into eternity.

'I like the expressions on the girls' faces,' said the Lagos Idiot, 'they are well-bred. Provocative with it, of course. I should say they were provocative, sir.'

'Do shut up, Bowkett,' said the DDT and O.

'Doves,' said Foster, 'you can't eat *them*.'

'They are pigeons,' said McIntish grimly.

'A strange laundry,' Mrs Foster said.

'I wish you wouldn't keep harping on that sheet, I mean that laundry,' said Foster aside. He said to McIntish, 'Picked them off while they were on the roof, did you? What a shame.'

'You are eating pigeon,' said McIntish.

Two of the subalterns were now addressing themselves to the yam on their plates with gusto, as though a display of enthusiasm for the veg might conceal the fact that they weren't touching the pigeon. The third subaltern said, 'If this is dove, give me dove every time.'

McIntish said to him, 'David —'

'Sir.'

'Call me *George*, in the Mess. Go down to my bungalow and get my dictionary of birds.'

The subaltern went out. The Lagos Idiot took a pull at his brandy and soda, continuing to stare at the pin-up pictures as he chewed his way through his whack of the pigeons. The DDT and O was drumming on the table. Foster had laid down his knife and fork and was looking at his plate as though it were a mirage. McIntish picked up a bone between his fingers and carefully sucked the meat off it.

Mrs Foster said, 'I revelled in every mouthful,' in about the time it takes to read the Queen's Speech.

'I wouldn't mind,' said the Lagos Idiot, 'I really wouldn't mind making love to any of 'em.'

'But they're only PAPER, Bowkett,' roared the DDT and O in an ecstasy of impatience.

McIntish's boy appeared in the doorway.

'Mr Smith, sir. He send message. He say he only find bound copy of *Children's Newspaper*.'

'Sheet!' screamed the parrot.

'Well, say what you like about doves,' said the Lagos Idiot, 'you can't beat a parrot for companionship.'

The Flat-Dweller as Deviant

MY suspicion of flat-dwellers is inherited from my mother. She associated flats with people who ordered their groceries by telephone and ran up bills (when Dedman's ran out of ginger-snaps she'd sneer at the manager. 'All put aside for your *telephone customers*', and the manager, a Mr Bowry, would smile but also blush, as though he shared her reservations and suspected the telephone was something he too easily deferred to).

Then I got the notion that people who lived in flats were rich and frivolous and often secretaries, because an aunt of mine who lived in a flat had twenty-three pairs of shoes, a cocktail cabinet, and a relationship with her boss that was always about to be marriage but kept on not being. I also felt flats were the first signs of Huxley's brave new world, a dangerously avant-garde way of life that you had to be very clever and probably unbalanced to be able to take up successfully. Above all, I thought of flats as incomplete, a fragment or caricature of the real thing, whose inhabitants would exhibit the same lack of bottom as the places they lived in.

On the other hand, houses went all the way down to the ground, they had the air of having been around long before actual people were ever thought of, and later in life I found they'd become the focus of strange dreams – extra rooms appeared in sinister visions of the house I grew up in, while outside the windows, streets ran into poisoned landscapes where once-friendly cinemas stood dark and empty. I've never heard of anyone dreaming about a *flat* in just that way.

Of course, all systems of keeping a roof over your head look a little sad, in the face of the universe, with all the contents of all the rooms in the world – puny attempts at self-assertion – no more than an inaudible squeak as Chaos rolls over them. But if, on bad days, houses look like hiding-places, flats always remind me of shelves on which people have been left.

Epiphany

SLAP at the traffic lights, a chap in a Daf Variomatic drew into the kerb, stopped the car and got out. The man behind him in a Jag hooted and the Daf man walked towards him with a sort of inquiring expression that had a hint of the inverted commas about it. 'Move up, how can I pass you?' shouted the Jag man. 'Rowlocks,' said the Daf man quietly, no respecter of persons, 'I'm parking here. You move back.' Jag man nearly had a seizure. Alongside the Jag was a large lorry, waiting for the lights. The driver, feeling like it, leant out of his cab and said in a languid way to the Jag man, 'You silly old sausage' (or words to that effect) 'why don't you do what he tells you? All the same you Jag drivers, think you own the bleedin' roads.' Jag driver stares at the lorry driver in amazement – lorry bears the name of firm of which he, the Jag driver, is Managing Director! Bereft of speech. Lorry driver continues in same leisurely vein, 'You miserable old turtle, driving them big cars goes to your 'ead, ain't they?' Managing Director gets out of Jag and walks slowly up to lorry driver, steam rising from the top of his head. 'Would you be speaking to me like that if you knew who I was?' I heard him cry.

Driver of lorry says, 'I don't care a footle who you are, big 'ead.' 'In that case,' says the Managing Director, 'let me tell you: I am Managing Director of,' and he told him. 'Oh, Castor and Pollux,' exclaims driver, 'goodness me, sir, I really must apologize, don't know what came over me,' etc. 'We won't go into that now,' says the Managing Director, still suffering from what looks like terminal frustration, but plainly amazed at his stunning good luck in having the universe deliver over to him a victim when he was most in need of one. Gets back into his own car, emotionally dislocated, and backs straight into a taxi waiting patiently behind. *Exeunt omnes*. I nearly got out and gave him the tenner I'd willingly have paid for the seat I'd enjoyed for nothing. The whole thing was a sort of vision.

Irony

A FRIEND of mine leant forward and boomed 'But my dear fellow, you don't know how famous I am.' And I replied, 'I do know how famous you are.' And irony being a mode in which the voice of one is heard in the voice of another, to its disadvantage, I thought my reply was an almost pure example.

The ironic voice incorporates the voice of its victim, but without distortion: if either of the voices is distorted, you don't have irony, you have sarcasm. I was well pleased with this little bit of analysis, rather doubting whether it had ever been put quite so deftly before; only to find that, yes, it had, quite often, and the best of the various definitions are included in D.J. Enright's essay on irony which he calls *The Alluring Problem* (anyone who enjoys a bit of a brood on style and meaning, especially when it's witty as well as thoughtful, shouldn't miss it.)

I like Empson's formulation, which postulates that both parts of the irony must be capable of being true: when I respond to my friend and say 'I know how famous you are' the words must be intelligible in terms of his own boast, as well as my reductive application of it. So when Johnson says irony 'is a mode of speech in which the meaning is contrary to the words' his definition is inadequate: he had better have said it was a mode of speech in which there are two meanings, *one* of which is contrary to the words. But this is put most charmingly by Kierkegaard: irony, says Kierkegaard, is like a riddle and its solution, possessed simultaneously.

I'm drawn to irony, but not without wondering if it isn't the instrument of the non-combatant. Enright offers Mr Bennett in *Pride and Prejudice* as an example of a henpecked husband for whom 'irony is the self-awarded consolation prize of the defeated'. But to have been defeated, you have to have fought: my own feeling is that all ironists so much fear defeat that they never pick up the sword. They are content to *mime* the possibility of combat. This would account for the winningness implicit in irony, which invites the onlooker, if not the victim, to reward the ironist with the right sort of smile. The audience is indispensable to the ironist, if his translation of conflict into charade is to be registered as an authentic option. Otherwise he may simply feel he has been evasive.

Enright urges that the ironist isn't saying he knows better, only that he knows otherwise. But he who says he knows otherwise, says he knows better, but is saying it politely. Friends were surprised when Herbert Read, the socialist critic, accepted a knighthood: he said, 'I'm not important enough to refuse a knighthood'. This perfect irony doesn't say it knows better. But it doesn't say it because it doesn't have to.

A pity the word itself is so abused; journalists use 'ironic' when they mean novel or unexpected. But getting it right isn't simply a matter of pedantry, of classification; irony is more than the merely linguistic. It is a style, a temper, a way of looking, that bears witness to the possibiltiy of being in and of the world without replacing it with yourself.

Viz: a young lobster wished to marry a crab, and her mother said My dear, they're so common and they don't have any money, and moreover they walk sideways. You couldn't marry anyone who walked sideways. Meet him, mother, said the lobster, and she turned up with the crab who shook hands politely and walked in a dead straight line into the drawing-room. But I thought crabs always walked sideways, said the mother. They do, said the crab, gravely accepting her premise, but I'm drunk.

The Middle-aged Booby Abroad

THE second morning at the ski resort, I woke up and looked out of the window and was shaken by a spasm of rage.

'See what I see?' I asked my wife.

'What?'

'The snow.'

'Well?'

I turned to the window and shook my fist. 'You should ski down it once, and it should all go away.'

I caught the sound of my own voice, and found I objected to it. What I'd said was no more than the revealed truth about holidays: what everyone can't stand about holidays is the way you do the same thing every day, without anything happening. But there was a kind of edge on the way I spoke that made me sound like someone whose company I wouldn't want to keep.

Then we went to Moscow for the weekend (makes a change from the Cotswolds) and when we got back I started telling people it had been like spending four days at a post office with all the positions closed. And for the second time I caught an echo of myself, and I sounded like a man who'd been to Paris and couldn't get a cup of tea.

No one's going to deny I'm absolutely right about the food in America, nobody's going to argue about it being absolutely tasteless, but when I went round announcing that the national dish of America was menus, I think I heard myself saying it like journalists do when they're trying to pass off some personal inconvenience as a symptom of someone else's economic malaise.

In many ways I qualified for the VC in sending back a steak in a reputable but unsympathetic two-star Michelin restaurant one quiet day in Clichy, when all I had between myself and my naked desire not to eat what I couldn't swallow was the fraying selvedge of my grammar-school French. Yet though I got full marks from my chum (who hadn't helped the cause by eating all his, plus the plate as well), I couldn't like myself very much as we walked away – I'd been right, but somehow that wasn't enough.

Seeing myself as I appear in these small histories is like suddenly having the view blotted out by a fat woman in a cinema. As time wears on and I travel further, there's one bloody old fool I'd like to leave behind, one fearsome old bore whose luggage slows me down, one fatuous tourist who won't let somewhere else be somewhere else, one damned old idiot who thinks Abroad has to prove itself, one ageing noodle who constantly gets in his own way, and of course I'm talking about me.

I seem to have crept up on myself so that now when I travel my own presence is a sort of static, distracting me from the Pyramids, the Taj Mahal, the Salt Lake Desert. I'm like a pirate station I can't tune out, a ludicrous mutter which keeps on asking 'Did you really want to come? When do you start enjoying yourself? Is it time to go home yet?' I hang around my own holidays like Marley's ghost, looking for someone to accuse.

When I was nineteen, I felt Abroad was some joyous conspiracy I'd been let into, a place that excited me because it had always been there while I hadn't. Now Abroad is the American I sat next to on the way to Washington who in a bagpipe monotone briefed me in the art of folding a jacket so that it should not crease, repeating his instructions not once but twice, even contriving by some sleight of hand to get me to say it all back to him. To prove to his wife that he had absolute power over me, he actually forced me to my feet between the seats so that all three of us could celebrate the holiday he had just enjoyed by drinking a toast to my lovely Queen. One way or another I always get this man because, poor bugger, he always gets me. In a dreadful sort of way, we need each other.

On the rare occasions I'm prepared to be surprised, I think I have the decency to feel remorse for the middle-aged philistinism through which the surprise has to crash. As for example, one hot morning in Malaga we walked into what looked like the coolest and oldest of hotels. Punkahs rustled in the brown gloom and an aged waiter bowed as we gave our order. The room was full of seigneurial males, one of whom rose slowly to his feet and approached us. In a tone which combined gentleness with an entire absence of reproof he said, 'You have made an understandable mistake. This is a gentleman's club. You are now my guests.'

Or the *garagiste* mending a motorbike in a lane full of bees and thyme, not far from La Devinière. I asked the way, wondering if he could tell me if there was wine to be bought in these parts. Pausing with the inner tube in his hands, he said he personally had no wine for sale, but would like to show me his collection. He took me into his *cave* – literally that, a vast antre within a rocky scarp – and standing there in his bicycle-clips pointed to rack after rack, fifteen years of growths from the Loire. We sampled the Chinon and the Ligré, the Montlouis and the Bourgeuil, through a long afternoon. He looked upon the wines of Bordeaux as illegitimate, scarcely potable on the grounds of their alcohol. He brought forth a curiosity, one of a dozen bottles so powerfully corked that in fact it tasted like the most exquisite vermouth. He laughed as he drank a little of it. He was amused. All this was his hobby. He was an *amateur*.

I do not deserve such treats, and as those very words go down on the paper, slap, slap, from the typewriter, the telephone rings and I am offered my true deserts. A man invites me to go to Marbella and there for a consideration chair a seminar of what in his own words he calls 'the older and wiser heads in Hardware'. Marbella is to echo to the voices of men who make self-adhesive tiles, and I shall be free to suck at the same dug as the sons of Polyfilla. The open-handed man on the other end of the phone urges the weight of the occasion by candidly admitting his first choice had been Frank Bough – 'to give you some idea of the level at which you would be operating'.

I honestly felt some wag had been looking over my shoulder and had been laying for me with a moral in the shape of a blunt instrument. After all, if I don't like my own company as a traveller because I tend to exclude what I should include, where better to complete the sealing-off process than that concrete grove, Marbella, and what better to grout in the edges than a high-class product like Polycel? I might almost have gone, if I hadn't had to travel with myself.

Marmalade

On a morning when the whole of Russia was changing hands, and the cosmic layers were shifting, I returned thanks for the news that Sir Michael Tippett was going to judge a marmalade competition. I looked again, uncertain for a moment whether it wasn't Sir Michael Tiptree, but no, it was the great composer, Order of Marmalade. There is a lively energetic vibration about the phrase 'marmalade competition', as though the stuff was going to be thrown like a javelin. Or perhaps it was to be a new sort of 100 yards dash in special marmalade spikes, through fathoms of the stuff. For the indoor event, dozens of marmalade Grand Masters would crouch earnestly over jars of the home-made variety supplied by their wives, struggling to remove the elastic-band without crumpling the transparent paper top, Sir Michael deducting marks for sticky fingers. At the viva, a sort of confessional, he would put it to the competitors individually: have you ever bought shop marmalade when no one was looking simply because it has a lid you can put back on again? And that extra disc of grease-proof paper that is placed on top of the home-made stuff – have you ever been able to throw it away without feeling faintly guilty? The winner gets a holiday for two in Broadstairs, where there is a café which sells Virol sandwiches.

The Last Interview with Nabokov

WE arrived in February. Wintry laurels and the bare willow trees made the path at the side of the lake seem melancholy, and there was a curious feeling of taking a walk in an old photograph. We were calling on Nabokov to let him know we were there, and also to tell him he'd given us rather short measure. The Nabokov interview is an entirely structured affair: the questions are sent a fortnight or so before the event, the answers are composed and returned, and then all you have to do is get in front of a camera and *serve* the interview, like iced cake. But it was to be a 25-minute programme, and he hadn't given us quite enough.

He had been very ill. When he came into one of the public rooms of that slightly left-over caravanserai, the Montreux-Palace Hotel, he was leaning on a stick, his face was pale, and his collar was now a size or two too large for the neck. Mme Nabokov was with him, and because she too had been ill she had a bent and hooded look. I felt rather scared, I don't quite know why, and to my surprise, after we'd been talking for a few minutes and I'd said how agreeable it was to know the interview had already taken place, frozen on paper before the cameras arrived, precluding the possibility of anything unexpected, Mme Nabokov murmured in a low voice, 'Were you frightened?' I jumped and cried, 'Oh no, not at all, not a bit,' but I suppose in accepting the premise of so strange a question, I gave myself the lie.

As far as the length of the interview was concerned, it was plain that Nabokov had said all that he wished to say and wished to say no more. So it was decided that he would read one of his poems, and immediately, like a chef measuring out his ingredients in extraordinarily careful spoonfuls, he began to weigh the poem in terms of time – 'So many *strophes* at so many seconds a *strophe*, let us say fifteen *strophes* –' 'No, it is twelve,' interjected Mme Nabokov – 'twelve, then say thirty seconds for each *strophe*, multiplied by twelve, that gives us an extra six minutes, yes, it is quite enough –'

We weren't allowed into the Nabokov quarters – six rooms on the top floor of the Hotel ('those *attics*', as Nabokov drily apostrophized them). We were excluded on the grounds of there not being space enough, but it would have been odd if a man who had devoted his life to holding the world entertainingly at bay should not have protected his privacy. So a faint social hiccup developed – we were calling on business, but they actually *lived* at the Hotel, so that when Nabokov said, 'We could go into the bar, if you wished to offer a drink,' I thought he must have meant 'If you wish to *be* offered a drink'; but not only was this a slightly absurd indulgence to extend to a writer who always takes pains to say precisely what he wants to say, it just didn't feel as though the Nabokovs were 'At Home' . . .

We drank some vodka ('Crepkaya, if it is for M. Nabokov', the waiter murmured) and Nabokov explained that he would like some vodka on the table in front of him when the interview was filmed the following day – 'but because I do not wish to give a false impression and have people think I am an old drunk, let them put the vodka in a water-jug'. In short, he was saying that the illness had laid him low, and the camera and the bright lights would tax his strength. When we got up to go, he said, 'Who is the potentate?' and I realized – again with a faint twinge of embarrassment – he was saying, 'You pay.'

The next day a room at the Montreux-Palace was lit for the cameras, and Nabokov seated himself at one of those Louis-the-Hotel tables and propped his notes against the carafe which held the vodka, and we did the question-and-answer as I imagine Elizabethan actors conducted a duologue – moving stiffly through a sequence of conventional gestures and inflections which had been devised to relieve the participants of the idiocy of pretending the exchange was spontaneous. Neither Nabokov nor I made any attempt at *mime*, we lifted the cards to our eyes and read the words we had already exchanged on paper, aloud: at the end of the dance, I as it were handed my partner back to his seat, and put on my glasses to read the words, 'Thank you, Mr Nabokov.'

When the film ran out, by times, we conversed. Nabokov said, 'I once had an interview with a man who suspected that my feelings for Lolita were something other than a father might feel towards his child.' His tone, his manner, as he spoke, seemed coquettish. Was he coaxing me into the banality of an inquiry? I said, referring to the journalist he was talking about, 'That was a bit crass of him.' But Nabokov looked a little sulky, a little disappointed. 'Oh no,' he said, 'not crass, not necessarily.' I said spinsterishly, 'I don't think it's a question I'd want to ask you.' Nabokov said, 'Oh, I think *I* would. I think *I* would.' And smiled, but not engagingly.

After a while, Nabokov said, 'Do you think Lewis Carroll actually did anything with those little girls he photographed?' I found the question alarmingly anecdotal, from a member of the Pantheon. I said, giving the matter a second or two's thought, 'I doubt it. If he had, he wouldn't have needed to write the books or take the pictures, would he?' Again I felt I had given the wrong answer. Nabokov shook his head. 'No, no, no. There was something going on.' I said, 'But I could imagine the works, the stories, the fantasies, were *instead* of all that?' Nabokov smiled a smile that was full of bad news. He said, 'There was a lay in it somewhere. There was a *lay* in it somewhere.' Throughout the interview, throughout the asides, Mme Nabokov had sat in a quiet corner of the room, her hands clasped on her walking-stick, quite silent. I sensed her presence behind me throughout, and as I faced Nabokov, I felt her absorption too, he was all her care. The Nabokovs moved slowly out of the room, and I had some idea they were returning to a chess game they had left unfinished upstairs.

R.R.: First, sir, to spare you irritation, I wonder if you will instruct me in the pronunciation of your name.
V.N.: Let me put it this way. There exists a number of deceptively simple-looking Russian names, whose spelling and pronunciation present the foreigner with strange traps. The name Suvarov took a couple of centuries to lose the preposterous middle 'a' – it should be Suvorov. American autograph-seekers, while professing a knowledge of all my books – prudently not mentioning their titles – rejuggle the vowels of my name in all the ways allowed by mathematics. 'Nabakav' is especially touching for the 'a's. Pronunciation problems fall into a less erratic pattern. On the playing-fields of Cambridge, my football team used to hail me as 'Nabkov' or, facetiously, 'Macnab'. New Yorkers reveal their tendency of turning 'o' into 'ah' by pronouncing my name 'Nabarkov'. The aberration '*Nabokov*' is a favourite one of postal officials. Now, the correct Russian way would take too much time to explain, and so I've settled for euphonious 'Na*bo*kov', with the middle syllable accented and rhyming with 'smoke'. Would you like to try?
R.R.: Mr Na*bo*kov.
V.N.: That's right.
R.R.: You grant interviews on the understanding that they shall not be spontaneous. This admirable method ensures there will be no dull patches. Can you tell me why and when you decided upon it?
V.N.: I'm not a dull speaker, I'm a bad speaker, I'm a wretched speaker. The tape of my unprepared speech differs from my written prose as much as the worm differs from the perfect insect – or, as I once put

it, I think like a genius, I write like a distinguished author and I speak like a child.

R.R.: You've been a writer all your life. Can you evoke for us the earliest stirring of the impulse?

V.N.: I was a boy of fifteen, the lilacs were in full bloom. I had read Pushkin and Keats. I was madly in love with a girl of my age, I had a new bicycle (an Enfield, I remember) with reversible handlebars that could turn it into a racer. My first poems were awful, but then I reversed those handlebars, and things improved. It took me, however, ten more years to realize that my true instrument was prose — poetic prose, in the special sense that it depended on comparisons and metaphors to say what it wanted to say. I spent the years 1925 to 1940 in Berlin, Paris and the Riviera, after which I took off for America. I cannot complain of neglect on the part of any great critics, although as always and everywhere there was an odd rascal or two badgering me. What has amused me in recent years is that those old novels and stories published in English in the Sixties and Seventies were appreciated much more warmly than they had been in Russian thirty years ago.

R.R.: Has your satisfaction in the act of writing ever fluctuated? I mean, is it keener now or less keen than once it was?

V.N.: Keener.

R.R.: Why?

V.N.: Because the ice of experience now mingles with the fire of inspiration.

R.R.: Apart from the pleasure it brings, what do you conceive your task as a writer to be?

V.N.: This writer's task is the purely subjective one of reproducing as closely as possible the image of the book he has in his mind. The reader need not know, or, indeed, cannot know, what the image is, and so cannot tell how closely the book has conformed to its image in the author's mind. In other words, the reader has no business bothering about the author's intentions, nor has the author any business trying to learn whether the consumer likes what he consumes.

R.R.: Of course, the author works harder than the reader does. But I wonder whether it augments his — this is to say, your — pleasure that he makes the reader work hard, too.

V.N.: The author is perfectly indifferent to the capacity and condition of the reader's brain.

R.R.: Could you give us some idea of the pattern of your working day?

V.N.: This pattern has lately become blurry and inconstant. At the peak of the book, I work all day, cursing the tricks that objects play upon me, the mislaid spectacles, the spilled wine. I also find talking of my working day far less entertaining than I formerly did.

R.R.: The conventional view of an hotel is as of a temporary shelter – one arrives as a traveller, after all – yet you choose to make it permanent.

V.N.: I have toyed on and off with the idea of buying a villa. I can imagine the comfortable furniture, the efficient burglar alarms, but I am unable to visualize an adequate staff. Old retainers require time to get old, and I wonder how much of it there still is at my disposal.

R.R.: You once entertained the possibility of returning to the United States. I wonder if you will.

V.N.: I will certainly return to the United States at the first opportunity. I'm indolent, I'm sluggish, but I'm sure I'll go back with tenderness. The thrill with which I think of certain trails in the Rockies is only matched by visions of my Russian woods, which I will never revisit.

R.R.: Is Switzerland a place with positive advantages for you, or is it simply a place without positive disadvantages?

V.N.: The winters can be pretty dismal here, and my old borzoi has developed feuds with lots of local dogs, but otherwise it's all right.

R.R.: You think and write in three languages – which would be the preferred one?

V.N.: Yes, I write in three languages, but I think in images. The matter of preference does not really arise. Images are mute, yet presently the silent cinema begins to talk and I recognize its language. During the second part of my life, it was generally English, my own brand of English – not the Cambridge variety, but still English.

R.R.: At any point do you invite your wife to comment on work in progress?

V.N.: When the book is quite finished, and its fair copy is still warm and wet, my wife goes carefully through it. Her comments are usually few but invariably to the point.

R.R.: Do you find that you re-read your own earlier work, and if you do, with what feelings?

V.N.: Re-reading my own works is a purely utilitarian business. I have to do it when correcting a paperback edition riddled with misprints or controlling a translation, but there are some rewards. In certain species – this is going to be a metaphor – in certain species, the wings of the pupated butterfly begin to show in exquisite miniature through the wing-cases of the chrysalis a few days before emergence. It is the pathetic sight of an iridescent future transpiring through the shell of the past, something of the kind I experience when dipping into my books written in the Twenties. Suddenly through a drab photograph a blush of colour, an outline of form, seems to be distinguishable. I'm saying this with absolute scientific modesty, not with the smugness of ageing art.

R.R.: Which writers are you currently reading with pleasure?

V.N.: I'm re-reading Rimbaud, his marvellous verse and his pathetic correspondence in the Pléiade edition. I am also dipping into a collection of unbelievably stupid Soviet jokes.

R.R.: Your praise for Joyce and Wells has been high. Could you identify briefly the quality in each which sets them apart?

V.N.: Joyce's *Ulysses* is set apart from all modern literature, not only by the force of his genius, but also by the novelty of his form. Wells is a great writer, but there are many writers as great as he.

R.R.: Your distaste for the theories of Freud has sometimes sounded to me like the agony of one betrayed, as though the old magus had once fooled you with his famous three-card trick. Were you ever a fan?

V.N.: What a bizarre notion! Actually I always loathed the Viennese quack. I used to stalk him down dark alleys of thought, and now we shall never forget the sight of old, flustered Freud seeking to unlock his door with the point of his umbrella.

R.R.: The world knows that you are also a lepidopterist but may not know what that involves. In the collection of butterflies, could you describe the process from pursuit to display?

V.N.: Only common butterflies, showy moths from the tropics, are put on display in a dusty case between a primitive mask and a vulgar abstract picture. The rare, precious stuff is kept in the glazed drawers of museum cabinets. As for pursuit, it is, of course, ecstasy to follow an undescribed beauty skimming over the rocks of its habitat, but it is also great fun to locate a new species among the broken insects in an old biscuit tin sent over by a sailor from some remote island.

R.R.: One can always induce a mild vertigo by recalling that Joyce might not have existed as the writer but as the tenor. Have you any sense of having narrowly missed some other role? What substitute could you endure?

V.N.: Oh, yes, I have always had a number of parts lined up in case the muse failed. A lepidopterist exploring famous jungles came first, then there was the chess grandmaster, then the tennis ace with an un-returnable service, then the goalie saving a historic shot, and finally, finally, the author of a pile of unknown writings – *Pale Fire*, *Lolita*, *Ada* – which my heirs discover and publish.

R.R.: Alberto Moravia told me of his conviction that each writer writes only of one thing – has but a single obsession he continually develops. Can you agree?

V.N.: I have not read Alberto Moravia, but the pronouncement you quote is certainly wrong in my case. The circus tiger is not obsessed by his torturer, my characters cringe as I come near with my whip. I have seen a whole avenue of imagined trees losing their leaves at the threat of my passage. If I do have any obsessions, I'm careful not to reveal them in fictional form.
R.R.: Mr Nabokov, thank you.
V.N.: You're welcome, as we say in my adopted country.

Chopsticks

'SHOW me a man who asks for a spoon and fork in a Chinese restaurant,' said a friend of mine who lives in East Molesey, 'and I'll show you a man who orders sweet and sour pork.' I bridled self-consciously. 'Look here,' I blurted, 'its simply not true – I may have a weakness for crispy beef –'. But he cut in decisively. 'I go further,' he said, 'I say a man who can't use chopsticks has no business entering a Chinese restaurant.' 'You mean,' I quavered, 'man without chopsticks allee samee Philistine?' 'I'm not at all sure,' he said reflectively, 'that he should even be allowed into a Chinese laundry.'

This was radical stuff, and as one who using chopsticks only ever picks up his own middle finger, I felt rather defensive. My friend had been strutting about like a piece of rare old Ming ever since he'd heard the Queen used chopsticks in China and was a dab hand with them – he felt it secured the social standing of gastronomic Sinophiles everywhere.

I said he ought to bear in mind that the top chopstick man – the Olympic Gold Medallist – had been drafted in to instruct the Queen, who set aside half an hour each day in order to get it right before setting off for the Land of the Rising Sun. 'And something tells me,' I said, 'the Duke of Edinburgh's a spoon and fork man.' He laughed derisively. 'You'll be telling me next he orders the food by number.'

Of course, the East Molesey Strict Baptist position on all this isn't just a fantasy brought on by the MSG. There's a rational basis to my chum's insistence that the food tastes different with chopsticks, because you only take small mouthfuls of the individual dishes – your fork and spoon man does tend to load the stuff in bulk. And I have to admit that sometimes when I ask for the irons I have a dreadful feeling the waiter will bring a bib and a high-chair as well.

But the chaps with the chopsticks do have a desperate air of passing themselves off as Old China Hands. And yet I notice they never go the whole hog, you don't see the chopstick wallahs lifting the rice bowl and nipping at the stuff, as the Chinese do. The Chinese dip their faces elegantly downwards, and the passage of the food is scarcely observed – birdlike, as though pecking up seed. But if a Western face were to try it, chopsticks or no chopsticks, it would simply look greedy.

'All right,' said the man from East Molesey, giving me one last chance, 'when was the last time you ordered ants-in-a-tree with fish-lip bang-bang?' 'That's easy,' I said, 'it was up-country at a little place called Zeeta's, and we had scones to follow.'

Drinking Near Mellstock

WHEN the lanthorn shone through the cracks of the barn the stringy cats fled over the straw. Men came in and lit the candles and the shadows of the butts – the big barrels sitting against the wall like monks in their stalls – rose to the ceiling and leaned across the room.

'Not from the small barrel, for that do taste like maidens' water,' said one of the men, who wore a cap and was the oldest of the four.

'Well, maidens' water ain't bad,' said another, who had a blue nose and hair like bracken on his cheekbones.

'You won't find none in Mellstock,' said the youngest with a laugh.

He took a jug to the tallest butt and drew off a quart of the cider. Then he picked up a cup made from a cow's horn and filled it. He handed the horn-cup to the oldest man who drank the cider in it and handed it back to him. Then the youngest filled it again and handed it to the man with the blue nose who stood next to the oldest man and on his right.

'I'm in a bliddy awkward position here,' said the fourth member of the company, whose features looked as though they had been cloven in his red face with a cleaver, and who was last to be served.

'Thee does know we must pass the cup the way of the sun, or the weather mid change,' said the oldest man.

The youngest drank last, for he was butler to the company, and served the rest all evening. The cider he poured was cloudy and zestful, five months old, bland but not insipid, cold and dense. The drinkers had made the drink themselves, and drank it at work and in the evening, and drank it again on Saturdays and Sundays. They were the last men in Dorset to make drink for themselves as the Tranter Dewy had made it in the days of the Mellstock Quire, long before television.

'Every house in village had tackle in my father's day,' said the old man, 'and my father drank a gallon before his breakfast while he sharpened his tools.'

'A drop before breakfast,' said the man with the blue nose, 'be better than none all day.'

'But taps in barrels do freeze,' said the red-faced man, whose ears extruded at right angles as though pressed out by thumbs when the face was molten. ''Tis hard in morning, burning candle under spigot.'

The cider mill stood a man's height in a corner of the barn, and next to it the cider press. In the autumn the apples were put in the mill and mashed and the pulp was spread on beds of straw under the press, and the press wound down by the four men. Along the top of the press was a sentence carved in the wood: *Squeeze me tighte, yet be polite.*

'The better the apple for eating, the worse for drinking,' said the youngest man. 'A Bloody Butcher or a Sweet Harry do go well –'

'But best cider be made out of thik apple they do call a Moonlight,' said the man with the blue nose, and the company laughed obscurely.

'A Moonlight or a Starlight or a Shoulder Pippin,' said the oldest man, 'led out of orchard when all do sleep. But the real old ancient cider apple be dying out. Who have heard now of a Sheep's Nose or a Sweet Acombe or a Bobby Roper?'

The horn-cup had come to the old man again and he drank from it, putting his head back, his eyes wide apart and mild as a child's. 'Twill keep four or five years, but tis best palate at four months. Some mid put a bushel of wheat in barrel or a joint of beef or muscatels, but good cider needs nothing except sweet straw and nice apples.'

'Juice pressed straight out of apples be sweet as honey, even though the apples be sour in the flesh,' said the man with the red face.

'So long as fence-wire ain't dropped in barrel,' said the butler. 'We spoiled a butt with dropping some in accidental and had to feed the liquor to the cows. They gave black manure and I did know a man who dried it out and kept it for firing in the winter.'

The man with the red face took the cup, drank, and said, 'What'll make ye bad'll make ye better.'

'And to think,' said the old man, looking at him, 'you was once teetotal. No kin to *him*,' he went on, nodding at the youngest, 'who I do recollect as dancing drunk at four year old – it was after spud-hacking, I do remember –'

The butler said, 'I lay down under spigot and drank. I knew no better, and was cussed for it.'

'Well,' said the old man, 'thee needed the loan of my wold donkey. When I fell senseless in a field after coming from pub at Bridport, thik wold donkey pressed his wet nose on my face and so revived me. He smelt the lik-*ure*.'

The ex-teetotaller said, 'I never touched a drop till I was twenty-two. Then I drank nine and a half pints and knew no more till I woke up and saw a frosty moon above me and right next to my head two words in capital letters – CAPTAIN MOLYNEUX. Bless me, I were dead drunk on the Captain's grave.'

'And thee only a Private,' said the blue-nosed man.

The horn-cup was filled again and the butler drank. 'A good butler do drink first and last,' he said.

The old man said, 'Once we did sing "The Mistletoe Bough" and "The Two Irish Labouring Gentlemen" to the tunes of fiddles and tambourines. But now tis mostly tale-telling.'

The butler put the horn-cup on the lid of the barrel and doused the lights, and the company left the barn, while a dog barked in a field a mile away.

Saucepan Universe

I FIRST noticed the sky was littered with saucepans when I was a small boy, and I didn't bother to mention it to people because I thought they all knew. Wherever you look in the sky there are six or seven stars in a cluster, and you simply join them together and you've got a saucepan.

It was about the time I first noted all this that it also occurred to me that if everything is made up of atoms then perhaps the stars themselves are atoms, and that all the stars in all the galaxies in *our* universe are simply the constituent atoms of some small object in somebody else's universe.

It didn't worry me that atoms were supposed to be small and stars big, because size is only relative and proportion would vary from universe to universe. But I did wonder what the object that the stars in our universe were the atoms of might turn out to be.

Sometimes I thought it might be a bicycle-pump or a shirt button, but walking down a moonlit lane on the Blackdown Hills I realized how very slow on the uptake I'd been. If the constellations ended up in the shape of saucepans then the object our universe simply exists to supply the atoms for must itself be a saucepan!

As I walked home I realized that the billions of years that had already elapsed, and the billions that were to come, were only the time it took for a saucepan, sitting on a gas-ring in a man's house in another universe, to boil an egg.

Arm in Arm with Borges

I GAVE Borges my arm and we walked through the park at the top of the Avenida Marcelo T. d'Alvear. We walked very slowly for Borges was blind, and though he has been blind for more than twenty years he treads timidly, as people do who are not blind but close their eyes trying to imagine what it would be like. I was shoulder to shoulder with an oracle, for people ran up to Borges and put questions to him with the half-smiling faces they would wear when they told the story at home: 'I was in the park, and you know, I saw Borges – and I asked him, Borges why have you not committed suicide as you said you would in that article you wrote for the newspaper? And – you know what he replied? – Borges said, "You must not believe all you read."'

What looked like the entire population of Buenos Aires was on its knees repairing holes in the pavement in time for the World Cup, and of course there are some things which if they are not done for a silly reason are not done at all. A band of soldiers in lion-tamers' outfits were playing wind instruments, while a visiting general laid a wreath at the foot of a statue which, whatever it commemorated, was a monument to hysteria. There were real soldiers with single hairs sticking out of chins that had never yet seen a razor, patrolling in their jungle-greens at the periphery of the celebrations, aiming their machine-guns at the stomachs of passers-by. I had been reading aloud to Borges from Sir Thomas Browne, later exchanging with him a shout or two from *Beowulf*, and now I had some sense that time had fallen out of its conjugations just as it does in a Borges story, and everything that *had* happened, and everything that was going to happen, was taking place now – instantaneously. A man came up to Borges and asked him to remind him of the first line of *The Odyssey*, saying, 'It is so long since I composed the poem I have forgotten it.' Or so I dreamed.

But this is the Borges effect. A story by Borges swings like a bright glass in front of your eyes, and through it you may see the theologian Swedenborg dreaming that though he is dead he is unconscious of the fact: until, opening a familiar door in his own house, he finds, within, a tropical rain-forest. Or a man seduced by the daughter of the caretaker of a great house, waking one morning to the sound of hammers, and finding as he walks into the next room that the noise was produced by the carpentry necessary for his own crucifixion, which then takes place.

In Borges, the dreams dovetail, the geometry is reciprocal. Lying in his garden by a well, beneath a tree, in Cairo, a man dreams his fortune is to be found in Isfahan. But when he arrives in Isfahan he is beaten by the chief of police there, who abuses him for his credulity, telling him that *he* dreams that his own fortune is to be found by a well, beneath a tree, in a garden in Cairo, but he is not so foolish that he pays attention to dreams. The man returns to Cairo, and by his own well, in his own garden, beneath his own tree, he finds his treasure.

A bishop calls on a magician and pleads to be instructed in the magic art. The magus bids his maid prepare some partridges for supper, but gives her orders that she is not to cook them until he tells her. Then he says to the bishop that he fears great men are sparing of their favours once they have what they want, but the bishop assures him of his good will, and the magus instructs him. The bishop is made a cardinal, then becomes Pope, and all the time the magician follows in his train, waits upon his favour, but is brushed aside, and is at last dismissed. 'Will you at least give me food for the return journey?' he asks, but the pontiff brusquely refuses. 'Then,' says the magus, 'I must roast the partridges I ordered for supper.' Both bishop and magus stand once more in the magus's library: the moment has been suspended, no time has passed at all.

The glass swings in the fingers of a hypnotist, and readers of Borges – 'A good reader is rarer than a good writer,' Borges says – find the incidents of their actual lives moving into patterns that are distinctly Borgesian (Borges says of Kafka that Kafkaesque traces are to be found in Browning and Kierkegaard, but that these strains would have been unidentifiable had Kafka never existed). As I shuffle with Borges along the formal pathways that evoke those labyrinths in his stories which grow until they fill the universe, in this park which gives me the illusion that it transects time, as though it were a sepia photograph of long ago joining the moment it was taken to the moment I find myself within it, I begin to think of a picture that hangs on a wall at home.

It is a picture of a country house, painted in the seventeenth century by Samuel van Hoogstraten, and when I brought it home I wondered what it was that made me uneasy. Then I realized. The picture was not of the actual house, it was of the gatehouse. The house itself remained unpainted, save for a single column at the edge of the canvas, and I as the onlooker was standing inside it. Then one day, in a gallery in another country, I saw a second picture by Hoogstraten. A woman with a dog walked within the colonnade of a country house. She was looking in my direction, and this seemed natural, for the first column in her picture is missing – and it is the last column in mine. When I discover all the other pictures, and the house finally has its four walls, will I be able to find a door in the canvas and open it into the enormous face of Hoogstraten? And as his brush hovers over his palette, will he agree to let me out before he paints me, irrevocably, in?

I repeat: it is the Borges effect. His stories hang in the glass he swings before your eyes like the brightly lit moments of a consuming fever. And his poems, conjuring the suburbs of Buenos Aires, have so successfully dreamed the dream on everyone's behalf that when I ventured into Palermo, the outlying district of Borges's youth, with its cobbled streets, neglected pillarboxes, and abandoned tramlines, I felt I must have been born here too but had somehow forgotten my old address. Every opening door and narrow passageway, every rusty balcony with a singing-bird hanging in its cage, every secret courtyard, spoke of something familiar, and I could not tell if this were the furniture of a poem or of reality:

> *The garden's grillework gate*
> *opens with the ease of a page*
> *in a much-thumbed book,*
> *and, once inside, our eyes*
> *have no need to dwell on objects*
> *already fixed and exact in memory.*
> *Here habits and minds and the private language*
> *all families invent*
> *are everyday things to me.*
> *What necessity is there to speak*
> *or pretend to be someone else?*
> *The whole house knows me,*
> *they're aware of my worries and weakness.*
> *This is the best that can happen –*
> *what Heaven will grant us:*
> *not to be wondered at or required to succeed*
> *but simply let in*
> *as part of an undeniable Reality*
> *like stones of the road, like trees.*

That day I returned via the Recoleta Cemetery, where Borges looks forward with satisfaction to occupying the family tomb. The cemetery is a sort of Mayfair of the dead, the most expensive real estate in Buenos Aires, each sepulchre a wild confection of urns and angels, pediments and cupolas, an architecture of Babel on whose pinnacles stone generals are carried into Valhalla in full evening-dress. It was lunchtime when I arrived, and sharp black shadows lay across the paths as though the sun itself were carving the entablature, and workmen retired into the tombs to feast, spreading tablecloths on the coffins of their betters. But now in the park Borges said to me: 'About half an hour ago I felt sure I was about to die. I tried to become curious about the event, but I failed. I wanted only to get it over with.' We moved slowly across the road. Borges said: 'Perhaps half an hour ago, we both died, and very soon now we shall realize it.'

The Tail of the Dinosaur is in the Early Edition

THE Chinese came over to collect the dinosaurs they'd lent to the National Museum of Wales and the Curator sounded very wistful when it was time to dismantle the huge creatures and say farewell. 'We shall miss them,' he said, 'the place is going to seem awfully empty without them.' While they were being crated-up, someone told a reporter that they'd disappeared from the earth because they only sired male off-spring, and this appeared in the paper over the weekend.

But by Monday an American professor from the University of Oshkosh was saying no, what actually happened was that dinosaurs were very tall, which meant that the leaves they ate from the tops of trees took so long to reach their stomachs that by the time they arrived there they'd fermented. This meant that Tyrannosaurus Rex was so drunk after every meal he found it hard to stay upright, and leaning heavily against the trees he tended to push them over, thus depopulating the forests and starting the next ice-age.

But the truth is the word dinosaur with all its variants was coined by Badger and Fairdale, a small Liverpool firm of toy manufacturers who in 1842 marketed the first construction kits for boys. The skeletons were designed by Aelred Fairdale and ranged from kit No. 1 – a small ichthyosaur – to kit No. 7, the Rex, which a serious boy who could be relied on not to lose the parts was given for his fourteenth birthday.

When Aelred diversified into steam laundries the firm went bust, and the dinosaurs vanished from the earth because the spare parts simply weren't available. Baden Powell appealed to all those whose dinosaur-sets had helped keep them pure in thought word and deed to send what remained of their kits to the V&A so that an interesting period in social history should not be forgotten. Unfortunately, the van-men delivered the stuff next door, and the models were set up in the Natural History Museum, where they stand to this day.

I sent this to Reuter marked Rush, but the night-subs ignored it, stumbling out of El Vino to tell the reading public that a giant footprint, two and a half million years old, had been unearthed near Mansfield. Measuring about a yard across, it had the power to turn hacks into palaeontologists eagerly explaining that the North Sea once lapped round Mansfield when the place was alive with amphibious squirrels, eighty feet high and bounding about like kangaroos.

This was to ignore the facts. Natives of Mansfield have always boasted large feet, and the footprint was none other than that of Albert Talbot, mayor of the town in the delightfully warm summer of 1907.

The Road to Athy

I WAS driving through Ireland when a man stepped out of a hedge and walked into the road with his arms stretched out. I was feeling like starch-reduced bread, very weightless, a consequence of spending the night before with some people and a lot of little tots of whisky which if you'd poured them all into a bath would have washed a baby. I couldn't run him down, so I stopped.

He was brown all over and he had a cap six inches thick on his head, like a cake. He put his head through the window, but I couldn't understand what he was saying, so he kept repeating himself until I got myself into the flow of the words – he was a Corkman – at the same speed as the current. He wanted to go to a place called Athy.

I'd been rehearsing the pronunciation of this word for some time, covering a lot of ground but just missing 'A Tie', which on this man's evidence it turned out to be. It was twenty-two miles ahead on the direct route. I hadn't even the guts to lie, so I told him to jump in.

But I didn't tell him to jump in off-handedly like that, I said, 'Of course, of course, step in, step in,' like a zombie in a television commercial pretending to be hearty. I opened the door and he got in, but instead of crouching fearfully in his own corner like an Englishman he sat bang in the middle of the seat and crowded me hard over to the side. Decent man, he didn't want to ask someone a favour then embarrass him by being stand-offish.

But the mock-welcome didn't fool him, he got the stink of my separateness very quickly, it must have got up his nostrils like acid, so that in the first thirty seconds or so of the companionship he was forced into thinking up some polite general topic – a manœuvre he wouldn't have put upon his worst enemy – inside which I might feel easy enough to communicate.

'Have ye got falsh teeth?' he roared.

The current was running strong. I felt in mortal danger of dashing myself on the rocks and drowning.

I said, 'What? What?'

'Falsh teeth, falsh teeth,' he shouted, for a Corkman always speaks accusingly, 'have ye got falsh teeth?'

I thought, good God, he's spotted them. I've got false teeth, two of them, they show up in ultra-violet light, I know they do because it happened once at an exhibition at the Science Museum, two nasty black gaps.

I said with a blush, expecting him to hit me or throw himself out, 'They are all mine, except two.'

I thought wait a minute, it isn't the false ones, it's the nasty look of the others. I should have said they were all false and only two real.

He reached into his mouth and pulled out two sets of the biggest teeth in the world and banged them sternly on the dashboard.

'With those in your mouth,' he said, 'you wouldn't know the difference between a Friday and a Monday if ye hadn't the aid of a calendar.'

We drove ten miles in silence. He'd made the effort. I was whirled this way and that in the deep stream of the man's presence and I hadn't been able to respond.

I grabbed an overhanging branch at the ten-mile mark, I said, 'You haven't had them long.'

'Eight years,' he replied.

We spoke hardly at all after that. I said had there been snow and he said yes, last Thursday. Then he threw me a life-line, a second chance to behave like a human being. 'And where were you last Thursday?' he bellowed. But my humanity was paralysed and all I could say was, 'Ah – at home.'

He didn't bother with me any more, he must have seen me as a poor sort of creature, an odd man out such as ancient mariners marooned on desert islands. At one point on the outskirts of Athy he pointed to a place in the hedge where a double-decker bus had fallen twenty feet and landed on its wheels so that the driver had driven on across the fields to the next crossroads. But I knew he was feeding me novelty and my guilt increased.

'And now you see Athy,' he said as we drove into the middle of the fair day there. He asked me which handle he pulled to let himself out and after one or two false starts he got the door open.

'God bless you,' he said, and I said the only proper thing I'd said in all the twenty-two miles – 'Good luck.' I think I said it in the way the Irish often say it, which is to say I meant it. He was down in the road by this time and as I drove off I spotted him in the driving mirror, watching me go, as if for the first time he knew there was a human being at the wheel.

I watched him and knew that he'd shown me the prized false teeth, offered me his individuality, in the way he'd thought I'd understand, and I'd been scared. I thought these thoughts as I drove on, and they are the reason the road to Athy will always be a sad road for me.

O to Scz

SOME thirty years ago I wrote a nine-word sentence to put into the mouth of a rather nervous inspector of police. This was in a detective novel I called *Landscape with Dead Dons* and although it's in print to this very day I little thought that the sentence I'm talking about would have its immortality ensured, even to the crack of doom.

What were these spectacular words? Something worthy of an imperishable condition, something on the lines of 'The world is everything that is the case' or 'An ounce of civet, good apothecary, to sweeten my imagination'? Some pithy apothegm of the Schopenhaurian order, something grandly opaque after the style of 'Get with child a mandrake root'? Judge for yourself when I tell you the nine magic words were 'Pity we got off to such a duff start'.

I could do better, I *have* done better, but it isn't quality that gets you walled up alive in the Oxford English Dictionary, just provenance. The sentence was quoted as a source, to bring heartsease to all who were worrying about the currency of the unresplendent word 'duff': their anxiety could be allayed by turning to the word and noting that one R. Robinson gave it a bit of a push in 1956.

That was supplement A to G, and I was rather tickled when Robert Burchfield, who has now brought the entire new edition of the OED to triumphant completion, pointed the fact out to me. There are a few other shards from the same book scattered through the Dictionary, but he has no record of their location: one day I'll set out with a metal detector to see if I can find another lucky ha'penny.

Shall I come across myself among the rude words that were first admitted via the supplement O to Scz? My own feeling is that language is indivisible, and that hiving the rude words off into specialist dictionaries not only divides communication, it divides the people who communicate. But then again, I'm not quite easy about the rude words being given this on-the-record status: *off* the record is their natural state – how rude can a rude word go on being, once its been taken account of? C. T. Onions, an earlier editor, wouldn't put them in because he said it wasn't possible to know their derivations, which was another way of saying the rude usages are here today and gone tomorrow. But all language is an eternal flux, and dictionaries being museums of language, all the words should be gathered up and put on exhibition. Dictionaries are histories, not guides to usage.

Slang was once perceived as a separate entity, the lingo of a tribe you didn't belong to but which you could patronize. When O to Scz came out I thought I detected a touch of this lingering on, in that the colloquial being suddenly so much in evidence, was it being sucked-up to? Disc-jockeys do it all the time, recommending themselves to the customers with absurd calcified variations on the way they think ordinary people speak – had the OED fallen prey to the same promotional values, anxious to let purchasers know it contained *their* sort of word?

But again, what is a dictionary to do? It could be argued that it exists to record the indispensable words, the ones which are in common owner-ship because nobody can do without them. Does this mean it leaves out the specialist words which 90 per cent of us have no use for? Certain variants of the meaning of the word 'pussy' will find no place in the vocabulary of the Archbishop of Canterbury, and some of the more rari-fied theological terms won't be much use to the rest of us. But this is ridiculously exclusive. Part of the function of a dictionary is to satisfy mere curiosity: you just might want to look up aposeopesis because the whim took you. But if on this ground specialist words are to be included, are *all* specialist words to be included? Is this even possible?

Not so simple. And how is the line drawn when it comes to foreign words? Why is the locution 'put-on' included, when its sources and its currency are exclusively North American (would you expect to find 'leg-pull' in an American dictionary?) Further down the page we find 'puttony' to be a Hungarian word for a basket made of staves and wickerwork that is used to transfer grapes from the vineyard to the wine-press. But why don't we also have the Hungarian word for bicycle or even sexual intercourse, which in a purely utilitarian consideration might be of more help in that country than the right word for a basket in which grapes are carried?

Sometimes successful new candidates cause as much pain as the

debutants admitted to *Who's Who*. *Not* old so-and-so – God, he's unbearable! For instance, 'ongoing', a fancy piece of plastic which is accepted
as legal tender in some circles, when coin of the realm is the word 'continuing'. And the unspeakable 'parameter', which once had a specific meaning
in the science of crystallography and was robbed of it in 1976 by a
jargonizing secretary to the Cabinet. Yet time has poulticed the eruptions
of earlier days. Who could bear 'rimbellisher', a neologism of the early
Fifties descriptive of circles of chrome that supposedly embellished the
rims of the wheels of motor-cars? Now, with the nerve of its currency
extracted, it seems perfectly harmless.

All the variations of 'plonk' are in, save Stephen Potter's excellent
'plonking', descriptive of a flat blancmange-like interruption designed
to spoil the flow of someone else's conversation. If the OED is going
to include useless Hungarian words, it should strive first to get in all
the useful English ones. And in a book so attentive to coarse usage I
take the omission of 'pork sword' and 'mutton dagger' to be an oversight.

Am I unduly touchy in finding the exclusion of 'sardony' somewhat
officious? I once publicly inferred the existence of this noun on the basis
of the adjective 'sardonic' – had to, since no suitable substantive is available – hoping to give it currency. But what we have in the OED is
the ridiculous coinage 'sardonicism' which is, in the precise sense, preposterous since it is derived *backwards* from the adjective, thus breaching
the dictionary's own rules. Marks have been deducted.

Of all the arrant beggarly lousy stinking linguistic rip-offs (*qv*) the
very worst of all finds its place in 'workshop', as debauched by the PR
gang. 'Class', 'lecture', 'seminar', 'talk', 'play-reading' are thought to be
terms that are too woolly for comfort and are abandoned in favour of
'workshop' with its aura of skill and precision. Enthusiasts find the word
irresistible, especially those who like to dip a toe into the composing
of verse or the putting on of plays, or even fatheads seeking to improve
their conversation with a touch of the sociological. The object is to mask
simple incompetence. 'Workshop' with its suggestion of something tang-
ible that can be measured, hints artfully at an end product when it doesn't
exist, and the use of artisan terminology is felt to confer special authenti-
city. 'Workshop' is the worst sort of theft, in that it is counterfeit.

Picking up my metal-detector, I set off for the interior of the OED,
knowing I shall encounter any number of such Gorgon's heads before
ever I run across another lucky ha'penny.

Lost November

I WAS in a stationer's shop where I was buying, on the strict understanding it was the poorest and cheapest, a ream of typing paper. In came a small mouselike lady bearing in her hand a small dog-eared pocket diary. She waved it in front of the white-haired whiskery beldam in a flowered overall who should by rights not have been running a stationer's shop but offering slightly too little for slightly too much in a tea-shop in Knutsford, and then spoke up in a timid thin South African voice: 'I'm sorry,' said Miss Mouse, waving the book about under the nose of the lady stationer, who now I think of it looked like Admiral Jellicoe, 'I'm sorry, but this diary you sold me has no November.' The Admiral, sensing mutiny, said, 'Well what's the good of bringing it back now when you bought it last January?' Miss Mouse said, smiling sadly, 'I'm sorry about that too, but when you buy a diary you don't read it through to make sure it's got November – you assume it's got the full twelve months, not eleven, and what can you do when you get to November and find it isn't there?' The First Sea Lord leant over the counter in her pinny and said sepulchrally, 'Happily, nothing whatever happens in November – at least,' she added, 'not in South-West One.' Miss Mouse burst into tears, and I made an excuse and left. I can't think which moved me more – the vulnerability of Miss Mouse (eleven-month diaries only happen to people like her) or the cheek of the Admiral.

The Fête

Every Saturday afternoon, all through the summer, the Member had to go and open a fête.

'I don't know whether you've ever seen one of those chromium-plated cake-stands, have you? Only at Zeeta's – quite. Well, we won one. Not exactly the sort of thing you can give anyone as a present, so we thought we'd donate it to the next fête. And do you know –' the Member studied me keenly, wondering if I was going to grasp that what he had to tell me next lay at the heart of the matter – 'We won the bloody thing again.'

We drove on through north Oxfordshire. Some spring of melancholy had been broached, and the Member said, 'I remember them all in terms of fuchsias. Loads and loads of fuchsias in pots, blowing over in the wind. You always have to buy one. Sometimes,' he said, 'they give you a great big carnation with five feet of fern adhering. They jam it into your buttonhole, and the fern tickles your chin all day.' He paused, dwelling on what he'd said. 'Fuchsias first, then women behind tea-urns, festooned in steam.'

We made for Charlbury. The fête was being held at the Marquis's place. He wouldn't be there, but he let them use his grounds.

'I once tied with the Marquis's butler, you know – bowling for the pig. Bowled and bowled, and finally got it. We fattened the pig, and then –' a spark which had kindled at the memory of the contest flickered and died ' – we gave the proceeds to Party funds.' He glanced briefly at me again, as though we'd run up against another of the basic principles and he didn't want me to miss it. 'If you win anything good, you've got to give it back.'

Then he said, 'Jam. Jars and jars of jam. We're not a jam-eating family, as it happens, but you have to buy it. You have to buy everything,' he said, 'but my wife and I have a special sort of basket, sort of long boat-shaped affair, and our tactic is to stuff two big cauliflowers either end and a jar of this jam in the middle, and really it looks as if you've swept through the place like a locust and bought the lot.'

There was a spatter of rain across the windscreen, but the sun shone through it. 'I do a five-minute opener, and about half-way through a child disconnects the amplifier, or a Voodoo jet with re-heat on comes over just as I get to the punch line. The vicar kindly leads the laughter. I keep the politics general because nobody is listening – it's a bit like a cabaret, only instead of the clash of knives and forks you get the eager hum of females settling on the jumble.'

We bumped across the Marquis's pasture. His nice house had shutters over the windows, and the swimming-pool was roped off, but his shaven lawns were being walked on by people who seemed delighted just to be doing that.

'Even get Labour people – can't resist a peep behind the lodge gates. Half the fun of it, really. Don't walled gardens make you curious? Here we are. You'll see me smiling at people rather a lot,' said the Member, getting out of the car. 'Hullo, ha, ha, ha,' he said, good as his word.

Music was winding out of the loudspeakers with that peculiar outdoor effect of being heavier than air. The Member walked across the sward, shaking hands with ladies from the village who kept laughing among themselves as though the business of encountering each other in public were somehow inexpressibly saucy. Someone wrenched the needle off the record, and it made a noise through the tannoy like a pair of trousers tearing. The Member walked on to the terrace in front of the long windows, and stood behind a trestle-table that was draped in a volum- inous Union Jack.

Said he was glad to be there. Hoped they were too. Felt sure that occasions like these were good for morale. Thought all Conservatives had a duty to go out into the highways and byways and spread the gospel. Urged everyone to lose no opportunity of 'widening the family in the good old Conservative way'. Had pleasure in declaring the fête open. Applause.

A small band beneath a mournful cypress struck up, and the rain rustled in the Marquis's elms. All the pennies at the roll'em stall clattered to the back when rolled because the stall was on a slope. 'Conditions are not ideal,' shouted a man through a megaphone, 'for weight-lifting, but Fred is going to attempt a snatch of a hundred and forty pounds.'

The Member approached the hoop-la stall. 'Sometimes you can't get away from the rostrum after the opening because an earnest, deaf, elderly constituent who has strong feelings on Afghanistan presses you up against the microphone and keeps his face very close to yours.' The hoop-la combined frivolity with perfect utility – prizes included a tin of Smedley's Golden Swede Turnips, a packet of Typhoo, and a bicycle-lamp. The Member won some Elizabeth Lazenby Portuguese Sardines. 'Actually, they were the only sort we were allowed as children.'

In a light rain, the folk-dancers waited patiently with their heads raised, while the tannoy ground through two wrong tunes and started on a third. 'I'm very sorry, ladies and gentlemen, but I keep getting it on to an inappropriate section of the record,' the announcer said. But one of the dancers ran off and fixed it for him, and then they did a dance, dressed in orange skirts and velvet waistcoats, while a small child took a picture of them, using a Box Brownie left over from the days when radio was called the wireless.

The Member ate a large dog-eared egg-sandwich the size of a pocket handkerchief, and tucked under his arm a bottle of Super-Active Nimbus, a pair of socks, and a coat-hanger covered in yellow knitting. The grass had a sweet, mashed smell, and it blended with heavier, more languorous exhalations rolling across the pasture from the hedges of box. The band, with unaggressive devotion, played 'Ye Banks and Braes of Bonny Doon', and the sound that came out of their silver instruments was pleasant for its very diffidence. Everyone smiled, pleased with their own presence, and pleased with the presence of everyone else.

I bought the Member a jam-sponge, and left with the sort of regret I could never have predicted.

A Room with a Leak

I HAD to go to New York to interview some people, and the hotel I stayed at seemed as unlike a natural shelter as one of those giant toadstools pixies sit under. Built on a scale to dwarf the Grand Canyon, the foyer was lavishly equipped with marble grottoes, brawling streams and so many enchanted groves that as I passed through one of them I stumbled across a man with goat feet trying to find a nine-hole golf-course.

My billet was on the top floor of this ziggurat, a modest single apartment featuring, in addition to the bedroom, two bathrooms and a drawing-room which was a stretched version of the *grand salon* at Londonderry House. It was all terribly dislocating, like living in one of those frigid labyrinths that Borges writes about, but one night I was sitting at the edge of the three-acre carpet, gibbering with anomie and agoraphobia, when I felt a splash of water on my nose.

I looked up, and saw to my intense delight that the roof was leaking! I leapt to the door to lock it, in case the management should appear with a plumber and by plugging the leak extinguish my only link with reality. For the rest of my stay I slept like a baby, falling asleep to the comforting sound of rain dripping into a waste-paper basket.

I did the decent thing when I checked out. 'Your roof leaks', I said to the man who was conjuring my bill from the computer. He turned pale. 'How can we ever apologize?' he cried. 'No, no, you don't understand,' I said, 'I simply wanted to thank you.'

Landscape with Water Diviner

THE dowser cut a hazel fork from the hedgerow. 'My brother lost an eye in a hedge, the twig snaked out like a long little finger and his eye ran out down his cheek.' The Shropshire hills sat up in the blue distance like a romantic landscape, lacking only the broken columns and the ladies with the uncontrollable garments. The dowser gripped each end of the fork with his palms inward, as if he were trying to push something back into a box.

'These here underground streams run out towards the rising sun, but why it is, is a question I can't answer.' He walked jerkily, as if one time or another he had been cut out of a hedge himself. He had a smallholding on the next hill, but his long face would have looked right on a painter. He had hair on his cheekbones.

'I've had dozens and dozens of watches, I have a silver watch upstairs this minute. None of them go. They go a couple of days then stop. I clean them and oil them, but they won't work.'

The diviner stopped where the grass was lush. The angle subtended by the two branches of the fork rose imperceptibly from the horizontal.

'There's water in this old field, but where's the best place for it?'

He stood still in the field while the countryside went on making its alarums – lambs whirred like self-starters, cows bawled, bees were supplying electricity to the hemisphere. Even the blossom effervesced on the trees like fireworks and the dandelions were too loud.

'It was many years ago when I was in poor health. I was sitting on a bank behind the hawthorn with Harry Styles. We were hedging and it was ever so hot. I picked up a bit of wire. "Harry," I said, "it's so hot this here wire's sticking to my hand." Harry said, "Turn that bit of wire round into a horseshoe, there's water under here."'

The diviner walked to the corner of the field. 'The ravens and the car'on crows have been killing my lambs. They dash 'em in the eye then stick their bills down the soft part of the sheep's head like a knife right down into the brain. I had two killed while I was at my dinner middle day.'

The birds whistled coarsely like old-time errand boys.

'When Harry and I went back for our tea I was shaking and trembling. I felt sort of hazy for an hour or more. That's the only way I can describe it. I said to Harry afterwards, "Did I spill my tea?" After that I found water on four farms but I can't tell the depth. I'm only an *armateur*.'

In the middle of the field, the fork came up. 'Push it down, sir, push it down, see if you can push it down.' The diviner bit his lip as if he were trying to close a suitcase against heavy odds, but the fork rose. There was a pressure under the twig as if all the water in Shropshire were rising through the earth against it.

'It's by feeling the pressure on the rod that you can tell whether there's a lot or a little. There's a lot in this old field.'

The diviner was sweating. He held the twig down at either end, but above his fists the fork was striking up at him. A couple of seconds later the torque became too strong, the upper sections of the rod twisted against the lower sections which were held in the man's hand, and there was a snap as both limbs splintered.

'I've seen diviners use television aerials. Whalebone does it. I used a whalebone but he was so sensitive on me he jerked all the way down the road and broke before ever I got near the water. Some hold the rod up by their shoulders' – he held the twig like a lyre – 'but I never got the knack.'

Electricity of some sort? Water being a good conductor of electricity. But does that mean that there is electricity wherever there's water? Even then, there is earth between the man and the water. Is hazel a conductor? And if to him, why not to me?

'I never learnt a trade,' said the dowser, 'but I can lay a brick, shoe

a horse or carpenter with any man. I can slaughter. I can crop and pleach
and stake and pleach, I take pupils in hedging. There are few jobs I
detest, but of those few, picking potatoes is the worst.

'I have divined silver. I divined a half-crown that had been buried
in a mole-tump, buried for the purpose, of course. But I found it.'

We stood under a glaring, brumey sky, where trees surged down into
a small valley and squares of red plough alternated with green pasture.
The land didn't belong to the dowser, but he belonged to it. My status
as spectator gave me but little satisfaction.

Oddity

DETAILS of the edible Japanese credit card are now to hand. They cost
eighty pence for two, and come in eight flavours, shrimp, beef, jam,
honey, apple, banana, cocoa and coffee. I thought – and I still think
– coloured lavatory-paper to be the weirdest option ever to have suggested
itself to the human mind, but a digestible credit card runs it close. Here
we have the consumer society made manifest – you actually eat the money.
The creators of this novel titbit ensure continuous consumption because,
as your mouth waters and you prepare to devour the succulent plastic,
you must first use it to buy other cards before falling to, then use each
of the new cards in the same way so that the process is perpetual. I
foresee theses on the peristalsic cycle of the Japanese credit card : 'Dangers
of combining bankruptcy with stomach ache' – A Doctor Writes.

What is so appealing about oddity is its completeness. It can't be translated, reduced or enlarged. As dawn broke over the television set the
other morning I heard a lady presenter say 'I wonder if you've ever
thought about hernia?' *Hernia – sa plage, son piscine, ses vues pittoresques.*
And at lunch time that same day a man leaned across and said, 'I was
walking through Soho just now and I passed a door with a brass plate
on it, and on the brass plate were inscribed the words 'The Holy Roman
Empire Pension Fund'. I cried, 'You made that up,' and he said, 'Sir,
we both know such things are beyond the power of anyone to make up.'

Perfectly true. For only the previous week, I had bought an ice-cream cornet from a stall on a Dorset beach, and taped to the window there was a notice written in italic script which announced 'Ice-creams cannot be exchanged.' Would anyone have gone to the lengths of producing such a notice unless attempts to exchange ice-creams had become epidemic? But on what grounds would you seek to exchange an ice cream? That it was the wrong size, you didn't like the colour, it didn't go with the curtains? And by the time you brought it back, it would have started to drip.

The television director who was my companion on that occasion said it was the unassailable self-sufficiency of the odd which defeated any attempt at explanation, and he referred me to the notice in Shepherd's Bush which simply says 'Learn to dance quickly'. He said he liked that, and so do I; there is something about the words that rises above either of the-two possible meanings, and seems to be trying to say something that cannot be said.

As when an actor friend told me how he was listening to the conversation of two American women in Kensington High Street in 1968. Pontings was still extant, along with Barkers, and Derry and Toms, and as the two women stood taking in the noble facades of these unforgettable shops, one turned to the other and said, 'I don't know what Mildred was talking about – its not a bit like Venice.'

'Probably the same two women I flew up from Miami to New York with,' said my lunch time companion. 'They had the two inside seats, and when the steward came round to ask whether they'd have red wine or white, the one nearest the window said, "It makes no difference to me, I'm colour-blind".'

A Touch of the Elemental

THE air on the Quantock Hills is full of grey. Where does it all come from? Perhaps that's what Stonehenge is for, a secret factory making greyness which is distributed via the cows who breathe it into the air on cold mornings. It sticks in the hedges and a man with a hedging-knife beats it out like dust from a carpet.

In this mist on a common an empty cement bag hangs on a piece of rope tied for no clear reason to a tree, and it swings like a hanged man. This is not a day when we shall feel our spirits challenged by the sunshine, this is a day we shall all easily be better than.

The stag-hunters met at a lane's end, sitting on tall horses which weren't really tall but being part of a world – such was the quality of the morning – which had been stripped down to the elemental, shared with the ragged farmyards, the hillsides, the woods, the bracken dying in a brown welter, an illusion of extra size. The riders sat like statues and if they wore black jackets with slits up the back and clean breeches and shiny boots, yet there was a something about the day which translated the clothes into shaggy bearskins and wristbands of copper and the bowler-hats put out wings and were helmets.

The hounds grouped, sad, not elevated, feeling the single claim of their blood, to hunt a stag. There was a black wood beyond and as the hounds moved down into the valley with one horseman there was more of Beowulf than Jorrocks in the scene –

> *It is not far as miles are marked that the mere stands.*
> *Where rime-covered woods rooted in earth*
> *Hang over the dark water –*

'There,' said a boy who stood like a sentinel on the opposite hill, waiting for the hounds to draw the holt-wood, 'that hole in thik hedge – he will come out of the wood and up the slope and bound through that hole until he can reach the common above. But if he reach the common where the mist do lie, they've lost him.'

Earth was scattered in the lane where the stags had crossed in the night.

'A stag will run all day,' said the boy, 'a stag will run fifty mile and then stand to bay with his head lowered. A hind stamps, but a stag to bay faces the hounds with his horns down.'

There was no sound from the black woods across the valley. Then a roaring – 'Haaaaa – ' that resounded like the clang of metal through the mist, and the hounds screamed. Had they found, not a stag, but Grendel – the shadow-ganger, the marsh-stepper – had *they* been flushed?

'The huntsman is after a hind, not a stag. They want to keep the breeding in balance,' said the boy. 'If they kill the right one – they call it "taking" not killing – they preserve the beasts and that's a fine thing,' the boy said, 'for they'm lovely animals provided they don't get too mischeevious.'

Then across the valley the hounds trailed through the trees like a skein of sausages and out at the water's edge ran a hind with her calf –

> *Though the heath-stepper by the hounds sore-pressed – harried*
> *from far, the hart strong of horn –*
> *may fly into the forest, he will faint on the brink,*
> *let his life go, ere he enter that lake –*

The hind skirted the water, and raced up the nearer slope.

'Quiet,' said the boy, 'get your bliddy head down or she'll jump on it.'

Hind and calf sailed through the hedge, loped up the top half of the nearer hill. The hounds came after, fifteen couple. 'Bigger than foxhounds,' said the boy, 'why, some of these hounds might eat a fox for breakfast.'

The boy said, 'The calf will drop out soon enough.' He looked at the horses following. 'A blood horse from the Shires couldn't get up these slopes – fourteen two, or up to fifteen, say, that's the size you want.'

The boy went round by a cart-track to get to the common on top of the hills. Half-way up he stopped to listen. A brook sounded as if it were digesting the stones it ran over. Birds flew up out of some trees near the skyline. 'That's where they are,' the boy said.

He had a greyhound with him, he used it for coursing hares. The greyhound nosed into mildewing woods, dark colonnaded halls, vistas of dark green columns that regressed into infinite gloom where, when the greyhound scratched the bark, the onlooker thought 'I have seen this picture before.'

The mist hung in stalactites from what depths in the sky. On the common, on the top of the hill, the horn wound into the air from the horizon where the horsemen moved slowly away until they sank below the rim of the world and the boy and the greyhound and the onlooker stood in a cloud of their own steam, watching the light go out of the sky and the night-helm come down.

'Thik hind has gone,' the boy said. 'They won't catch it now, though it live for a thousand years.'

Laughing in the Wrong Place

LAUGHING is at its most delicious when it is strictly forbidden. Dacre Balsdon, archetypal Oxford-don, was once reminiscing about his days as a schoolmaster. He was on the staff of a school whose headmaster was a man called Weech. One day a chap came down to lecture on bird-song, interspersing his narrative with imitations of the sort of sounds the birds made, every one of which was a modulation of the headmaster's name.

The Greater Crested Woodhatch went '*Weechy-weechy-weechy*' in a low insinuating coaxing tone, the Lesser Tufted Spadger insanely warbled '*Wee-HEE-eech – wee-HEE-eech*', and the Spotted Cootbill, more peremptorily, bellowed like a Sergeant-Major '*WEECH! WEECH!*' Not a boy so much as smiled, and Balsdon said he felt the whole school should have been given a medal.

How different from my own youth, when hobbledehoys as we were we would cruise from girl's house to girl's house, where everything said by their parents seemed capable of double or even treble meanings. We had to have a banal joke at the ready to refer to quickly before the incipient laugh took over – what a feeble sense of humour the parents must have thought we had, as we roared away, the tears rolling down our cheeks. That the parents always seemed to be voicing sexual innuendos of which they were entirely unaware was a product of our own shameful knowledge that our intentions were impure and dishonourable, and the laughter was hysterical.

But when it's forbidden, it always is. A friend of mine, lately arrived from Hungary, got a job reading the news in the Hungarian service at Bush House. One evening in the office he was running through the script which he saw contained an item about a newly-developed Chinese rocket. It was not a nuclear device but one which had ordinary explosive in the warhead.

It happens that the word for 'explosive' in Hungarian is very nearly the same – differing by one letter – as another word which means something else. He made a joke about this to the girl who was typing the script, and she said you shouldn't have said that, you might say it while you're reading the news.

And, of course, he did. He said 'A new Chinese rocket has been developed which does not have a nuclear warhead but is filled with ordinary horse shit.' Well, the man kept on reading, sweat pouring from him in his efforts not to collapse with laughter. As he said, what made his inclination to laugh all but uncontrollable was saying *ordinary* horse shit, as though there were also a special sort they hadn't got round to using yet. At the back of his mind as he read on, this began to seem more and more convincing; Chinese culture being a very ancient one, what was more likely than that they'd known of the explosive properties of horse shit for thousands of years and were looking forward to conquering the West by smothering it in a new and improved variety!

When he finished the broadcast, he actually passed out with the strain of containing his hysteria, but he says those were dark days in Hungary, and he liked to think of the citizens of Buda or even Pest, rolling round the streets and for a few happy minutes, crying with forbidden laughter.

Of Myth and Men

C*APITALISM* in all its naked purity was stationed outside the Royal Festival Hall in the shape of a man who offered me a ten-guinea ticket for £200. His coat came down to his ankles, a garment – he explained – which kept him warm o' nights when he was rounding up cats for the vivisectionist.

Boys and girls, one lad in a crash-helmet, thronged the forecourt and the halls and the staircases, waiting for reality to put forth flowers, or explode. A gang of sports with no tickets were leading a stealthy assault on the scenery-block, but were headed off by the bogies.

Within the auditorium the atmosphere was strongly revivalist, though smelling of scent. 'Show me your tickets, show me your tickets,' screamed an excited usher as they played the National Anthem. 'Look here, my old sir,' said a lad of seventeen standing at the back, 'you don't think I've come all the way here just to show you my ticket, do you?' The front rows were black with mohair, where the celebrities sat.

Down went the lights and the musicians came on. Up with the lights again, pink, yellow and blue, and a comedian ran up to the microphone. 'He's going to Norfolk because he's heard so much about the Broads.' A lady sang, the comedian joked, a disc-jockey said it was the proudest moment of his life, and along alone at last came Frank Sinatra, while the people clapped as though a fairy-tale had come true.

I once went to Monte Carlo with a bunch of journalists who thought they were going to meet Frank Sinatra. He was singing at the Sporting Club and we filed obediently in under the red eye of Bluff Hal, the PRO. Well, I heard him sing, but the closest I came to making contact with him was a pale-faced supernumerary who accosted me with the kindly query, 'Are you getting enough to drink?' Then we all flew back again, like a herd of cows.

I saw him again, crouched on a chair in a tiny room in a London hotel, surrounded by journalists. It looked like a sort of crap game, with Sinatra the human dice, refusing to roll. I could just see the top of his scalp, gleaming pinkly through the hair, as I stood tiptoe and craned over the shoulder of an eager colleague. Then he got up and walked out.

In private life if someone turns his back on you I don't suppose you give him a chance to do it twice. But though show-business reporters grumble when they are snubbed, at obscurer levels they are experiencing an intestinal shudder of satisfaction – preparatory to lying down and letting the man do it again. For they know – obscurely – that they are playing their part: the perpetual holding-off, the continuous distancing of public contact, is essential to myth. Myth is the staple of a certain kind of journalism.

It is easier to write about myths than to write (or fail to write) about men. Myths are added to, subtracted from, without any one minding dreadfully. Myths are staged at a moment's notice, like circuses. Performer, journalist, PRO, feel in their bones that it is their mutual interest to expand or contract the myth – the muzzy article of belief – which is found in the cuttings: but heretical to question its premises. Over Fleet Street and the posh hotels the *muezzin* rises, and fabulous, spellbinding, mink-lined, controversial, glittering, no comment, secret, angry, stunning, lovable, open-necked, million-dollar, rhubarb, signals the green surrender.

People seek attention indiscriminately when they first become performers, they seek ratification of their identity from anyone who will give it to them. Later, they have taps installed, and the public is turned on and off. Later still, they start to hoard themselves.

They are surrounded by portable societies, collapsible worlds – managers, secretaries, front men, fixers. The performer feels he must save himself for the performance, keep himself in the emotional bank until the time for expenditure is ripe. But the saving spirit is contagious, and those on the periphery of his affairs become emotional misers. The fixer who a week ago might have contested the title of Most Available Man in Town is suddenly incommunicado.

I think Sinatra has the sort of voice which always sounds as if it will be better the day after tomorrow. At the Festival Hall, he seemed to hold the mike too close so that the voice blared from the amplifier at fairground pitch. But what he has got is the capacity to call every last fraction of himself in from the four corners of his consciousness and deposit the concentrate instantaneously.

To find out what you are, then be it. I think this is what all performers are trying to do, whether they cut figures of eight on the ice or offer their Lear in modern dress. Success at this sort of thing depends on how much real self you can lay your hands on. But if, like Sinatra, you are utterly present, for that moment you are the only person in the world.

Placement

ONE weekend the editor's notes in *The Spectator* entertained me more than usually. The editor – a Mr Moore – and his wife had gone to stay at a posh hotel in Morocco, and were pleased to find their choice of accommodation endorsed, in that there were also present a Member of Parliament and his wife, the editor of the magazine *Harper's & Queen*, and Mr and Mrs John Profumo. In letting you know the class of person he found himself hobnobbing with, Mr Moore did not, I think, wholly succeed in removing the reader's suspicion that – delightful as his fellow guests must have been – they weren't quite the First Eleven (even though Mr Moore pointed out that when swimming in the hotel pool Mr Profumo rather dashingly wore a tweed hat).

Then one morning the servants were observed feverishly blancoing the coal in the gas-fired ingle-nooks and putting a fresh coat of whitewash on the outside lavatory. I regret, said the manager to the two editors, the Member of Parliament, and to Mr and Mrs John Profumo, you will all have to clear out tomorrow, pronto, because the King is giving lunch to the President of the Cameroons and he wants the place to himself.

Sensation! Card-carrying members of the 071-*gratin*, all of whom might count on being greeted by name at the Groucho Club, treated as though their bona fides were so many Green Shield stamps! 'Does the King think he *owns* this hotel?' cried an enraged *goddam*, and the manager, snapping his fingers at the staff to get the luggage down, replied 'He thinks he owns the whole country.'

Like so many Irish immigrants newly arrived in Hammersmith, the guests were put up in temporary accommodation elsewhere. It is not clear that the Profumos availed themselves of the facility, or chose the alternative option, which was a free coach-trip. Perhaps the latter, for when they arrived back at the hotel they found their room had been ransacked. Plainly, the King had heard about Mr Profumo's tweed hat, and had sent in his meinie to see if it would fit him.

Meanwhile, the MP and his mem, opting for the inferior quarters, suffered the ultimate affront: seated by the pool at the hotel to which they had been forcibly transferred, they saw ordinary holidaymakers *arriving in charabancs and queuing for the lavatories.*

I can't remember when I've enjoyed an issue of *The Spectator* so much. Surely Mr Moore didn't expect the King of Morocco to behave like the editor of a weekly review? And yet his indignation provoked by the Monarch not according him the deference to which his contributors have accustomed him does suggest he doesn't know the old story about the tailor Henry Poole who was once invited to Chatsworth. The following Tuesday Poole was measuring up another noble customer and telling him of all the grand people he'd met at the weekend. To which the nobleman replied, 'But what did you expect, Poole? A bunch of bloody tailors?'

The Strolling Player

THE sun lit up the frosty landscape, melted the surface of the snow so that it shone like sweat on the flanks of the White Horse Hill. By the roadside six mice danced to the strains of the Savoy Orpheans as they played 'O Sing to Me, Gypsy' on a gramophone record which sounded as if it had been recorded through somebody's nose.

The mice twirled on their hind legs in a little brown cage, advancing and retreating as they auditioned under the eye of a big black dog who may have thought he was Lord Delfont. There was no human being, no member of the race in sight. Three donkeys stood at gaze under the hedgerow.

Then the record repeated itself and went 'The moon's high, the moon's high, the moon's high' and underneath a green tarpaulin which shrouded a two-wheeled trailer – the sort of trailer which people who have oil-fired central heating attach to their Vauxhall Cavaliers when they wish to transport their canoes to Ruislip Lido – something stirred.

A needle ripped across the grooves, the music stopped, the mice subsided, and a man with a beard stuck his head out of the tarpaulin as if he had just swarmed up from the centre of the earth.

After a decent interval – he had been in night-attire, that is to say fully dressed, but minus his trousers – he pulled the rest of himself from underneath the tarpaulin and was followed out by a little brown dog who may have been working the gramophone. The donkeys threw back their heads and creaked for joy like the swings in a child's playground, and the brown dog and the black dog flailed about on the snow like untended hoses, as though all the high spirits in the universe were being temporarily channelled through them.

'I play very old-time tunes to them, and they dance, see. And then the mice work the wheel,' said the man with the beard, whose name was Fred Abel, 'and I get the rats to walk the tight-rope.'

Fred Abel put his overcoat on and tied a piece of string round the middle of it.

'I get the rats to sit on the dog's nose.'

He pulled a piece of sack from another cage and lifted out two white rats. He laid them both across the muzzle of the big black dog who by this time was certain he was Lord Delfont. The dog sat there without moving and the two rats winked at each other.

'I've been stuck here the last six weeks because of the snow,' said Fred Abel. 'It gets very boring as I ain't much of a scholar and don't do no reading.

'Summer was very bad for business – I done a few flower-shows, but what's flower-shows? I did take seven quid one afternoon at a gymkhana in Farringdon – of course that was donkey-rides included as well as the performing. But generally it was nasty wet days. I had a bit by me – spend a shilling, save a shilling – otherwise I don't know what I'd have done.'

He took corn to the donkeys and they nodded excitedly.

'My mother was a very shrewd woman, so was my father, he was an engine-driver and was in the Boer War. I had an uncle was an old-time fair-man, he had a five-legged pony show, but he was rough, very rough, rougher than what I am. I've always wandered. I started with the donkeys, then I set up with two piebald rats and started myself as a proper one-man circus.

'I prefer performing in halls in towns, there ain't much money in the country. No, not pubs. I never perform in pubs – some people like it, some don't, see. No, I don't play no instrument, though Mother played the accordion, but I do dance with Towser. Towser's the black 'un, he's eight now and he's as good as gold.'

The rats, whose names were Ruth and Jacob, were walking up and down Towser's back.

I just go through the country at three mile an hour never going up the hills when I can go round 'em. My life is hard but regular. I have an ambition to get a four-wheel trailer and then I wouldn't call the king my uncle.'

Mr Abel hummed abstractedly, looking askance over his shoulder every now and again in case he should spot anyone sneaking up on him with any of those burdens that he had devoted a lifetime to side-stepping.

He picked the rats off the dog's back and put them back in their box.

'Rats go thin when they're old. I don't think about old age. Not really. Anyway, I might be lucky.'

The dirty black sky, which had been screwed down on country and city like the lid of a coffin, had fallen away that morning, and when Fred Abel danced with his dog at the roadside the sun shone as though it were the resurrection of the world.

Washing the Wigs

A SLIGHTLY surreal experience stays with me. I contrived to enter the apartment of a publisher in Paris by way of the cellars – looking back, this must have taken a bit of doing, but at the time I saw no other way in, and concluded the man forced his visitors to pass through a sort of hulks that dripped like Wapping Old Stairs, and then ascend in a sort of dumb-waiter designed to hold garbage, in obedience to some interior-decorator's whim. But of course I'd just got it wrong, and when I fell out of the dumb-waiter into the kitchen I was greeted by a man-servant in black trousers and green apron who – no doubt to distract me from my embarrassment – resorted to general topics, and said in a kindly way – or at least I thought he said – 'I have just been washing the wigs.' Shaking the cabbage stalks out of my turn-ups, I followed him to the drawing-room, wondering if he meant his own wig and that of his employer. Or was it that his employer had many wigs, one perhaps for each day of the week? Would they be steaming in front of the drawing-room fire? My host laughed politely when he heard of my odd entry, no doubt supposing that in entering via the waste-disposal unit I had been exercising a peculiarly English form of humour. My mind running on the wig problem, I suddenly wondered if it wasn't the word 'peruke' I'd heard but the word *'perroquets'* – perhaps what the man had said was 'I have just been washing the parrots.' This seemed even less likely until I looked down and saw one of these amiable birds shambling towards me over the Aubusson. It looked purposefully at me, hopped on to my knee, and whistled the Marseillaise from first note to last. When I told someone about these events, he simply said, 'No, not parrot – parakeet,' as though this was the only bit that interested him. But when I left the apartment, I felt I was walking out of a picture by Magritte or Delvaux.

Ivy

I'M not sure whether the word *was* a misprint or not, but in an article about Ivy Compton Burnett I think they meant to say the word 'books' when they said 'Her books are as perfect as pieces of music – you couldn't improve them.' But what actually got printed was 'Her *looks* are as perfect as pieces of music – you couldn't improve them.' As I say, it might not be a misprint, but when you recall that Dame Ivy looked like Austen Chamberlain wearing a bird's nest, there is room for doubt.

Don't Lose the Receipt

I IMAGINE anyone entering the Playboy Club feels he isn't quite as other men are, and on going into the gift shop – one of those vast silent places selling items in raffia and glass alongside the pedestrian walkways of provincial cities – I found I turned my collar up and pulled my hat well down as though my errand was somehow shameful.

What I wanted was a paper cup to drink out of while I was eating my sandwiches, and there was just a chance they had one. But once I was inside the atmosphere was so inauspicious I lost my nerve and found myself muttering to the girl as though I was trying to buy condoms. She pointed vaguely through the acres of perspex shelving, lit by the sort of strip-lighting that throws no shadows and in whose cold glare the best of friends become strangers.

I walked across and found a tea-cup in the form of a jar of Marmite, and beside it a tumbler into whose integument a pink liquid had been sealed; when the glass was raised to the lips a snowstorm of white flakes floated up the sides. There was another which came complete with a straw; the straw was stuck through the base then coiled round the outside of the glass until it ended in a snake's head at the rim – you filled the glass and sucked the snake's head and the liquid swirled up like venom. I thought sod it, I'll drink from the bottle.

On the way out I saw a table-sized version of a French onion-seller's bike, cast in pewter complete with onions, and was struck with wonder; what facial expression would be appropriate to the receipt of such a gift? 'Phyllis, Phyllis, come quick, someone's sent us a model of an onion-seller's bicycle', and I picture Phyllis's worried frown as she hurries into the dining-area, hoping the excitement won't be too much for Jim's asthma. There was a second version of this particular gift, another bicycle, but this time with a tiny ladder and a bucket and a cloth, and I hesitated – there was a risk that the window-cleaner's bike might seem to hint at Jim's humble beginnings, whereas even Phyllis couldn't think I was suggesting he'd once been an onion-seller. Better play safe, though – perhaps one of those miniature toasters you put your finger-tips into to dry your nail-varnish.

Yet a certain wistfulness lingered about some of the items – how hopeful the man who thought-up the decorative pin for your kilt! In vain they warned him of the narrowness of the market – even among those who actually wear kilts how many will be willing to break new ground with a pin that has Dumbo as its principal motif? I see the creator smile with quiet confidence as he reminds them that there were those who doubted the staying power of the musical toilet seat.

Moving past the battery-powered spaghetti forks, I thought there was something wrong with a shop that retailed a category as though it were an article, and since gifts cannot be pre-selected such places exist for those who won't accept the danger that giving something entails. To buy something already labelled 'gift' is like going to the Zoo to shoot tigers.

I bought a pencil-holder in the shape of a pair of buttocks, just to prove I was a gentleman, and the thought that went with me as I left (you get one free with every purchase) was that it must be very lowering to the spirits to work in a shop where you sell nothing that any customer is going to keep for himself. I passed on the buttocks with the pencil sticking out of them to a cab-driver in lieu of a tip, and to judge from the honest fellow's wholly unfeigned response, it was a present he wasn't expecting.

Non Sequitur

I DEARLY love a non sequitur if it's operatic enough, and, marooned overnight in the city of Washington, I turned on the television and caught the opening lines of one of the commercials. The scene was a bus-stop and it was raining, and the man standing there with his umbrella turned to the camera and said, 'In weather like this, diarrhoea's no fun.' For sheer quality, no programme was going to match that, so I turned it off and went to bed.

Hundreds of Old Felt Hats

WHEN the ancient newspapers you've asked for are trundled up to your desk the first thing you do is read the small ads. It doesn't matter what you've come to the British Museum Newspaper Library to look up, the small ads are the reward you give yourself for trekking all the way to Colindale. And setting up the file on the reading stand I saw on the front page 'Hundreds of old felt hats wanted for wartime purposes. Guy's Hospital.'

I kept going back to it, or rather it kept re-appearing as I turned the pages, and I was hoping there would at last be some additional message which would explain the request. But no. Other small ads seemed strange in different ways, but through the long drowsy day even after I'd begun to concentrate on the matter in hand the need for hundreds of old felt hats invaded other considerations like the cawing of rooks from distant fields.

The file I was leafing through was nearly half a century old, dating from a period when small ads appeared on *The Times* front page and no one could then have imagined it being otherwise. I noted such entries as 'A few good hunting polo saddles wanted' or 'Needed urgently, bottles for infantile whooping cough. Good condition essential'. These announcements were plain enough, and though their style was antique no exegesis was called for. But there were others which invoked the period more distinctly, in all its fading melancholy.

'Lady wanted – no front door, telephone or rough work.' 'Guests received at charming Elizabethan manor house. Billiards, dancing and bridge. Five and a half guineas.' 'Wanted – lady's Charnaux belt. Long model D preferred.' My impression is of something on the wane. A Mr Fortescue-Gange, expert picture restorer (retired) 'is willing, during the summer months, to recondition fine oil paintings, depreciating under wartime conditions, at owners' residences' – the last faint gasping sound of a voice that in a year or two's time would be extinguished in an almost religious revulsion against conventional deference. Soldiers who leaned obediently out of railway carriages giving the thumbs-up sign

were on the turn, as polite youths from the suburbs flocked to gramophone recitals at the local headquarters of the Commonwealth Party,
whence in a glow of disinterested fervour they would announce that
the Kingdom of Arcadia was at hand; a fiefdom, it was understood,
that was to be run in perpetuity by clever high-minded grammar school
boys.

Meanwhile, the way it was, the way it used to be, hung on, at any
rate in the small ads. 'Quiet country home offered to slightly backward
young man: gardening, poultry and supervision provided' – how strange
(I daydreamed, as the Colindale sunshine fell athwart the papyri) that
there were so many slightly backward young men you could set up an
enterprise to cater solely for them. And why would poultry be supplied?
No odder, perhaps, than 'Unwanted artificial teeth urgently needed' –
the adjective 'unwanted' thoughtfully slipped in to damp the patriotic
ardour of those who might tear from their mouths their wanted artificial
teeth, madly despatching them in brown paper parcels.

Two old favourites were featured: Nurse Olivier and Miss Gem Moufflet. Nurse supplied colonic irrigation, which was described as 'stimulat-
ing', and Miss Moufflet taught dancing, adding always that she 'partnered
out'. Who would have dared to hire her as a partner? She would be
so expert, and anyway, everyone else would know.

Grandpa Kruschen was prolonging his serflike existence by obediently
ingesting the salts, and Mr Barratt, with his air of solemn humility, was
on a perpetual stroll, dressed cap a pie in bowler, wing-collar, and toothbrush moustache, continuously being pounced on by neighbourhood
madmen who babbled of bunions and his wonderful shoes. Mr Barratt
was the ad gang's last stand in the fraudulent battle to persuade the
punters into believing shops were run by the people whose names
appeared above the door.

The felt hat mystery remained, until my bafflement reached the ears
of a correspondent who then wrote to me from Bristol. He said the
old hats were made into slippers at Guy's for the patients to wear while
they slopped round the wards. Ho hum. Isn't there something a bit
inconclusive about this explanation? What happened to the slippers when
they, too, got old? Did someone make small felt waistcoats for budgeri-
gars out of them, and when these fell apart or the birds died did someone
snip the felt into tiny discs for sticking under porcelain ornaments placed
on polished surfaces?

Its warm and cosy in the newspaper library, it smells deliciously of
floor-polish, and the long blameless day lapses across the printed page
as hour follows hour. Could I have dreamt it?

Debbie

I WAS in a posh hotel on the Welsh border entirely staffed by Debbies. The first one said 'Anything at all you require please don't hesitate to let me know'. I thought rather grumpily I don't imagine hesitating, the prices being what they are. A bit churlish, and I felt a little ashamed, but over my solitary dinner the thought wouldn't go away and I started to tease out the source of the faint irritation her words had promoted.

In urging you to accept what you might think you were entitled to anyway, isn't Debbie managing to suggest it *could* be withheld? Paranoia, no doubt induced by dining alone in public, but I have to say Debbie looked rather hard at her watch when I sat down and gave her my order. When she cleared away and said 'Coffee in the lounge', I replied 'Oh don't bother, I'll take it at the table,' – Debbie looked worried and said she'd ask Debbie.

She came back with the coffee and said Debbie had okayed it. I poured out the coffee, and in the way of conversation said 'No telly in the rooms, then?' and Debbie sent this back with top spin, saying 'Oh dear me no – our guests come here to get away from it.' To the possibility of paranoia was added a feeling that a Sky television dish was growing shamefully out of my head, like a cuckold's horns.

I turned the telly on in the empty lounge and Debbie put her delicious snub little nose round the door and said impishly 'You won't have it on too loud will you, there's a lady in the room above and she's got an early start.' And she said she's got an Early Start as though it were a gumboil or other painful inflammation.

The one I think of as the original Debbie was in charge of our party the time we went to Russia. After our arrival had been celebrated by a lunch of rubber elk served at half past eleven in the forenoon, accompanied by a bottle of mineral water flavoured with iron filings, I mumbled to my wife 'At least they'll give us a glass of vodka before dinner.' Debbie leant across and said 'Oh Mr Robinson, I can see you're not going to fit in.'

I began to tell some of this to a chap who was eating crisps noisily in the bar of the Welsh hotel, but he said 'Are you looking for a punch on the nose, my wife's name is Debbie.'

Whose Idea was it, anyway?

IT came as a surprise to me to learn that wire coathangers were invented. I'd always thought they simply grew, mostly on the back of bathroom doors where they jangle like out-of-tune door-chimes every time you go in and out. And I was fairly clear – without giving the matter much thought – that they reproduced, since every time you see two of them you turn round and there are four, and next time there are eight, sixteen, thirty-two and so on.

There must be more wire coathangers in the world than any other single manufactured article. Clinging to the rails of self-assembled wardrobes in hotels, they dance a mad jig if you so much as walk across the room, and when you pull open the doors they crash spitefully to the floor. In the oases of Arabia Deserta they hang from the palm trees, they litter the igloos of the eskimo and the caves of the banditti, and the reason the world is festooned with wire coathangers is because it is impossible to throw them away. Designed specifically to distort the shoulders of suits that would otherwise sit smoothly, and wrinkle the legs of trousers by means of a cross-bar which malevolently sags, the wire coathanger is also a ju-ju that people stick on cars to receive radio programmes and ward off (or possibly attract) succubuses.

As I say, I'd always thought they were one of the great natural scourges, present since the dawn of time along with dandruff and marzipan. But lo, the thing emerged from the tortured brain of one Albert J. Parkhouse who, returning from lunch to his labours at the Timberlake Wire and Novelty Company, fell into a spasm of rage because there wasn't a spare hook for his overcoat, and grabbing a bit of wire that would otherwise have been turned into an innocent pipe-cleaner, laid a new curse on mankind.

I got the information from a book called *But Whose Idea Was It?* by

Eileen Hellicar, a title you feel could do with *Anyway* tacked on to it when you're reading about the bonehead who invented the musical cash-register or the sadist who dreamt up the carpet-sweeper. I think the carpet-sweeper is more of a sworn tormentor than the wire coathanger itself, since it nearly works – it picks up *nearly* everything, and personally I'd sooner have a machine that didn't work at all than one that doesn't work every time. How cleverly it alternates not picking cotton threads up with picking them up and putting them down somewhere else. But what it enjoys most is wondering how many times you'll run it over the same bit of fluff before you bend down and pick it up yourself.

Oliver Herford celebrated the inventive quirk when he wrote –

> *Here's to the man who invented stairs,*
> *And taught our feet to soar;*
> *He was the first who ever burst*
> *Into a second floor.*
>
> *The world would be downstairs today*
> *Had he not found the key;*
> *So let his name go down in fame,*
> *Whatever it may be . . .*

The inventor's gift is being able to see what is invisible, then making it visible to all by defining it. But supposing what the inventor thinks he sees isn't so much invisible as just not there? I once met a man who'd invented a hammer it was impossible to bang your thumb with. This was achieved by having a slot in the head of the hammer into which you fitted the nail before you began so you didn't have to hold it with your other hand. Brilliant! So why did nobody take it up? The inventor couldn't understand it and neither could I, until one night I woke up and saw the snag. How could you be sure the *point* of the nail would hit the exact spot the first time you banged it?

It was rather sad, but not as sad as Bootsy, of Bootsy and Snudge, when he was daydreaming about the worlds that would open up to him if he could invent something like the paper-clip. Suddenly he grabs one, twists it, and holds it up in front of Snudge. It's a shape no one has ever dreamt of before, it's different, it's new! Spellbound by the sheer originality of the object, neither of them get round to wondering what it's for.

But it wouldn't be the first invention whose practical application is simply taken for granted. Miss Hellicar lists Baden-Powell as the inventor of the Boy Scouts, but neither she nor anyone I've asked can tell me what the invention is for. What function has a boy, as a scout, when he is surrounded by brick and mortar criss-crossed by bus-routes? Why do you need patrols when there isn't a war? And if hostilities broke out, how would knots help? If it's all for fun, what boy needs an organization – much less a 'movement', whatever that sinister word turns out to mean – to supply him with that? So you have a real mystery, an invention everyone accepts, but whose uses no one can ever describe.

It was nice to be told potato crisps were George Crum's idea, and that the petrol pump came to Sylvanus Bowser while he was chatting to Jake Gumper. But the inventor who came closest to home with me was the chap who dreamed up dry-cleaning in 1855. Apparently he set about inventing dry-cleaning because he'd spilt paraffin on his suit, and his name was Jean Baptiste Joly. The name rang a bell.

There is a picture on my wall, and the signature reads H.B.P. Joly. Had he spilt the paraffin on his suit while washing his brushes? Did he mess his initials about to distance himself from the dry-cleaning side of things, or was he anxious to preserve his secret life as a painter from the Rotarians who met weekly at the Hotel des Gourmets? Of course, Rousseau was a customs-official, but will people look at my picture and say 'Ah, not bad for a man who invented dry-cleaning.' On reflection, I think I'll keep it quiet.

Hockney and his Dad

HOCKNEY was telling me his dad does imitations of the Emperor of Japan and actually takes his teeth out to get the proper effect. At the end of the performance, which is a fairly disobliging one, Hockney's dad puts his teeth back in and says (of the Emperor), 'Ah well, I suppose he can't help it.' Hockney says his father keeps several pairs of false teeth, one set in a jar marked BEST PAIR, another marked NEXT BEST and a third marked NOT BAD. He also keeps things other people might not and has a collection of dud batteries. He gave Hockney a fibre-tipped pen refill which he had labelled PARTLY USED.

Now, I'm very fond of this sort of information; what I like about it is its irreducibility. You can stare at it till the cows come home and it won't get you a degree in sociology. You can't use it for secondary purposes, you can't generalize it away, it isn't *like* anything. I find this cheering because it really is quite easy to walk out into the street and see nothing that isn't a reference to something else which isn't a reference to something else – you wouldn't call it a code because you can crack a code, it's much more an endless jargon, a sort of equation that simply refers to another equation.

So on those odd occasions when you do seem to have arrived at a destination, it's very reassuring. While Hockney was telling me about his dad, I was feeling like our Mr Satchell who used to do the electrics for us. Once he'd got the flex sticking out of the little holes in the plaster where he was going to put the wall-lights, Mr Satchell made sure the electricity was getting through by grabbing hold of the bare wires. 'Ha-a-a-ah,' he would cry – it was a noise midway between a shout of delight and a groan of satisfaction – 'the supply – it's there – it's there –' I had exactly the same feeling when hearing about Hockney's dad's false teeth. Hockney stood looking at the canvas he was working on and for a moment seemed to speak with his father's voice when he said, 'I sometimes wonder if this is a way for a man of forty to pass his time.'

He'd been talking about Bradford (he's a Bradford man) and art school, and I said that reminds me of the first picture I ever bought. I got it from Bonham's when they were hammering off canvases that had accumulated over the years in the basement of the Royal Academy, a great pile of pictures people had said they'd buy but never got round to paying for, or stuff the painters hadn't bothered to collect when the exhibitions closed – sort of *salon de refusés*, in a way. The one I bought was a big tall picture with two little girls and a mum. They're standing in a road under a bleached-out winter-evening sky, and the perspective is staked out with black telegraph poles all the way down to the dark warehouses at the end of the street. Now, the street is a Bradford street because it says so on the back, and I've always had a feeling – something about the carefulness of the way the painter brought the thing together, the hint you get of an anecdote or story in the way the three figures are standing – that this is exactly the sort of picture people at art schools paint, full of feeling but a touch literary. God knows who the artist is, he's got his name on the back too: D.S. Stafford. Hockney looked incredulous. 'You're joking aren't you? D.S. Stafford was my teacher …'

Now, if you were making that story up, you'd have to tear the edges a bit, make them ragged, it's too neat, too pat to be anything but the truth. Hockney's coming to see the picture and he's bringing D.S. Stafford with him. It's rather odd that I've been intimate with D.S. Stafford for twenty years yet never thought of him as a person. Will he mind about the way I came by the picture? Will it enrage him that I only gave eight quid for it? ('You ought to be ashamed of yourself,' J.B.P., another Bradfordian, growled when he heard the price.) Well, I do believe such clear, round, flawless coincidences don't roll out of your turn-ups half often enough – I keep putting off making an actual date with the two painters because after that it will all be over.

The Magic Rectangle

WHEN I wrote a television film that tried to anatomize the business of being a Television Personality I made the point that whatever the condition turned out to be, it had little to do with fame. Fame meant you left something behind.

I was thinking in particular of Gilbert Harding, the *ur*-Personality, the very first one, a presence who in his day loomed over the popular consciousness like a geni out of a bottle. All he's remembered for now is bursting into tears on the *Face to Face* show (which, as a matter of fact, he didn't) and for his irascibility (what Harding couldn't bear was the idea of the audience feeding off the single facet of himself that seemed to be the Personality, but what he could bear even less was the prospect of giving this up. No wonder he was bad-tempered).

Anyway, I saw how things actually stood one evening when I walked into the foyer of the Vaudeville Theatre in the Strand. Harding was a few steps ahead of me. 'That Gilbert Harding?' asked a respectable matron from Weybridge (might even have been Berrylands). 'It is, it is,' cried her companion enthusiastically. 'Right,' said the First Murderer, 'now I've seen him, you can take him out and shoot him.'

For the sort of attention you get if you're a Television Personality is massive, but weightless – it comes in units like Co-op tallies or Green

Shield stamps, you get lots of it, but as much as you get you always feel you'd need a couple of million more before you could exchange it for anything useful, like a fried egg sandwich.

Of course, the sheer volume disturbs your emotional compass. How pathetically grateful I was thirty years ago, sitting in the Lyons at the corner of Gray's Inn Road, to be approached by a stranger who said I looked like the man who the night before had presented a programme called *Picture Parade*. 'But it *was* me!' I cried wildly, 'I mean, it was I!' And walking out into High Holborn in a trance of self-love, I with difficulty restrained myself from asking passers-by if they'd like to be touched for the King's Evil. Nor was my narcissism one wit diminished by my barber, a straight-faced man in those days, who half way through the haircut said sourly, 'I wouldn't have guessed you had it in you.'

Ah, but where is that wholesome, swollen-headed lad these days? Can it be the old ratbag in the Millet's hat and the dark glasses who edges boot-faced into Waitrose's and looks as though he'd bite anyone who looked speculatively at him? Yes, it is. Odd the way wanting to be known turns into not wanting it; odd the way being known is never quite enough, that the natural curiosity of others comes to make you feel like a white mouse taken out of everyone's pocket. I have a suspicion this means I am an addict. In registering irritation at the attention I get, in fact I am asking for more, I'm asking for a higher class of curiosity. Show me a Television Personality and I'll show you a fathead.

That's why they all resist the title. 'Television *person*,' says Frost. 'I never think of myself as *famous*,' says Rippon. Well, no. Fame happens to people who aren't thinking about it – Celebrity is what the magic rectangle bestows. And as someone once said, Celebrity comes to those who think about nothing else. But whatever you do on the telly, if you do it often enough, you're a Television Personality, and you dine with the governess, not the family.

You're the one who is looked at. The Oblong Halo is placed round your neck, and you're the focus of attention. It's another form of the wreath of garlic, as long as you wear it you are protected from the curse of anonymity. Once upon a time to get this sort of mass attention you had to be able to do something the audience might feel it couldn't do for itself. Playing the nose-flute, say, or doing conjuring tricks. But somewhere around the early Fifties the phenomenon emerged. Suddenly, all you had to do was turn up.

Well, turn up, and not fall over. But the faint mystery is that for the first time in history people were getting an audience of millions to watch them do something the audience might easily feel it could get up on stage and do for itself. What took place didn't look as though it was *trained* for. So anyone could be a Television Personality – yes?

Miss Rantzen lowers her voice and with a winning smile softly emits an ever-so-regretful negative. 'No-o-o-' she breathes. But the late Macdonald Hobley contradicts. Anything but the bland figure his black tie and dinner-jacket might have made him seem, he said, 'If you pick your nose often enough on television, you'll become a Television Personality. Mind you,' he added, 'there are amateur nose-pickers and there are professional nose-pickers. And I,' said Hobley, with justifiable pride, 'was a professional nose-picker.'

In the short history of the Television Personality only one person ever took off the Magic Rectangle and gave it back. Marghanita Laski, novelist and critic, found herself a star turn on the original panel-game, *What's My Line?* After some months of what she felt was spurious celebrity, she quit. 'I felt,' she told me, 'I'd been taken up to the mountain top and offered the kingdoms of the world far too cheap.'

The audience doesn't so much applaud as take you into public ownership, letting you go on doing what doesn't look like very much, almost as though they *were* doing it themselves. They stare easily into your face, as though recognizing features that belong to them – as though *your* identity were a vacant space, in which they find their own.

Does this mean that the little rectangle, in turning a real person into a Television Personality, deprives him of something? In turning him into a version of everyone, has it turned *him* into no one?

Everyone, and no one. A new fate for Narcissus.

The Rumanian Sports Jacket

A correspondent wrote to tell me he owns a Rumanian sports jacket and he said as soon as he looked inside the collar and saw it came from Rumania he started to wonder what was wrong with it.

I know what he means, indeed as I read his letter I found myself conjuring up the image of a Rumanian sports jacket as being very short, with the square look that jackets have when you see them hanging on poles in fields to scare birds, woven from some dark synthetic fibre, and shot through with gold lurex to ward off the vampires. I see a Rumanian sports jacket as incomplete without pegtop trousers and winklepicker shoes.

The label telling you where the article comes from is a powerful conditioner of expectation: who has not noted the shoes that come from Yugoslavia, and just for a second visualized a man in a bear-skin and cross-garters, painfully sewing the uppers with a needle made out of a sparrow's ulna? Stranger yet, when I see Portuguese footwear advertised I assume it to be made of pot – I associate Portugal with everything ceramic, and my internal vision of Portuguese shoes is of chimney-pots that you can wear on your feet.

People say Belgian chocolates are the very best, and I believe them. Easy to imagine heavy-looking Flemings tirelessly labouring to create those exquisite little domes of chocolate with pink inside and crystallized violets on top, because only foreigners would toil to produce something that takes three seconds to swallow – energy which the British have always reserved for sterner activities, like treading the swedes for HP sauce or knitting bedsocks. Even when M. Charbonnel found a British partner called Walker to join him in manufacturing chocolates, Walker insisted the business shouldn't be called Charbonnel *and* Walker, it was to be Charbonnel *et* Walker, so Walker (who was ashamed of having invented the nut-cluster) could pretend the whole fancy enterprise had little or nothing to do with him.

All this goes with feeling its strange that the Japanese are no longer small persons who are clever at mimicking the grown-ups. It's the other way round now. However, their past status as people who never originated anything is still traceable in the way they make the best cars but don't get the name quite right. There's something about the Cherry or the Sunny which suggests clockwork rather than the internal combustion engine.

How does Sea Island cotton differ from cotton *tout court*? I perceive it as stunningly pure, redolent of the sea-breezes of some undiscovered island in the most sparkling of oceans beneath the most limpid of blue skies; woven by pre-lapsarian innocents, themselves entirely naked, whose life work is to supply the fallen, corrupt, outside world with the finest possible fig-leaves. Whoever dreamed up the label was a marketing genius.

But C & A have an inbuilt disadvantage; the minute you learn it's a Dutch firm you start trying to remember when you last saw a well-dressed Dutchman. And perhaps even worse, you begin to think of C & A as the place a visiting Africaaner might naturally come to find a replacement for his big black suit and black cardboard hat. As absurd as supposing that anything with the Israeli label was manufactured by earnest men and women living on principle in uncomfortable kibbutzes, and is therefore enormously hard-wearing, though the colours might be a touch on the muddy side.

Is Spanish leather stiff because the cows look skinny? Why are trousers from Italy made for dinky little numbers with 23-inch waists, and even when they are in your own size why are they too small? I offered a glass of British wine to a Hungarian friend. 'As Rumanian sports coats go' he said, holding it up to the light, 'I wouldn't wrap a dog in the one, nor wash my bike in the other.'

The Affair of the Eight Chinese Racing Pigs

WHEN the sparkle goes out of life some people read a book, go on day trips, take to drink. John Dash, of South-West London, suffering a *cafard*, initiated a correspondence.

> Dear Sirs [he wrote to the Ministry of Agriculture and Fisheries], I have recently been left eight (8) pedigree pigs in the will of a Great-Aunt who kept a pig farm at Ongar. They have been delivered to my flat and I was wondering whether you would like to have them? I know at Whitehall the poor creatures would receive the care and attention my Great-Aunt was so anxious to obtain for them.

> Dear Sirs [he wrote to Qantas Airways Ltd], I am emigrating to Australia in March and I wish to take with me eight pedigree pigs left to me in the will of a Great-Aunt who kept a pig farm at Ongar. I wish to charter a private plane for the pigs, myself, and an old friend who is a veterinary surgeon.

> Dear Sirs [he wrote to the Architect's Department of the London County Council, dating his letter from his flat in Tregunter Road, Kensington], I have recently been left eight pigs in the will of a Great-Aunt who kept a pig farm in Ongar. I propose to keep them on a plot of land adjoining these premises.

John Dash, the blood now moving less sluggishly in his veins, felt the tonic beginning to work. He received replies as follows.

> Dear Sir [wrote the Ministry of Agriculture], Thank you for your recent letter about pedigree pigs. The Ministry regrets it is unable to accept your kind offer, and suggests you communicate with the Secretary of the appropriate Breed Society.

> Dear Sir or Madam [wrote Qantas], With reference to your letter concerning the chartering of a fully-pressurized aircraft to Australia

for the conveyance of two people together with eight pedigree pigs, we wish to advise the following: We do not carry any livestock whatsoever on our aircraft. However, we have sent a copy of your letter to BOAC.

BOAC wrote,

Dear Sir, We regret we are unable to help you charterwise. However, should you decide to send the pigs to Australia by sea, and fly out yourselves –

The Architect's Department wrote,

Dear Sir, In respect of your proposed erection of a pig-sty in Tregunter Road, I enclose without any prejudice, form T.P. 1 –

Then John Dash, throwing in a *bouquet garni* so to speak, wrote to the Ministry of Housing and Local Government,

Dear Sirs, Mr John Dash who occupies accommodation below my own has recently acquired eight pigs, which I understand were left to him in the will of a Great-Aunt. These dreadful creatures keep me awake at night but when I complain he tells me if I don't like it I can go back to China. Trusting this matter will receive your early attention. I remain, yours truly, Fang P'ing.

An Inspector called when John Dash was out and, though assured by the landlady there were no pigs on the premises, looked in all the wardrobes. In reply to a further letter from Dash inquiring about breeding possibilities, an Officer of the Pig Industry Development Authority replied, 'I would like to offer a word of caution before you decide to launch into pig-keeping in South-West London –'

Later Dash received leaflets entitled 'Breeding for bacon production', 'Pig feeding', 'Diseases of pigs', 'The housing of pigs', and was referred to standard works, viz., 'A modern guide to pig husbandry', 'Profitable pig farming', and 'The production and marketing of pigs'.

Already Dash was sleeping better, the colour was returning to his cheeks, and friends remarked on his cheerful demeanour. Finding the medicine was doing him good, Dash increased the dosage.

Dear Sir [he wrote to the Secretaries of the New Cross, Hendon, Wembley, and Stamford Bridge Greyhound Stadiums], I have recently arrived in the Old Country from Australia where several associates and myself have revived the ancient Chinese sport of Pig Racing. I am pleased to say I have brought a team of Racing Pigs with me and it is my intention to introduce and promote this sport in this country. Will it be possible to hire your stadium for any one night in January? For your information races are usually run over 600 yards –

An official from the Wembley Stadium replied,

I have received your letter of the 25th instant and in view of the extraordinary nature of your proposition it would be well if you gave us a ring –

From the Greyhound Racing Association Limited a reply came,

Although we are as a Company the biggest sports promoting organization in the country I have to admit that pig racing is a new one on us. Looking forward to a further insight into this Confucian pastime, Yours faithfully.

Scenting a correspondent after his own heart, John Dash replied to the last letter:

I regret I have been unable to reply earlier as I have been out of town seeking suitable training grounds for the pigs. I am pleased to report that I have found a likely site not too far from Ongar.

I was surprised to learn [he continued], that an experienced organization such as your good selves had not heard of Pig Racing. We find Fang P'ing referring to it as early as the first half or the sixth century BC, later it is called 'a royal sport', and its popularity only begins to wane in the third century AD when the great Chinese General and Emperor, Tseng Kuofan – 'China's Cromwell' (Klaeber) – proscribes it as 'barbarous'. May I urge you to do a little background reading on the subject of this superlative sport? Doubtless we shall then be able to arrange an appointment to discuss this matter further on more level terms.

Dear Sir [replied the Greyhound Racing Association Limited], I was glad to hear you have found suitable training gallops near Ongar. However, I do not intend to enter into historical research as this could in no way lead to a true assessment of the possible changes in 'spectator appeal' which may have resulted from the passage of twenty-five centuries.

I have in the past [continued this amiable correspondent], pursued the pig, culminating in a nasty tumble in the Kadir Cup of 1937. I have therefore been able to form a high opinion of him as a fleet-footed

and noble animal. I have not however discovered what it is the pig
pursues.

It should not, however [the writer concluded], be in any way beyond
the scope of our Engineering Department to fabricate and operate
an electric truffle.

With a cry of delight John Dash knew that his cure was complete.
The *cafard* had gone, life had regained its savour, and to the Eight Chinese
Racing Pigs and to the good people who had suffered them, he owed
a debt he could never repay.

Public Bath

YOU turn a corner and see your own bath standing outside somebody
else's front door. It happened to me – there it was in Christchurch Street,
Chelsea, the absolutely unmistakable object, the bath so big it never
looked quite right without a diving-board at one end, the very bath
to which over the many years each of my three children in turn has
been reluctant to go, but once in has resolutely refused to get out of
– there it was, with the two big taps that look as though they're holding
back the Aswan Dam, standing on its end outside some bright spark's
dinky new villa. It's a dream-like experience, seeing your own bath in
an unfamiliar context – it's like running across your mother in a nightclub.
'What's my bath doing in Christchurch Street?' I asked the builders when
I got back home. 'Ah,' said the painter, 'Mr Thing was looking for one
of those big old-fashioned ones, so we gave him yours. It's what they
call the nostalgia kick,' said the painter kindly. Now it's true I was having
this particular bathroom de-natured – an action equivalent to laying your
hands on all the fifty-pound notes you can find, stuffing them into a
Gladstone bag, and taking them to the zoo to feed the giraffes – but
what I hadn't bargained on was them levering out the actual bath and
giving it to someone, especially not someone who was going to use
it as a period piece. Think how you'd feel if your bath were being

patronized – how would you like it if you saw it standing outside someone else's house, surrounded by inverted commas? When your bath turns out to be *amusing*, what does that make you? On the other hand, of course, in not being too snooty to accept my cast-offs, Mr Thing is himself rather one down, wouldn't you say? And being a thoughtful sort of cove (I visualize him as the archetypal purchaser of reproduction pub mirrors) he will realize that since his bath used to belong to my children, every time I pass his house I shall be wondering whether he is at that very moment playing with his celluloid ducks.

Carpet Slipper Tango

WHY is it assumed to be axiomatic that a 're-shuffle' wonderfully renews the appeal of a government? The faces are exactly the same, they're simply changed round a bit, and lo, any slight misgivings the electorate may have had about the Government's competence are magically dispelled and the Head declares a half-holiday.

This would be more comprehensible if these re-shuffles involved some entirely new figure, clad in shining armour and riding a white horse, who was going to save us all: but what happens is that the same photograph of the same chap appears, translated to the Ministry of Woolgathering but wearing the same smirk he wore when he was at the Ministry of Aggravation and Fisheries. He even wears the same old suit. It isn't everyone who can distinguish a Kenneth from a Norman.

Before it all happens there have been unlimited supplies of 'speculation'. Sometimes there are reports that speculation is what there is a Mounting Frenzy of – but surely Mounting Frenzy (a peak in the Himalayas) is a mounting frenzy of impatience on the part of citizens as they are assailed by 'speculation', which is no more than a bunch of hacks telling you what they don't know.

I wonder if Prime Ministers who go in for re-shuffles have quite taken in what an unglamorous word it is? A shuffle is bad enough, suggestive of old carpet slippers, but a *re* -shuffle seems to add one of those plaid dressing-gowns to the carpet slippers, and you visualize ageing figures not only shuffling but re-shuffling up and down the corridors of Whitehall trying to find the canteen.

Over-prepared

In the glove pocket of my car I have a plastic box which contains pound coins and fifty-pence pieces for the parking-meter. As I shook out the necessary coins one morning the man I was giving a lift to said, 'You do realize a man who keeps parking money in a plastic box is the lineal descendant of the eunuch who kept his change in a purse?' I said, 'I don't think eunuchs have descendants', but he brushed this aside. 'You are *over* prepared,' he said, 'for something that doesn't matter.' Whereupon he got out of the car and went into Sainsbury's, and as he did so he pulled something from his pocket. I had to laugh. A man who goes shopping with a string-bag has no business lecturing anyone on the subject of over-preparedness.

String-bags, and then galoshes – I perfectly recognize their usefulness in keeping out the wet, I just can't see myself going into a shop and asking for a pair; you'd have to be wearing pince-nez and a cardigan under your waistcoat before you could make the purchase comfortably. Weirder than the galosh is the transparent plastic cover for the hat, as worn by cautious Americans. This is a specific *announcement* of over-preparedness since the hat protects, and should not itself need protection. If your hat wears a hat, why shouldn't the hat your hat wears also wear a hat? You could be strolling down Bond Street with a leaning tower of hats swaying above your head – serial headgear!

But how explain the fury that grips you when you see a man with each one of the three buttons on his jacket tightly done up? How explain the urge to rush up to him and cry Don't you know you aren't *supposed* to do up all the buttons? What unimaginable climatic onslaught are you over-preparing yourself for by doing up three buttons? Why not simply *stay at home*?

He may also be carrying an *undone* brolly on a bright Spring morning. If he is, it is a sure sign that he is wearing a cellular vest – I'm not quite certain what a cellular vest is, but the very words are dismal. Should you be standing behind this man at a cash dispenser outside a bank, it's a racing certainty that he will count the notes before he moves away. At that point you know he will pull hard at any glass door marked PUSH and hail taxis that are already occupied.

Some people are chronically over-prepared. I quite often see a nut-brown 65-year-old on the road near the town of Bridgwater, dressed in breeches, stockings, parka, stick and rucksack, striding purposefully towards the pedestrian precincts as though they were the summit of Kanchenjunga. Even his walk is a kind of slow lope, as though he were holding himself in for the last few furlongs, which in his case I know for certain add up to the distance from the charcuterie to the check-out. I once said to my son, as we drove past him, Can you guess what the most insulting thing is that you could do to that man? Of course I can, my son replied – offer him a lift.

But this instance of over-preparedness must stand by another. No sooner had a light fall of snow all but obliterated the dog-muck on the pavements of Chelsea one winter's morning than another oldster, lean and lithe and wearing the smuggest smile seen west of Bob Monkhouse, turned the corner of Cheyne Row, striding along on – you've guessed it – skis! It was my wife who made the sighting. 'I'm glad you didn't see it,' she said, 'you'd have had a seizure.'

The Great Cherry Omelette Conspiracy

THE lady at the other end of the line said, 'A regular feature where people say what their favourite recipes are. Interesting things with – with spaghetti. Or say something went wrong like putting chocolate sauce with herrings and – '

The man said, 'Chocolate sauce instead of what?'

'Instead of. Well, something like that with herrings and it turned out everyone thought it was marvellous. You know?'

'Oh yes,' said the man.

'We ask people like you. Personalities. Visiting Firemen.'

The man, standing at the phone in his cold kitchen, felt thigh boots growing up his legs and a ghostly helmet shining like a glory round his head.

'We visit your kitchen,' said the lady briskly.

'*Here*,' said the Fireman, aghast. A pregnant cat was sitting in a washing-up bowl made of yellow plastic. 'It's not really the sort of. I'm hardly ever in.'

'Or our studio. Tell us what the ingredients are and come along. Wear something leisual.'

There was a brief silence.

'Leisure clothes,' said the lady shortly.

The Fireman was wearing his underpants and a jersey that was frayed at the cuffs so that it looked as if he had mittens on. 'I don't think I've got any,' he said after a while.

'Everyone's got a favourite recipe, *surely*,' said the lady winningly, yet with a touch of worldliness which by-passed the humanity of both parties and suggested that all Firemen had favourite recipes when rung up by magazines.

'I was thinking of the clothes,' said the Fireman. 'I only have the sort of trousers you wear braces on.'

'Oh, anything at all,' said the woman. Then she said, 'It could be something you picked up abroad.'

'Ptomaine,' whispered the Fireman.

'Or scampi,' said the woman.

'The trouble is,' said the Fireman, looking at the draining-board where a jam-jar was half-full of milk-bottle tops and half-full of blue mould, 'I eat the stuff and forget it. I don't *collect* it. Mind you,' he went on, as if he didn't want anyone to go away with the idea that he was an idiot, 'I'm very fond of leek soup.'

'Mmm,' said the lady.

'I'm very fond of it.'

'It's a *bit* – You mean you have a special. You put –'

'Oh it's very good.'

The woman was silent, then she started to speak brightly, rapidly, enthusiastically, as though she had made a lightning decision to junk all the previous conversation and start again. 'Look here, what about a sherry omelette? If we got the ingredients. I'm sure it *would* be your favourite.'

'Good heavens,' said the Fireman.

'Delicious,' encouraged the lady.

'A cherry omelette.'

'Yes.'

'We'd have the Fraud Squad round.'

They compromised on a dish that the Fireman had actually eaten and he went upstairs to collect his leisuals.

The office was homely, considering the glossiness of the paper on which the magazine was printed. But in a space hollowed out among the type-writers they had constructed a kitchen full of pastel shades and continuous surfaces and looking as if a burglar-alarm would go off if anything organic like food were carried across the threshold.

But there was some meat and a bottle of milk and a frying pan by the stove. The cameraman was setting up his camera and there was a great big silver umbrella – an actual umbrella, painted silver – stuck on a tripod to reflect the light where he wanted it to go.

'Sometimes we use stones instead of potatoes,' said the lady. 'Sometimes they look more like potatoes than potatoes do.'

The Fireman said, 'One, two, three and I expose my braces.' He whipped out of his waistcoat like an escapologist, put the pullover on and turned the sleeves under at the cuffs to hide the hanging bits.

'Is there any reason why our friend shouldn't sit *on* the table?' said the photographer.

'Holding the pan,' nodded the lady.

'Salt in the other hand –'

'And balancing the bottle on his chin,' suggested the Fireman.

Then they gave him the equipment.

'Very happy,' warned the photographer looking into the viewfinder. The Fireman laughed and the photographer took the picture. Then they turned the bright lights off and the kitchen went inert like furniture in a shop-window when the shop is closed.

'This sherry omelette would have been gayer,' said the lady.

'I thought you said cherry,' said the Fireman.

They said good-bye at the lift and the liftman closed the doors.

'As far as food goes,' said the liftman on the way down, 'I don't think you can beat a couple of dumplings as big as your head.'

Slowing Down the Spider

'Too many parents have deprived their children of the joy of keeping ferrets' says a man writing a book on polecats, and I know that another indictment has been added to the long list my own children can produce against me – 'Buy us a ferret, Dad,' they would piteously mew, and how they wept when I replied 'Only if we can have it fried for breakfast, with mushrooms.'

But spurning the ferret lobby, I say such small nasty beasts will never catch on because their movements are unpredictable and sudden. I was proud when we discovered a little frog among our roses, and I wondered where it had come from. My wife said it must have hopped all the way up the combe from the river, and I said that's why it's so small and thin, all that effort, it's lost weight. But though we both preened ourselves because the frog had chosen our garden, neither of us would have stooped down to pick it up for a king's ransom. Frogs are too quick. Like spiders and silver fish and rats, frogs go from absolute immobility to total movement. They don't *start* moving, they are hideously transformed from one state to the other. That's what frightens people. The sudden-ness is unannounced, it sends no signals, one moment it isn't, the next

94

it *is*. Unpredictability is an immemorial threat.

And it is combined with a terrifying singleness of purpose. In the time that elapses in the movement of people you see the chink or gap necessary for a mind, a heart, an impulse, to change. But the movement of a frog, a snake, a polecat, a spider, admits of no such possibility for no time is seen to elapse; the cobra strikes, and between the intention and the act there is no second thought, no scope for modification, no chance of an alternative, no possibility of appeal. Let the spider be slowed down, let the frog learn to amble, and they might have a chance of getting on terms with human beings (though the frog's eyes would still be worrying; if a frog sneezed, the eyes would blast out of its head). Until then, even the cheese beetle which has so many tiny legs it's a wonder it achieves traction at all, moving slowly across the carpet like a toothbrush, has a better chance of arousing affection.

Birds embody the threat. A house martin bombs the bread and butter on the table at tea in the garden, and every time it dives you prickle afresh. Are the bird's attentions aggressive or flirtatious? But the real apprehension lies in not knowing when the dive will be repeated. Late at night in a manor house in Spain I sat reading by candlelight while moths rattled insanely round the candleholders and every now and then a small hard shiny black fly dropped like a splinter of treacle toffee on to the tiled floor. But there were cages in the room, containing birds, and their twittering presaged all that can't be predicted: it was as though they were arguing about what they would do if ever they got free. A rat rustled behind the skirting-board and terror of the unpredictable, accumulated in human beings over the millenia, made me cry out as instinctively as crows rise into the air when a shot is fired.

And yet when my ginger tom, purring against my hand turns suddenly and in a feral memory of the wild garden from which he was rescued, bites my finger, I smile, for the unpredictable has become merely the unexpected. His stripes go right down to the brain and interfere with the wiring, but his random behaviour is no threat, since it has long since been allowed for. Something you can never do for frogs and ferrets, spiders and bats.

The Theatre of Conversation

Someone in a play by Angus Wilson says 'Where's all this good talk we hear so much about?' as if the stuff you got round dinner-tables didn't quite live up to expectation and there must be a natural growth which had been stunted by being dragged into drawing rooms, not to mention television studios. As though in a state of nature, when you came to conversation you got the real thing. Is this true?

Coarse shout from the back of the gallery: give him an enema! Actor on stage playing the doctor looks up from the patient and replies It wouldn't help. Coarse voice from the back: It wouldn't hurt! Question: is this conversation? A report in *The Times* noted that Mrs Diane Evans, mother of three and married for seventeen years, called to her husband in the garden, 'I am getting divorced.' Mr Evans replied, 'If I don't get these tomato plants in soon they will die.' At Dover a customs-officer who was suspicious of a sealed container shouted 'Are you all right in there?' Back came the reply 'Yes' and twenty-two illegal immigrants were arrested.

Something was going on, but was it conversation? Glazing a six-pane window (I sometimes think of learning Greek and glazing a six-pane window seemed a sort of start) I was just tapping in the sprigs when a chap who gets his living doing that sort of thing walked out of the pub opposite and, picking up my pliers, pulled out the sprig I'd just knocked in and tapped it back at a slightly different angle. But kept on rapping the glass as he did so. I said: 'Oh thanks. But shouldn't I do it? Bit of bad luck if *you* broke it.' And still tapping he said 'Wouldn't be the first I'd broken, either.'

So I don't know – it was an exchange, but it seemed more important than a conversation. What about exchanges that seem *less* important than a conversation? There was once a fifteen-minute television programme called *Jim's Inn*. It was a sort of jumbo commercial, staffed by anonymous actors led by a particularly egregious performer called Jimmy Hanley. The actors were supposed to be in a pub, and what appealed to connoisseurs of sadistic theatre was the obligation laid on them to maintain their saloon-bar casualness while dragging into the 'conversation' the consumer durables whose agents had bought space in the script.

They had a fat man who leant on the end of the bar, wearing his blazer and puffing his pipe, who was the very spirit of promiscuous approval. 'What's that you've got up your nose, Jim?' 'Ah, you noticed it, did you, Jack – its a nose-flute.' 'Cost you a bit, I bet.' 'A lot less than you'd think, Jack – only a hundred and seventy five guineas from Tesco's, and you get a free music-holder that clips over your ears.' 'Can't grumble at that, Jim – give us Bonnie Scotland.'

Now, if this *were* conversation, the knack of it could easily be taught, and all those handbooks on How To Hold The Table Spellbound would come into their own. Such guides rest on the assumption that life is a sequence of 'situations' but they read as though the people who compiled them had failed as writers of soap-operas because they couldn't make the situations convincing.

So for instance one author advises the reader that if he's on the fringes of a group at a party the way to get into the conversation is to wait until someone stops speaking and say 'And what happened then?' Try as I may I can't summon up a final line to which this response would seem like a good idea. 'And so he said You'll either be hanged or die of the pox and the other chap said That depends on whether I embrace your principles or your mistress' (And what happened then?) 'There was the time Edward VII saw this old chum of his coming towards him in Piccadilly wearing – horrors! – brown boots and said Hullo Jack, goin' rattin'?' (And what happened then?) Still worse is the author's recommendation that you ingratiate yourself by saying 'That's a truly incredible story! How long ago did this happen?' Even men who are very easily pleased may feel that, as a tribute, the enquiry falls short.

No one speaks like this: is that why it is not conversation? And if so, is it a sufficient definition of conversation, to say that it is the way people *do* speak to each other? Here is a transcript of what I overheard one evening in a restaurant.

One woman said to the other, 'My first husband didn't last six months.' Then she said, 'He was a racing tipster, but I didn't know that and it came as a terrible shock to me.' The other woman said, 'What paper did he do it for?' and the first replied, 'No, he was on the Course. He had this educated voice. He'd been at Wellington, not much of a school, but as good as some.' After a little while, she went on, 'He dressed the part. He wore a gown like they do at Oxford, only it was white.' There was another pause, and then she said, 'He called himself the Great Gully,' and the second woman said, 'Why did he do that?' and the second woman said, 'Well, obviously, because he'd been a sergeant in the Egyptian army.' And her companion said, 'Mmm'.

There was a silence as the food was served, and the second lady said, 'Oh those candle-flames. So Louis Quatorze.' The other murmured, 'Really?' 'They're so steady. He was such a steady fellow.' Then the first one said, 'We have candelabra like that. We get them out of pawn at Christmas.' And the second lady said 'Mmm'.

You might get a lot of 'Mmm' if you overheard God looking round creation, and I sometimes wonder if the banality of overheard remarks isn't the music of the spheres. Whatever it is, it isn't conversation. The speakers are on automatic pilot, what they say is not to each other but to themselves. They speak because someone else is there, but only because this provides the excuse.

Such unstructured self-expression is certainly found in the wild, and it grows over the world like bindweed. What it puts a stop to is what conversation exists to facilitate: encounter. When two or more people acknowledge that a desire to say who you are is universally shared, a conversation is possible. Those present become an ensemble playing extempore on the same instrument. If this is so, then the answer to my opening question is clear: there is no conversation in a state of nature, any more than there is joined-up writing or wallpaper. It is wholly artificial.

And on what terms do people meet in conversations? Why, only the most engaging. The messenger who arrives to tell Caesar the war is lost does far more than converse, and is strangled for his pains. In conversation we are on stage, but in the most pleasing of roles, ourselves as we would be thought to be! We suspend the purely utilitarian functions of communication in favour of performance, and as performers we fictionalize ourselves.

Groves and thickets spring up around us as we move from one part of the forest to another, from drawing room comedy to bedroom farce to revenger's tragedy, the scenery changing as the pantomime of conversation carries us through an endless series of transformation scenes. The decor is as impromptu as the words which engender it.

In the fragment that follows, Trevor Breadnut, Old Mrs Fruitfly, Robert Robinson, Ann Leslie, Milton Shulman and Laurie Taylor are entirely fictitious, and bear no resemblance to any person, living or dead. Eric Blore, of course, appears as himself.

*

Prologue

THE talk was all of custard. Custard filled the air.

'At some point in their lives, everyone adored custard –'

'Rubbish!'

'And custard, which has a special claim on the attention of all who had proper access to it –'

'*Proper* access – to custard?'

'Without proper access to custard Proust would have found his madeleine-cake a very different –'

'You mean the custard his mother filled his hot-water bottle with –'

'And more than that, could Yeats have given us –'

'– all those wonderful melodies –'

'The Centre Cannot Hold, Boys and Girls are Level Now with Men, and there is nothing left floating upside-down in custard but –'

'Jesus H. Christ, I knew you were a philistine –'

'I suspected very early on in childhood that there was something wrong with custard, because every time my mother served it to me she said it tasted like something else – she said it tasted like cream, she said it tasted like ice cream, she said it tasted like –'

'You are thinking of prunes –'

'I said WHY, I said WHY doesn't it taste like itself? And she always replied –'

'You mean –'

'She always replied –'

'You mean you let her –'

'She always replied –'

'What kind of household was this, where everyone was discussing custard –'

'What she always said was, what she always replied was –'

'Come on –'

'What she always shrewdly observed, and when you think of it –'

'*Aaaargh* –'

'What she always said was, SHUTUP. But –'

'Doesn't it all depend on what you mean by custard?'

'No, it certainly doesn't depend on that, I think I can safely say –'

'– without fear or favour or hope of reward –'

'– right. I think we are all agreed, Trevor, that it absolutely one hundred per cent doesn't depend on what you mean by custard, if it depends on anything at all it doesn't depend on that –'

'Why has nobody made reference to the custard-tart?'

'Because the only use a custard-tart might have is as a cold compress to a black-eye or other contusion –'

'I cannot believe you have never taken a custard-tart –'

'– and plastered it round a boil?'

'– and counted the dear little brown freckles which form on the top and which were the guarantee – at least they were when I was a lad in eighteen I mean nineteen thirty seven –'

'– when you could have a night out –'

'– and change from a three-bob note –'

'But the interesting thing, the interesting, the ah ah ah, the, the, interesting, the eh eh eh, the interesting thing about custard is the way you would never turn up at a smart dinner-party and expect your hostess to serve custard. Which reminds me of the time Goldberg asked his wife what she'd like for her birthday and she said "Just once, I'd like you to buy me something retail" –'

'What on earth has that to do with it –'

'Not a lot.'

'Well if you're going to get worked up about custard, what about gravy? It's this lower-middle-class thing about not wanting to pour stuff over stuff, I mean if stuff is a bit on the dry side what's wrong with saying to your hostess Do you think I could have a little gravy –'

'Ha, ha, ha.'

'– well you can sneer –'

'Its just I can't see that phrase falling smoothly from anyone's lips – Might I have a little gravy, have you a touch of gravy about your person –'

'– middle-class people put the custard and the gravy in at an earlier stage, that's all that happens –'

'In what?'

'Oh come on, coq au vin, I don't know the names of all these *made* dishes –'

'I was put off gravy at an earlier, more serious phase of my life when I was judging a Glamorous Grandmothers' competition at a Butlin's Holiday Camp, and as we sat at lunch the gravy came round, and it was poured from a coffee-pot – to this hour the ogles of the grandmas and the brown stream falling from the long spout of the pewter jug, seem to combine and emulsify –'

'I don't believe there is a restaurant in London that serves junket. Has semolina been mentioned?'

'No, there are ladies present.'

'– or blancmange –'

'Shape –'

'Tapioca –'

'Condensed-milk butties –'

'Ah – I have information germane to all these things, and yet more horrifying than all. A correspondent tells me that any endeavours to keep British tables custard-free is doomed to failure, at least in Gloucester-shire. Happily for herself, she lives in Bristol, but in Gloucester she says there is a café which not only serves custard, but boasts a menu-board which lists Radio-Malt flan.'

Qu'est ce que c'est, ce custard qu'on fout partout? The babel of that particular conversation still seemed to hum in Robinson's head. The wrath of the custard lobby had been poured all over him until, in truth, he felt a bit of a rhubarb crumble himself. But he clung stoutly to his conviction – the steamy smell of custard was the smell of eggs, obscurely abused. There would be nothing of the sort tonight. Cottage-pie and a bit of cheese and a mouthful of burgundy, and then that nice pudding with caramelized sugar sitting in a shiny slab on top, and the peeled grapes and brandy and cream beneath . . .

ON certain Saturday evenings they met in surroundings that were essentially fictional.

For this reason, the park might have extended to the horizon, but Robinson felt that something smaller, with a little standing timber and a flock of Southdowns, would bear witness not only to his imagination but also to his modesty. Far within the mellow stone house – 1685, certainly not later than 1690 – the door-chimes (removed in a fit of piety from the bungalow of his mother) echoed like a set of inverted commas, and before the last strains of 'Danny Boy' had died away on the evening air, Eric had appeared on the terrace to announce the arrival of Milton Shulman.

Strolling pensively past the windows of the Old Library, and looking down from the terrace to the shaven lawns below, Robinson wondered whether a peacock or two might not add a touch of colour, a grace note that even the most derisive of his companions could admit was funny without being vulgar.

There was a shout, which came vaguely from the direction of the Orangery.

'Sorry, squire – lost my way.'

Laurie Taylor, pjink in black tie and light-reactive spectacles, crunched into view on the gravel path below, waving cheerfully with his free hand and bearing in the other a pair of tomato-coloured boots which he would afterwards explain were the occasion of his making an entry via the domestic offices, whither he had made a detour to beg the use of a tin of dubbin.

The clatter of a helicopter grew louder.

'Its Ann,' Robinson shouted to Laurie.

The plane came swooping in over the pasture, flattening the grass as it skimmed the pepper-pot roof of the gazebo, and hovered delicately as though unsure of its welcome, before lowering itself on to a tiny square of turf precisely at the centre of the parterre, between the salvias and the cinneraria.

As Ann Leslie was tipping the pilot, Eric appeared at the door which led from the drawing-room to the terrace. He was grimacing horribly, his lips undulating like two roller-blinds which had gone out of control.

'Mr Shulman is complaining that nobody takes him seriously. He says in a properly conducted household the butler would not have left a guest to fetch the host, the host would already have been there to greet him. He also asked me why I was wearing a white jacket instead of a black one –' Eric began to breathe formidably through his nose – 'I told him the black one was being *cleaned*.'

Eric gave the word 'cleaned' a dreadful emphasis, rolled his eyes and grinned with rage. His likeness to the late Eric Blore was uncanny, until you realized he actually was the man – after all (as Robinson reflected) why spoil the ship for a ha'porth of tar.

'Mr Shulman ought to have been late – he always is.'

Laurie and Ann walked up the stone steps together, and suddenly there was a blast of sound from the gnarled branches of the four-hundred-year-old Spanish chestnut, as though it had been roofed in slates, and they were all falling off – clearly, Robinson had made up his mind about the peacocks.

'*Can* they fly?' Ann turned sharply, and looked up at the tree.

'I'll get Eric to check with the Zoo.'

'And after that – ' a rather high piercing voice volplaned down from the mullions of the second storey – 'we might have a little bear-baiting on the lawn – eh?'

'Trevor –'

They all followed their host's gaze as he craned his neck to address the face which was framed in the casement above. But the features, which at first glance seemed to consist chiefly of a pair of pince-nez, were abruptly withdrawn, and Robinson said, 'Trevor, he arrived early of course, he told me he'd been back-packing in the area –'

But before he could finish, the man in the pince-nez sprinted out on to the terrace, having negotiated the staircase in record time, advancing on the others with a beaming smile which somehow his pince-nez instantly converted into yoghurt. He was wearing bicycle-clips.

'I do hope Eric found you a billet for your machine,' Robinson said. 'Plenty of room for the bike in one of the loose-boxes –'

'What bike?'

'Oh –', Robinson dragged his gaze away from the bicycle clips. 'Have you met Trevor Breadnut? Trevor – how shall I introduce you –'

'Just call me – Wordsmith.'

Laurie and Ann spoke nearly as one, though slightly out of synch.

'No, no,' said Robinson pettishly, 'his name isn't Wordsmith, his name is Breadnut –'

But the man – with a slight, but distinctly italicized, wriggle of his shoulders – had swung a pair of binoculars into play and was sweeping the landscape through the lenses with a wry twist to his lips, as though what he wanted to see had already been painted on the glass before he looked through it. 'Just the place for a – Wild Life Park. Or would you call it a – Sanctuary?'

There was a noise, as of a human-being imitating a machine-gun.

'Uh-uh-uh, ah-ah-ah, eh-eh-eh.'

The Breadnut figure whipped round, and jerking the long glasses behind him with a movement of the neck unappealingly reminiscent of a Burmese temple dancer, darted forward across the gravel, and confronting the man who now stood in the doorway, began to make signs to him in what looked like the language of the deaf and dumb.

Milton – for it was he – stared at the man.

'Were you talking about the Zoo?'

The man in the pince-nez fell back a pace.

'But you can speak!' he cried.

'Who are you?'

'Let's just say I'm –'

'His name is Trevor Breadnut,' said Robinson hastily, 'Trevor, this is Milton.'

'I masterminded a whole series of films about the Zoo, the Zoo, ah ah ah, I worked at the, at the, at the, I worked at the Zoo, and I want to tell you that an actual wild animal is worth a hundred images of wild animals on television, wolf spiders, Java fighting fish, there's an eyeball to eyeball contact, and, ah ah ah, and this contact, ah, this contact, you see children meeting the gaze of anacondas and in that very instant realizing they're looking at something real not something that is a picture, and I just want to say –'

Shulman raised his voice a decibel or two as everyone turned to follow Eric who had walked out of the house with a tray full of glasses and was now moving away towards the herb garden.

'Eh eh eh –'

Everyone was filing off, behind the butler, crunching over the gravel, then clattering down the steps at the east end of the terrace, and along a narrow paved path.

'You smell the beasts, you enter a reality that programmes about animals can't ever, eh eh eh, can't possibly –'

There was a small pavilion ahead, in front of it three round white metal tables, and a cluster of garden chairs, each with a cushion that looked a mite too small for its function.

'Only thing is,' someone ahead of Milton in the crocodile shouted over his shoulder, 'the animals haven't volunteered for this educative experience.'

The man called Trevor had paused, suddenly crouching down in front of Ann Leslie (who was forced to pull up short, but not so short that she didn't manage to catch him in the ribs, twice, delicately, as she stepped over his stooping figure) and let out a short series of laughs, each of which came out sharper than the last as everyone clambering over him seemed as clumsy as the lady, catching their toes in his anorak.

Trev sat on his hunkers in front of a patch of herb robert, staring keenly at the unremarkable plant as though discovering Newfoundland, and still emitting an occasional bark of laughter, as though whoever it was who had responded to Milton's thesis had managed to ruin what might have been a reasonably good point. The others spread themselves over the chairs, their irritation with Trev made manifest by the way they began to talk at random and with a hostility that was only accentuated by its facetiousness.

Eric, who had placed the *flutes* on the table, walked back from the pavilion carrying two bottles of champagne, retreated once more into the building and brought with him two more. Laurie began to struggle with one of the corks. Eric started to breathe audibly through his nose.

'If I may make so *baold* – sir.'

He stepped forward and treading with great accuracy on Laurie's toe, dragged the bottle from his hand, but as he began with one of his characteristic smirks to turn the cork, Trev bounded up from his not altogether uncritical inspection of what the universe in its feeble way was getting the earth to put forth, and with a cry of 'Give it here', pulled the already loosened cork free so that a plume of froth shot up the nostrils of the butler.

Eric blew back the foam like an enraged dolphin in a Bartolozzi print, but Laurie darted towards Trevor and grasping him by the shoulder, cried, 'We've met before.'

A murmur arose: 'Of course –' 'How silly –' 'You joined us –' 'Custard –'

Trevor simpered.

Robinson, who only ever remembered people he had privately elected to the status of blood relative, said importantly, 'How perfectly ridiculous – but today Trevor has his bicycle-clips on, and its surprising what a difference –'

'It does –'

'You wouldn't know him –'

'And he's changed his parting –'

'Eh eh eh, but the Zoo, where else could anyone find a collection of animals who, or I might say which, aren't just pictures but are really there?'

Trevor, who seemed to accept the fact of his late recognition not so much as a slight but as an accolade – as though being overlooked and then acknowledged was a distinction he shared with Galileo and one or two others – had pulled out a chair and was waiting for the butler to be seated.

He turned his head as Milton spoke and said, 'Don't you you know that what you have just said makes animals sound like the sort of cigarette-card you stick in an album?'

This was so like acerbic good sense, albeit emanating from a tainted source, that everyone started to say Rhubarb Rhubarb and nothing could be distinctly heard above what – if it were taking place on radio – would have called forth a flood of correspondence complaining that the conversation was not worth hearing at the best of times, but surely good manners required that each person spoke in turn.

'But they exist – Zoos I mean,' said Ann Leslie, floating energetically up to the surface of the static. 'I know when you walk through the gate there's more than a hint of the penal colony, a touch of the reformatory –'

'Something mechanistic and out-of-date,' Robinson interjected.

'But honestly, the suspicion the place is a sort of freak show, doesn't it vanish as soon as you set eyes on the animals?'

'You said it for me, Ann,' exclaimed their shameless host, 'one is always put off by the people giggling raucously as though it were the eighteenth-century and they'd come to visit Bedlam to laugh at the lunatics –'

'Yes, yes,' Ann fell athwart what threatened to develop momentum in a direction that might not have suited her purposes, 'but when you do see the animals are you not reminded that there is such a thing as wonder – and wonder is a good long way removed from simply staring –'

'I wish,' said Robinson, 'you'd been with me on Tuesday last when I wandered into the London Zoo and saw, to my own satisfaction at least, that the orang-outang didn't seem to like being on show in a cage that looked like a bijou maisonette – it was piling scraps of old cardboard on its head like a poor old lady abandoned in some geriatric nowhere – I say if you had been there you would have seen as I did that when the orang-outang walked to the side window of the plate-glass centrally-heated place it was marooned in, and looked moodily out, away from the people, it was at once so like, and so entirely unlike, the rest of us that I was spellbound by what you accurately identified – wonder.'

Eric had sunk down into the chair Trevor had offered, poured himself a glass of champagne, and as his employer came to the end of his statement, raised the *flute* to the side of his head and somewhat vulgarly made as though to pour the contents down his left ear.

'All the very best,' he crowed.

It was at once apparent that Laurie, who had been standing throughout the conversational exchanges, felt it necessary to put the butler at his ease: a work of supererogation (his host reflected) since to attempt to put Eric at his ease was equivalent to trying to help Einstein with his sums – as anyone who had seen the man's films would readily attest.

'Nothing like a mouthful of bubbly after you've been on your feet all day,' Laurie said, leaning towards Eric, having taken the next chair with the air of one who didn't mind who he sat next to.

Eric leered hideously.

'You're a sociologist, aren't you?'

'By way of,' Laurie chuckled.

'A professor of sociology.'

'They said I was Chair Material!' Laurie laughed hugely.

'Then perhaps you'll be able to tell me,' said Eric, emptying his glass, and refilling it, 'who it was who said there is no television programme that isn't improved by the *absence* of a professor of sociology?'

Robinson's lower-middle class heart was always rendered uneasy when people started to clamber out of their allotted roles.

'Quite a lot to be done in the house, Eric,' he said shiftily, like someone who had come across the phrase *au dessus de sa gare*, thought it attractive, but had never run into a situation where he had found sufficient confidence to utter it.

Eric looked despisingly at him.

'You must surely realize I am not sitting down *qua* butler. I am sitting down *qua* Eric Blore. I thought the distinction between fact and fiction was one thing at least that everyone here would appreciate –'

'Fiction is something we shall certainly be discussing on some future occasion, and when we do I shall require you to be on hand.'

'Yes – *sir*', said Eric, rising from his chair with a wriggling motion, and sticking each of his index fingers into the necks of two empty bottles, he set off whistling down the garden path, kicking his legs sideways before mounting the steps to the terrace.

'But Trevor,' said Laurie, 'I gather you don't approve of Zoos, and I don't think I do either, but what would you do with all the animals

– not compulsory repatriation, surely?'

'Ha!' Trevor, who had cast off his anorak to reveal the gleaming buckles on the shoulder straps of his boiler-suit, clapped his hand to his forehead and rolled his eyes as one melodramatically amused at the crassness of the company he was having to keep, 'Ha!'

'Well, come on, you can't just throw open their cages and point them in the general direction of the Brazilian jungle, can you?'

'But you know,' said Ann, 'if you've ever been in that giant palace of the pachyderms at the London Zoo you can see people do have crazy notions about animals – I remember Celia Haddon pointing out it was so high it looked as though it'd been built for elephants that roost at night –'

'And when the Victorians were wondering what might be suitable accommodation for camels they decided on mosques – I think it was Celia who said that too –'

'Celia's always felt strongly about zoos.'

'Well, but sometimes the animals themselves can be as odd as the people,' said Milton. 'That famous aviary they have at Regents Park has had some holes torn in the wire, and do you think any of the birds have tried to escape? On the contrary, a bunch of mad seagulls pecked those holes so they could get themselves inside.'

Robinson said, 'I wonder if the Victorians started zoos so they could contemplate the basic emotions in animals which they couldn't bear to contemplate in themselves –'

'Ha!' There was another delighted shout from Trevor. 'I knew we'd get round to the obvious if we stuck at it long enough.'

'Thank you, Trevor,' said Robinson sourly, 'it must be a terrible trial having a first-class brain. I was merely going to add that the idea of a zoo as a gallery of grotesques exhibiting all the primal passions would be very attractive to a society which felt it had somehow been obliged to rise above those appetites itself, yet still required them to be publicly proclaimed.'

'There may be something in it,' said Laurie. 'And if the animals began as grotesques which were simply to be pointed at, the next stage would be the awakening of a sort of conscience, a feeling that these unfortunate creatures were to be more the object of pity than anything else, and in the Thirties when I first became aware of zoos, there was a vague obligation to let yourself be heard being kind to the animals, people thanked the camel or the elephant after the children had had the ride, and used the very polite voice grown-ups always use when they're remind-ing children to say thank-you, and then there was the Chimps' Teaparty –'

'Regular feature of Pathe Gazette –'

'But it was always as if the animals were twopence short of the shilling.'

'Yes,' Robinson agreed, 'it was always as though the animals were not very effective attempts on God's part to get round to inventing *us*. I wonder if the next stage will be to see them for what they are, namely themselves?'

The sound of a gong from inside the house rolled round the park and through the trees.

'But it really is quite difficult not to see them as caricatures of people,' Ann said, as they filed out of the herb garden. 'I never see a camel but he reminds me of Lytton Strachey. The way it walks, I mean.'

Trevor, who had reinvested himself with his anorak, began to hum the Eton Boating Song.

'How does it go, Trev?' said Laurie, treading on Trevor's heels. 'I can't even remember the last two lines.'

The chance to correct, enlighten, inform was too much, and Trev smirked as he complacently quoted –

'Which accounts for the hump on the camel

'And the Sphinx's inscrutable smile.'

'Of course "smile" rhymes with "Nile",' Milton said. 'How does the rest of it go? "Now the something something sands of the desert, Are washed by the something of the Nile –"'

Trevor made an elaborately theatrical display of clearing his throat and actually nudged Milton in the ribs with his elbow.

'Herk herm – ladies, old man, ladies.'

'He shouldn't just spare the ladies,' said Robinson, 'he should spare us all. Almost nothing is more jarring than a man with a tin ear for scansion trying to remember a poem he has long forgotten. I myself certainly can't recall more than one of the verses, but that verse perfectly illustrates the scurrilous rhymester's essential grasp of epitome. As you know, I am in receipt of a voluminous correspondence from people who share our own interest in what might seem at first sight to be matters scarcely visible to the naked eye, but which on inspection turn out to be small but quite distinct doorways through which we pass into the rolling prairies of identity, not only our own but sometimes, when we are lucky, the identity we share with everyone –'

'I love it when you talk like this,' said Ann, 'it reminds me of how much we lost when the grammar-schools went comprehensive.'

' – and it was one of those correspondents, a lady of seventy-five, who passed the verse on to me – it had been imparted to her by a boy-friend, at that time a student of divinity, fifty years ago. It runs as follows:

'Exhaustive research, and enquiry,
By Darwin and Huxley and Hall,
Have conclusively proved that the hedgehog
Has no sexual relations at all.
And further extensive researches
Have incontrovertibly shown
That sexual safety in Egypt
Is enjoyed by the hedgehog alone.'

'Ow, no, no, *no* – it wasn't Egypt,' cried Eric irritably, standing on the terrace and holding a gong in one hand and a hammer in the other, 'it was Keble. And two of the earlier lines went –

'Now the camel considers these matters
In the light of a couple of drinks '

– and Eric, his lips curling contemptuously, struck the gong once, as though awarding himself the only mark.

'That certainly rhymes with "Sphinx",' nodded Milton sagely, as they all moved inside.

They were in the Small Dining-room that evening, sitting at the round patent red-mahogany table that had been made by Bridgett and Sursingle for the then master of Bagfox Hall (George Macadam Robinson) in 1811. One circular tier of its wooden leaves had been added, so that the space having been enlarged each of the five people who were dining might loll at their ease. Candles flickered cleverly in their sconces, and the silver glowed as Eric diligently breathed on the back of the soup spoons and having rubbed them briskly up and down his lapels, replaced them on the figured wood.

Ancestral portraits looked down from the linenfold – Erasmus Robinson, one hand brandishing a sextant, the other pointing towards a map of the Isle of Wight which he had recently discovered; Cadwallader Robinson, scion of the Welsh branch, known in Porthcawl as the Hammer of the Chaste; Prosperity Robinson, who managed a small Woolworths for Oliver Cromwell; Cosmo Wellbeloved Robinson, bishop of the Spice Islands, who had placed a charge of gunpowder in his fundament to cure himself of hiccups; and Horneyold Leadbitter Robinson, first Earl of New Malden, whose historical niche was stolen from him along with his cloak, when it was snatched off his shoulders by Sir Walter Raleigh intent on protecting Queen Elizabeth from the puddle.

Before they sat down, Trevor had been engaged in a struggle outside the Small Dining-room with Eric over the question of attire, and actually coming to grips with the butler in a rolling double-axel as Eric attempted to divest him forcibly of his anorak, staggered across the passageway and collided with the croquet-sticks in the umbrella-stand.

'Allow me to pull your coat straight, sir,' and Eric at his most insinuating had reached beneath the offending garment and, grabbing a handful of Trevor's baggy trousers in the mistaken impression they were his non-existent jacket, had them round his ankles in a trice.

A short sharp scream, followed by the cry 'Arse-bandit!' as Trevor re-positioned his dungarees, could not be repressed, but the contretemps had soon been smoothed over, and the conversation proceeded as dinner was served.

'It won't do', said Robinson, 'to speak of the many ways we have all seen the knife and fork held – I spoke once of a man in a Little Chef, on the A303, who managed to hold the handles of both implements away from himself, so that from where I was sitting it seemed as though he was not only offering the implements to an invisible third party seated opposite, but was actually operating them for him. But when I made a joke about this in public, I was roundly abused by someone writing in the *New Statesman* who said I was going on like Sir Owen Seaman "Teaching some swine, To sneer at a char with a washing-line" –'

Trevor, who was adjusting the buckles of his shoulder-straps while his soup cooled, said 'I wrote that piece. You sounded very much like someone who was trying to smuggle his own insecurity past the *douane* in the form of a joke.'

'You mean unless jokes are about Dukes, they are contraband?'

'Oh, everyone is vulnerable,' said Trevor eating his soup out of the correct side of the spoon to the annoyance of the entire company, 'but have you ever considered the option that is always available to you – not making jokes about anyone?'

Trevor's smile was as impermeable as polyurethane. Robinson ground his teeth audibly and said to Eric, 'Pass Mr Breadnut the croutons – I don't think those he has are quite as crunchy as he would like.' There was something about Robinson that let you know that the one thing he hated in all the world was to seem to be bested, in company.

'We'd be better off with peas,' Ann Leslie volunteered, 'as far as things that don't matter are concerned. How you eat peas –'

'None tonight,' interjected Robinson, who sounded surly.

'I claim,' said Ann, 'that the way anyone eats peas is, as a topic of conversation, restful. The sort of thing that can't matter to anyone, very similar in its effect to the question of how many angels can dance on the end of a pin –'

'Ow, I wouldn't say *that*, madam,' said Eric, who was leaning with one elbow on the sideboard, his other fist tucked into his hip, and his legs crossed negligently at the ankles. 'It was among others a question that bothered St Thomas Aquinas very much indeed, none of us goes back as far as he does, I'm sure, but not being *owld* enough to have sat at his feet wouldn't in itself be a good enough reason – wouldn't –' and here Eric grimaced sadistically, '– wouldn't be a *sufficient* reason, as the Angelic Doctor himself might have put it, to reduce his reasoned caveats to the level of mere dinner-table conversation – more wine, my Lord?' – he oared his way towards Laurie Taylor with the burgundy.

Robinson seemed to be recovering his spirits. 'I thought people had stopped worrying about how you eat peas,' he said, 'after Virginia Woolf made it plain you scooped them up on your knife, held your hand over them and cried 'How many?' –

But Milton interjected: 'Eh eh eh there was ah ah ah there was a worrying piece in the *Daily Telegraph* about which side of the fork President Mitterand of France had at them with, apparently there was I mean a general feeling that he ought to cram the eh eh eh on the back of the implement but ah ah ah that would ruin the pea, wouldn't it, pea's gone to a lot of trouble to get itself spheroid, and you ah ah you mash it up as though it were a mere banana –'

'Well I sort of wouldn't say a banana, I mean I'd say there was a sort of basic feeling, you know, that pea-eating ought to be a bit difficult,' Laurie Taylor began, 'because while they're struggling to get the things into their mouths people are too preoccupied to realize how sort of boring the bloody things are, I mean, scoop up too many peas too easily and you'll find yourself wondering why you bothered in the first place –'

'All very true,' Robinson nodded, 'I knew a man who ate at the same restaurant every day, and he was at last driven mad by the blandness of the peas and there he was, firing them round the place using the end of his knife as a catapult – just off Great Mersey Street, it was, not far from the Phoenix Mill, and if I haven't got it wrong, his name was Gooch – no, Geek – and he had a lisp, a slight impediment, rather attractive in its way.'

Trevor said insinuatingly to Ann, 'Might I trouble you for the condiments?' For a moment Ann looked startled, as though this were a sexual euphemism unknown to her. But then realizing what he meant, she pushed one of the salts towards him.

'Tar', said Trev, adding, 'When my father ate cornflakes I used to turn the Third Programme on and listen to organ music.'

Eric, who had his back turned to the company, and was rubbing the uppers of his shoes up and down each trouser-legged calf in turn, poured into a little silver cup a measure from the magnum of Chambolle Musigny les Amoureuses 1949 which he had newly opened. He said, without turning round, 'It was even worse with my father.'

He approached the table, hung his fat olive nose over the silver taster, took a sip, then drank off the rest. 'Yum, yum,' he said, then filled Ann's glass. 'It wasn't just cornflakes with him,' said Eric, 'it was the way he went out into the hall when he wanted to fart – it was a nice gesture, but you could still hear him. Know what I mean?'

'Eric,' said Robinson, 'You're a fan of Saul Bellow, I wonder if you can identify which of his novels this line comes from: "Do you have to tell me *everything*?"'

'*Mr Sammler's Planet*, of course.' Eric writhed backwards towards the swing-door which led to the kitchen. 'Ho, ho,' he said, and left to collect the cottage-pie.

'Some services are too intimate,' Laurie pointed out, 'like you know when the waiter offers to peel your peach for you, or when he says you know do you want your sole on or off the bone, its OK but it comes too close to what you might only want to do for yourself, you know, I mean, like when the barber offers to snip the hairs in your ears –'

One of the labrador/retriever-crosses which had been lying in front of the gas-fired logs which burned so convincingly Robinson always felt impelled to announce they were false before anyone who entered the room could be sure what object of his own the host (characteristically) was so instantly denigrating, lurched slowly to its feet and padding over to Trevor, pulled the anorak off the back of his chair and dragged it across the Aubusson to his master.

'Good dog!' Robinson patted the beast. 'I'm sorry Trevor, he has an instinct for quality. No, it isn't that Eric offers to iron *The Times* for me, its more that he was hired as staff but refuses to stay in character.'

'Great word,' Milton cried, 'staff, I mean. Whatever happened to servant?'

'Taken over,' replied Ann, 'by politicians who say they are servants of the public. Also by retired Field-Marshals writing to the same news-paper Eric has eaten his bran to the accompaniment of before ever he presents it to his employer – men who sign their letters Your Obedient Servant but who are not the sort of servant who are no longer called the servants, as you would very soon find out if you asked one of them to fetch your anorak –'

Trevor had risen, but only to squat, as he fondled the enormous dog who had stolen the garment from his chair (mahogany, simulated rose-wood). The dog, sinking down between his front paws, indicated the entire incident was closed, but Trevor made free with his ears and addressed him enthusiastically as 'Boy'.

'You just can't assume the relationship is as absolute as the word servant once suggested,' Laurie was pointing out. 'It's a word that said that what was happening between the two parties couldn't ever be otherwise, and of course such a distinct delineation of the two roles isn't now possible –'

Trevor, who was lying on the carpet as though insisting that a warm personal relationship had sprung up between himself and the dog, said 'Ha! So human relationships have to be reduced to mathematical formulae before they can be taken account of!'

Laurie said sharply, 'Which will exclude anyone who didn't get beyond his twice-times table.'

'No, no, the English are very nervous about those who attend them,' Milton chimed in, 'they don't feel they deserve it.'

Trevor made to rise, but the dog was lying on his arm, and he had to tug determinedly before he had it free. Robinson spoke, lowering his voice in case Eric should suddenly dive back into the room: 'I daresay you could imagine anyone wanting to be a sociologist or a drama critic or a journalist, but –' and his voice dropped even lower – 'can you imagine anyone saying he wanted to be a butler when he grew up?'

'Being a waiter would be all right. Who wouldn't want Goldberg in a restaurant to ask him what the time was and be able to reply, napkin over arm, 'Sorry, this isn't my table – eh what, eh eh eh, what what –'

The dog made a noise, half way between a snuffle and a groan.

A voice off, echoing like a character in an opera, came nearer and nearer. 'There are FAIRIES at the bottom of my garden – yes there ARE, yes there ARE –' Eric kicked open the swing-door. 'Sorry, boys and girls,' he continued in the same falsetto, 'the Bisto curdled.'

'Now I could have sworn you'd have had music,' Ann said. 'Apart from Eric, I mean –'

'Oh *madam*,' gurgled Eric, 'you and I could give them a few of the *owld* ones. "Lets all sing like the birdies sing, tweet, tweet, tweet, tweet, tweet –"'

'Do shut up,' said Trevor, to everyone's surprise, 'you've got a lousy voice and just because you're playing a butler doesn't entitle you to the forbearance that a real servant would command – right, Laurie?'

Laurie's sphinx-like look suggested that being addressed by the affectionate diminutive of his own first name by the man he didn't like incurred a response he would have put into words if he could have hit on an arrangement of them that would have made this clear without making something about himself even clearer. He contented himself for the time being by sticking the business end of a butter knife into his mouth, bending it with his fingers against the fulcrum of his teeth, then strumming the blade until it emitted the unmistakeable twang of a jews harp. Whereupon Trev dug into the breast pocket of his dungarees and brought forth, not a spanner but a harmonica, ramming the glittering instrument into his mouth endwise and – moving it round his lips as limberly as Clint Eastwood chewing a thin cigar – provided so lively a rendering of 'The Turkey In The Straw' that Ann and Milton and Robinson broke into spontaneous applause, while Eric – placing hot plates in front of all those at table, and evidently taking Trevor's disobliging remarks as a sort of tribute (sour, but undeniable) to his histrionic powers – turned his delivery of the utensils into a brisk but rhythmic *pas seul*.

'We could have had a Mozart trio,' their host said, when the applause subsided, 'something outside the windows, on the terrace. A little night music –'

'Calls for a full orchestra,' said Milton, whose musical sensibilities had been forged in the Toronto equivalent of the borscht belt, crooning in suburban luncheon-clubs where to the blue-rinse brigade he was known as Whispering Milt.

'I wonder what goes on inside a composer's head before the music comes out,' Robinson said vaguely, 'does he have a diagram in his mind which he fills with notes? Is there a skeleton of sound which he carries about in his imagination – something on which he drapes an arrangement of the notes? Does he invoke an invisible symmetry round which he slides the notes until a new symmetry emerges – you know, like a chess grand master perceiving a fresh pattern of moves? Or does he simply hear the stuff at the back of his head? What comes first?'

'What comes first,' said Ann, 'is a call from his agent. As Sammy Kahn once pointed out.'

'And Johnson eh eh eh,' Milton chimed in, 'you know Johnson said Had I learned to fiddle I'd have done nothing else for the rest of my life. And all that's true, you know ah ah ah, its true, its a gift, a gift for music, its either there or it isn't.'

'Glad its not here,' said Laurie, diving into the cottage-pie, 'if you've ever seen you know like a four-piece zigeuner band in a Viennese Raths-keller start climbing down off the stage where you thought they were you know like rooted and begin to move towards you like the Forest of Dunsinane, tipping their fiddles well up so you could see the high-denomination notes they'd stuffed inside the instruments to encourage the diners to tip lavishly – '

'Supposed to be romantic and special,' nodded Ann, 'but awfully aggressive – I remember a film where the hero hid a whole slew of gypsy instrumentalists in the hotel bathroom and when they came out on cue playing their ghastly fiddles the girl, instead of ringing instantly for the hotel psychiatrist, fell straight into the hero's bed.'

'Gypsy music is basically gloomy,' said Milton, prising off a segment of crisp brown scab from the top of his cottage-pie, crunching it up with relish, and washing it down with a deep draught of the delicious red burgundy, 'because the sound of it suggests that everything you hanker after is already over and in decay –'

'Like Wagner,' interrupted Robinson, 'where the orgasm is staved off for five hours, and at the end of the evening you're invited to come back the next night and hear it staved off again –'

Trevor gave a high-pitched laugh, and repeated the word – 'Orgasm', he pronounced, derisively.

'Yes,' said Eric, looking at him thoughtfully, 'those were the days, weren't they, sir?' He moved across with a bottle and placed it in front of Trev. 'Ketchup, sir?'

' – the consequence, of course, of the music being indigenous to Vienna,' Milton went on. 'But harps are worse – how gloom settled on the cinema when all the jokes and fun stopped and Harpo was discovered at the instrument – '

'That,' said Laurie, who had casually hooked the sauce bottle towards him and was abstractedly studying the label, 'was because the bastard played the thing as though he were showing an old lady across the road.'

'I'll give you a word for the harpist' – said Trevor leaning forward across the table, his face lighting up – 'plucky!'

There was a terrible rattling of knives and forks, under cover of which Laurie, as though in a fit of absent-mindedness, removed the screw-top of the sauce bottle and shook a dollop or two on to his plate.

'Spot on, Trev,' said Robinson, 'I don't think Stoppard could have bettered you there. But when it comes to promoting unease in a public dining-area to be terrorized by a gypsy-band is as nothing compared with looking up from your plate in a restaurant – as I did the other evening – to find that a lady with a harp has slipped into the next seat. To find as you're crunching up your deep-fried golden-brown scampi, served with lemon wedge and sachet of sauce tartare, that you're cheek by jowl with a lady and a harp is – as I think even Trevor will agree – the ultimate test of sang-froid –'

'Eh eh eh nonsense ah ah, no no,' Milton interrupted, 'the ultimate in ah in ah the ultimate in that sort of thing is sitting next to a man at a dinner-party in Eaton Square who takes a banana from the fruit-bowl, lays it on his plate, then takes two plums and places them each side of the bottom end of the banana, and actually nudges your wife to make sure she doesn't miss it –'

'And that,' said Ann, 'is outclassed by the man at a dinner-party in Kentish Town who just before we all went home did an imitation of a one-armed man trying to press the button in a lift which involved him sticking his finger through his flies and hanging his walking-stick on it –'

'Which can't hold a candle,' Laurie intervened, 'to the man at a dinner-party in Great Crosby –'

'*Sow* distingué,' chirruped Eric, passing the flageolets.

'– in Great Crosby, who actually took us into the downstairs loo to give us his imitation of Toulouse-Lautrec relieving himself, the tableau naturally taking place with the man on his knees, and achieving its climax with the seat of the lavatory clanging down and the man pretending to shout in agony –'

'What a church mouse you all make me feel,' Robinson mildly observed. 'Nonetheless, or anyway nonetheverymuchless, I think the circumstances I was giving you the broad outline of include sang-froid somewhere, I'm buggered if they don't. Had the lady offered us a tune on her mouth-organ like Trevor, we could all of us have hummed along, but you simply can't tap your knife in time to a harp – and even to smile encouragingly at a woman who appears to be doing more with her two arms than an octopus does with eight seems, or indeed seemed, woefully inadequate. Besieged as you may be –' he was warming to his theme, 'by gypsies making menacing movements with the bows of their fiddles in the direction of your *knoedls*, you can at least ask them to play something you're fond of, but you can't turn to a lady with a harp and ask her for 'Oh what a Beautiful Morning'.

'Oh it happened,' Laurie interjected, piling french beans on to his plate, possibly to mask the tell-tale red of the ketchup, 'it happened, or at least something very like it happened, at the Argyle Theatre, Birkenhead, when Joan Hammond I think it was or it could have been Evadne Girdlschoon was giving a recital –'

'Vocal gems from *Maritana*?' ventured Ann.

'Never heard of it, no – I really don't, you know, know what the programme was, but it certainly included the Flower Song from something or other like Faust and one or two things like –'

'One Fine Day?'

'Ave Maria?'

'Roselein, roselein, roselein, rot –'

'Love it!' cried Eric.

'– yes, yes, yes, why can't you all, you know, anyway, she'd got to the end of something or other –'

'Also sprach Zarathustra?'

'That's right, and there was tumultuous applause and this bloke got up and walked down the aisle and went right up to the orchestra-rail as silence fell, and he said, he said, looking up at her on the stage, he said, he said, 'Give us "Mother Macree"', and the mistake she made was actually replying to him, she said, 'I'm afraid that's not in my repertoire', and this bloke he said, he said – '

Trevor, his face radiant with malice, just got there first.

'OK, show us your tits.'

For the second time that evening there was an outbreak of rhubarb, rhubarb, and it was some moments before Robinson could draw the business about the harp to a peaceful close.

'Yes,' he said to Eric, who hovered with the second instalment of the cottage-pie, magnificent on a pewter trencher, 'a morsel, I think. But as I was saying –' the pie came beautifully to the spoon, moist enough, but as integral as a wedge of cake, 'I felt the instrument precluded casual requests, and by the end of the evening men were twining their hands in their hair and groaning dismally, and when the bell went for Round 12 the harpist wasn't even breathing hard. "My compliments to the chef," I told the waiter, as I finally threw in the napkin, "but I think the harp was a little overdone" – not something you could say about this cottage-pie,' he ended, turning to Eric, who was now leaning against the sideboard, plate in hand, having helped himself to a generous portion.

'Ambrosia, sir,' cooed Eric, his fat cheeks distended in the act of mastication, 'Old Mrs Fruitfly will be *sow* pleased the dish gave pleasure.'

'Nelly always gives pleasure,' Robinson said, rather sententiously, 'I shall make a point of telling her myself later on.'

Perhaps convinced that no one observed him, Laurie took a piece of bread and deftly swabbed the red smear from his plate, popping the evidence into his mouth before enlarging on the subject of food – 'The Concept Restaurant has you know much to be said for it, Mozart's all very well but what about being able to dial conversation when you're on your own, something to listen to while you're engaged in the rather you know boring act of eating' – the crust proving more substantial than his busy delivery of the words could for the moment accommodate, he was obliged to pause and jerk his jaw sideways, dipping his head in the manner of Stan Laurel eating a wax apple – 'there's a sort of chat show on the radio, I've often wondered why they don't start a restaurant, call it *Stop the Quiche*, and have their conversations relayed through table-mounted juke-boxes –'

'Clear the place like lightning –'

'Worse than ptomaine –'

'I'd pay an inclusive 15 per cent service-charge to avoid such a bunch of gallstones –'

'No, no, no' – Laurie swallowed definitively – 'a topless waitress at one elbow and a conversation machine at the other –'

'What a trio you'd make,' tootled Eric, 'no one knowing which of you to put the penny in.' Scooping up the dirty plates along with his own, he bustled merrily out through the swing doors to fetch the pudding.

'But you wouldn't be able to overhear what other people are saying,' Ann pointed out. 'I was eating alone at Joe Allen's, and I heard one lady in a twin-set say, "The world's full of violence" and her chum in the good tweeds and the pearls replied "Personally, I'm sorry we ever beheaded Charles the First –"'

'Now that's the way people really talk,' said Robinson, 'in riddles.'

Milton was chuckling as the example came to him: 'Well has Mavis reason to remember Nuneaton –'

But Trevor who had loosened his buckles and folded down the bib section of his dungarees to reveal the buttons on his combinations, held up his finger.

'Max Beerbohm,' he smirked, 'and it wasn't a restaurant, it was a railway-carriage.'

'Oh but the nicest was, how did it go, oh yes,' Laurie got the sentence in his sights, 'yes – "Mad I don't say, queer I grant you, many's the time I've seen her naked at the piano" –'

Trevor unbuttoned the neck of his comms, and with the air of a man with a hammer and an unlimited supply of the right sort of nails, immobilized the conversation once more. '*New Statesman* competition, August 1953,' he nodded, driving the nail straight and true.

As Eric re-entered bearing two dishes on his ample tray (at the last moment Robinson had added a bitter-orange tart to the simple menu as an alternative to the grape-brulée) Laurie, his teeth chattering like static, cried 'I don't suppose your unremitting study of ephemera allows you the leisure to stray out of the Poly and cock an ear to what real people might actually be saying –'

'Cock an ear!' Trev whinnied with joy, 'that's one for the archives, squire. But oh yes, yes, yes' – he paused to nod, redundantly – 'yes, yes, yes, yes', he continued, possibly not knowing that his host was looking about him for something inexpensive to throw, 'I was eating a bacon sandwich one afternoon in Reece's in Cardiff and a Welshman sitting at the next table said to his companion, "When they come to write the 'istory of the fuck, Jake Evans will be on the frontispiece . . ."'

Eric was deftly sliding the pudding dishes across the table in a miniature variation of the old winter sport of curling, but the last one clattered from his hands and he staggered back to collide with the sideboard, sobbing with mirth.

'Ow dear, ow dear,' he cried, mopping his eyes with a napkin, 'its the dropped aitch that makes it, sir –'

'Pity mice implicitly,' Robinson announced with the air of expecting someone to say something. 'No? Well, its mishearings rather than overhearings that appeal to me. Pitying mice implicitly was what we wanted Jesus to do when I used to go to Sunday school – mice need it, they are very small and get caught in traps and could be overlooked, so in that hymn about Gentle Jesus Meek and Mild we regularly urged him to pity mice, to pity them implicitly since he could hardly go round pitying them *explicitly* all the time –'

Eric had produced a glass-cutter from his waistcoat, and with its small diamond wheel was diligently scoring diagonals across the rondel of caramelized sugar which surmounted the noble dish that held the grape-brulée. Then he tapped the surface with the handle-end of the cutter, and the sweet brown disc fell neatly into segments.

'O pity my simplicity, sir,' he smirked, holding up the cutter 'I found it after they'd finished glazing the outside and I *knew* it'd serve a turn.'

As they helped themselves, Milton said, 'I've never really eh eh eh really never ah ah recovered from the time I telephoned in my notice for *The Merchant Of Venice* and when I opened the paper the next day I found the demand for a pound of flesh was being made by someone called Skylark –'

'Whoops, that Canadian accent,' murmured Trevor, picking his segment of toffee from the top of the pudding, and lobbing it up in the air towards the dog with a 'Here! Catch! Good boy!'

Badly aimed, the sweetmeat struck Robinson on the nose. 'Woof, woof, thank you, Trev. And then one of my correspondents writes to say that he told a piano pupil of his that Schumann had eight children, and the pupil responding in terror cried, 'But if he had ate them, didn't their mothers complain?'

Ann, crooning with delight over the flan, said 'One day I heard the girl next to me at school praying for us miserable offenders, and I realized that I'd always prayed for us miserable old fenders –'

'Used to do a lot of confessing to the Holy Impossibles, Peter and Paul, when I was about seven,' Laurie said, crunching up the hard-topped pudding like a platoon of soldiers marching through gravel.

'Our Father which art in Heaven, Harold be thy name –'

'Send her Victorias – plums, I always supposed –'

'One of my god-daughters studied for a while in America,' Robinson said, 'and in the English class the professor said There are two words you must never, never use in your essays – one is "nifty" and the other is "lousy". There was a second's brooding silence throughout the seminar, and then one of the girls burst out, Yes, yes, but what *are* the words?...'

The dog made a series of high yelping noises, then stood up with his forepaws against the back of his master's chair, balancing on his hind legs like some Queen's Beast.

'He's very quick on the uptake,' Robinson said, as the hound licked his bald head.

Eric collected the plates, clashing them energetically together, and Ann said, 'The small son of a friend of mine asked his mother who George Augustus Peppermint was. They'd been to a wedding and he wondered why the parson had said "If anyone knows George Augustus Peppermint, let him speak now or forever hold his peace."'

'Coffee in the Music Room, sir?' enquired Eric.

They rose, and Eric led the way, out across the Great Hall where a giant sixteenth-century knight astride a caparisoned charger was forever pointing his lance at the snuffbox carried by a surprised-looking Scotsman in bearskin and kilt – the latter adopted by Robinson when the lease of a tobacconist's shop, hard by Gamages, fell in.

'Oh, just sign my Visitors' Book, will you?' cried the host. They paused beside a large brass lectern, worked in the shape of an eagle with its tongue sticking out, on which the richly-tooled volume rested.

'Saucy bugger!' Laurie put his own tongue out at the bird.

'Absolutely right,' said Robinson, 'but don't look it too closely in the eye, you remember the way it hypnotized Augustus Carp's father. Comes from St James-the-Least-of-All, Kennington Oval –'

They stared at him.

'I got it before they turned the place into a bingo-hall,' Robinson said vaguely. 'Outbid a northern Caledonian of the most offensive type – name of Carkeek.'

Ann picked up the Visitors' Book and leafed through a few pages

– 'A home from home', Noel Coward, 'Hasta la vista', Greta Garbo, – and Eric proffering his ballpoint, they all signed.

The doors to the music-room stood open, and sighting the Bosendorfer sitting like a black-widow at the further end of the softly-lit room, Trevor elbowed Eric aside, broke into a trot, and with all the advantage conferred upon him by his rope-soled espadrilles took the highly-polished parquet at a run, and skimming the forty feet to the instrument in one irritating *glissando*, was into the first bars of 'The Pennsylvania Polka' before the others realized that once again he'd stolen the initiative.

From all save Eric. Not for nothing had Eric provided the comic relief in musical films starring Harry James and Tommy Dorsey – in the long tedious sequences in which the maestros held up the action by unloading the music, Eric had sat through re-take after re-take as the musicians slowly sobered up under the savage eyes of Gloria de Haven and Betty Grable, and by the time the director had been replaced, and re-replaced, Eric had as thorough a grounding in the skills of each individual instrument as ever the Juillard School could have hoped to instil.

Moving heel-and-toe down the room as though to show that speed was not inconsequent upon dignity, Eric seated himself amid a silvery grove of side-traps, and scooping up a bouquet of sticks and brushes, whipped the skins into a froth of sound that left Trev idling about on Crewe Station.

'Wow!' The exclamation was as genuine a compliment as any ivory-tinkler could bestow, and Trev put his foot down with the object of catching up.

Robinson claimed Ann for his partner, and Milton and Laurie had no choice.

'Will you rustle a muscle for this tussle?' Laurie asked the drama critic, and Milton hooted, 'Don't mind if I do.' Dashingly, the two couples whirled about the floor. 'It's not something you can serve an apprentice-ship to,' Robinson whispered into Ann's ear, 'like singing or making love – can't do it with one toe on the bottom – have to plunge in –'

'Ow!' screamed Ann, as Robinson scraped his heel across her instep.

'Natural rhythm,' breathed her partner, 'it can't be learned.'

'Sorry to say so, but you're doing it like the British Ballroom Dancing team when they were dancing against the Danes –'

'Against!'

'As though it was ballroom-wrestling –'

'Double Flying Arkwrights –'

'Exactly.'

Laurie and Milton swirled by, and Milton said, 'They've tamed the cha-cha, the tango is housebroken – *Ole !*'

At this moment the door of the music-room opened and a figure bearing a tray of coffee moved across the floor, threading her way through the dancers towards the Bosendorfer. As Trevor continued to play, his head bending over the keys like some Cornell Wilde whose health – not to mention whose wardrobe – had been miraculously transformed by anti-biotics, the lady slid the tray on to the draped glass-topped table adjacent to the little gilt chairs for sitting-out. Her movements were demure but sinuous, and as she turned round to face the room she clasped her hands before her.

Robinson approached with Ann, but Milton and Laurie whirled on, encouraged by the romantic arpeggios of the denim-clad maestro and the mooing sounds of the saxophone for which Eric had now abandoned his brushes.

'Do you reverse ?' shouted Laurie to his partner.

'Like a bird,' yodelled Milton.

A modest smile played about the bee-stung lips of the female who had brought in the supplies. She wore a Laura Ashley top-and-skirt whose billowing chintz seemed deliciously at odds with something firmer under-neath.

Robinson paused, arm-in-arm with Ann, and pressed a button in the wainscote.

A glass sphere lowered itself from the ceiling, and as it began to revolve, splinters of light from its myriad small surfaces flickered across the room to touch with fire the gleaming black hair of the handmaiden. Now she bent over the coffee cups, and as Ann and Robinson approached, she set down the coffee-pot (John Cafe, London, 1758), lowering her gaze, her long eyelashes veiling for a moment the large and lustrous brown eyes. When she spoke, her voice was a vibrant sweet contralto.

'Well, Mungo,' she said softly to Robinson (who was appreciating, not for the first time, her unique blend of Esther Williams and Jane Eyre) 'I knew you were broad-minded, but I should have thought you'd have drawn the line at a couple of poofs.'

Milton and Laurie skipped across the floor as Eric and Trevor mashed the music into a sort of tinned-fruit ecstasy.

'Did we win the spot prize ?' they breathlessly enquired.

All converged on the coffee-tray (Paul de Lamerie, London, 1742) and there was a roll on the drums as Eric picked up the sticks again, ending with an enormous kick in the region of the tympany.

'Up the wooden hill to Bedfordshire,' he carolled, 'early start in the morning.'

'Mungo ?', echoed Ann, unbelievingly.

Even Trevor's grin was ingratiating as he took his cup from the coffee-lady, first removing his horrible pince-nez, then putting them on again, uncertain which afforded him the better view.

'Dinner was well up to standard,' Robinson said, 'which is something I've come to expect. May I present Mrs Fruitfly on whose *coup de main* I gratefully depend.' He smiled benignly at the lady. 'The bitter-orange tart in particular is her speciality. Old Mrs Fruitfly, housekeeper extraordinaire.'

'I'd like to see her free bus-pass!' chuckled Laurie, who with a great notion of doing the genteel had somehow managed to draw in his waist and hunch up his shoulders like Mr Turveydrop.

'The next twenty-eight I shall see,' Mrs Fruitfly said pensively, 'will be on somebody's front-door. It may not seem a great age to someone like yourself who is on the wrong side of fifty, but there are those of us who burn out early.'

'She's frail, of course,' Robinson nodded sympathetically, 'but she still gets about. Nelly, have the warming-pans been applied?'

'All except your own, Mungo,' and this time she dropped as it were the ghost, the elegant phantom, of a curtsey.

'Good girl. Eric will show you to your rooms. Breakfast at eight, we must get the best of the day.'

Mrs Fruitfly glided across the parquet, prodding the button in the panelling which took up the revolving sphere.

'I feel a mite guilty at times,' murmured their host, 'her sense of the Protestant work-ethic – well, prodigal is the word. Nelly!' he cried, raising his voice as he followed her swiftly across the floor, 'you are not to carry it youself – you may slide it between the sheets, but I insist I carry it upstairs –' Mrs Fruitfly pirouetted round the jamb of the door, and Robinson followed, the very picture of a practical man who was about to change a fuse – 'Night all,' and as he disappeared, Ann turned to Laurie whose face bore a worried frown.

'Mungo?' she queried, this time as though checking an inventory that was one item short, 'what kind of a name is that?'

'Scottish, madam,' said Eric, fiddling with the satin-finished dimmers which their host had had installed to commemorate his defeat by an aunt whose confident use of the word 'lounge' he had spent thirty years attempting without success to undermine.

'You don't really think she thought – I mean, it was a joke, wasn't it? She couldn't possibly think you and me –' Laurie turned to Milton.

Milton pulled Ann onto his knee.

'Well you know what Goldberg said about his old friend Cohen? Everyone knew that Cohen had been accused of having carnal knowledge of a horse, and when someone asked "Was it a mare or a stallion?" Goldberg replied –'

'A mare of course, there's nothing queer about Cohen', and without dislocating his pince-nez or his hands touching the floor, Trevor skidded energetically across the parquet, flipping into a forward somersault that only years of dedicated fell-walking allowed him to perform.

Eric managed to get the better of the switches and as Trevor cried, 'Who's for a pickle sandwich and a cup of Bovril?' the lights faded, and Bagfox Hall was silent.

*

Four Hundred Horses Wedged in Chimney

BEACHCOMBER gave up his column believing the world had caught up with his most outlandish fantasies, so that he felt he could no longer compete. And when I read an earnest letter in *The Times* pointing out that birds get sea-sick when swinging on nut-dispensers, I saw what he meant.

It was only a day or so later that a science correspondent devoted a whole article to the subject of firing treacle tins into outer space. He'd begun by comparing man-made satellites to treacle-tins, but by the end of the piece the comparison had taken over. 'When the first space colonies are established it will be a simple matter to keep them supplied with tins of treacle.'

Morbleu! Bataclan de tralala! I hear Beachcomber despair as his territory is usurped and the authorities announce that they will hire clowns to soothe fractious travellers held up at airports – what an inspiration, clowns, when more humdrum minds might have settled for tarantulas or green mambas.

A plague of pink frogs terrorized Cirencester, and the Gloucester Trust for Nature Conservation worked day and night for six months before they cracked it. The frogs had been sucked up from the sands of the Sahara and transferred to the Cotswolds by what the Trust in its report called 'freak winds', landing in Cirencester in a rain storm. But in selecting this solution, what others did the Trust discard? Dr Strabismus (the Trust's consultant) reports that some of the frogs were carried on as far as Brize Norton where they queued for return flights.

Even Mrs Gromyko seemed a reincarnation of Beachcomber's Mrs McGurgle. She was hauled out of the boot-cupboard as a substitute for Mrs Gorbachev during the Reagan visit to Leningrad, and was detailed off to join the visiting firemen at the Hermitage. Here they all raced through the place as though Ron was settling a bet with Gorbachev that it was possible to get from one end to the other in three minutes flat without looking at a picture.

Stitched into the sort of sailcloth they bury people at sea in, Mrs Gromyko was lying about tenth but was pulling up nicely even though carrying extra weight, when a reporter asked her if she was tired. 'Tired?' cried this splendid woman, flooring him with her handbag as though he were a recalcitrant lodger at Marine House, 'I'm seventy-seven years old–why *shouldn't* I be tired?' And seeing the back-markers disappearing across the parquet she slid out through a side door and took a No 19 back home.

Beachcomber once published a letter from a quondam lodger at Marine House, where Mrs McGurgle reigned supreme. 'All we old timers want is for your place to stay as it was. We long to return to your sermons about gravy-stains, and to hear you say, in a voice that reduced us all to dumb terror: "No lady or gentleman, I presume, wishes a *second* portion of Yorkshire?" And do you remember when a novice held up his hand and said, "I could do with another go"? The way you affected to be unaware that anybody had spoken was magnificent. And how about when Eames, the steam carpet beating clerk, threw a potato at the cat Mibbins? And the old gent who said, "If this is curry, I'm the Emperor of Iceland"? And Wedger, who pinched the cheese from the mousetraps? What days! May they soon return. Yrs gratefully, Monty Clowdes.'

Those days are with us. At Saffron Waldron a point of etiquette arose that would have held Casa McGurgle entranced: viz, how much are you allowed to take when you are invited to help yourself? Tempers flared, reported the local Cambridge paper in a perfect pastiche of the Beachcomber News Service, when a customer took advantage of the help-yourself service at the buffet of The Eight Bells.

'The girl at the display table told me I could take as much as I liked,' said the customer, a Mr Walker, 'but only on one plate. So I paid my £4.95 and took a piece of beef weighing three and a half pounds, one third of a salmon, ten chicken drumsticks, and half a dozen slices of ham. I didn't have any salad.' The landlord turned him out and added that his table-manners were disgusting. Mr Walker commented rather loftily, 'I was eating with my fingers, like I always do.'

From time to time, Beachcomber used to print the words '400 HORSES WEDGED IN CHIMNEY' and add, 'The news story to fit this headline has yet to be found.' Not long now.

I Mean That Very Sincerely

RON Widdershins the disc-jockey indignantly rebutted suggestions that his job could be carried out with equal efficiency by a drunken child of five:

'Look here, old boy, I don't want to get pear-shaped about it, but I've got a pleasing personality. I don't steal bicycles or throw bottles in church, I'm an archetype of good behaviour, I put records on like a man who is so well behaved he doesn't even vote. I sound as if I've never differed with anyone in my life. If someone sandbagged my mother and the mike was live I'd grin and say "Well, everyone's entitled to their own opinion." Oh no, either you've got it or you haven't. Be fair.

'And that's only for openers. Talent? Well, if behaving like a general favourite on mere assumption doesn't take talent, I don't know what the word means. You've heard me in the mornings, haven't you? *Hallo, welcome, and chirribirribim.* I always say that, that's how you know it's me, I behave as if I was everyone's best friend. Some envious bastard said if he ever ran in to me in the street and I said chirribirribim he'd bite me, but some people aren't happy unless they're knock, knock, knock.

'See, what you've got to do is get on the same wavelength as the nellies who write in the requests, but stay different. If you don't stay different one morning they'll be in there at the microphone and you'll be out there listening. So you speak a different language, you bring a touch of sophistication to their grey little lives, and when you end your programme you don't say "Good-bye", you say, "It's good-bye from me".

'Chat 'em up. Lapse into comic showbusiness-cockney – it makes them feel superior. Watch you don't mispronounce the names of the towns – I had a lot of trouble with a place in Ireland called Kirkcudbright, you'd think people'd have something better to do.

'If they're old or infirm, that's a bonus. "Get well soon", "Many, many happy returns of your eighty-ninth birthday and I mean that very, very sincerely". Call them by their first names. Remember, you're sort of congratulating them on being alive.

'Of course you never *play* a record, you spin one, you give it a spin, you give it a whirl, you give it a twist. A record is a disc is a platter is a biscuit is a waxing is a label. There's no such thing as the other side of a record, there is only the flip, the flipside, the flipover, the coupling, the B-side. And if watering the currency of expression, neutering communication and adulterating the nature of experience like *that* doesn't call for the skill of a master-forger, my name isn't Widdershins.

'You're like a hypnotist really, it's a sort of ritual with key words. "Relax" is one of them. "Just relax." Relax from what? Don't ask me. "Fabulous" is another, but I have my own variation on that, I sometimes say "fantabulous". That's a coinage. I use the suffix "-ville" – "this one's heading straight for Hitsville". Americanisms that have been left standing a bit make them feel knowing, most of 'em think America is the promised land.

'Look, have you ever thought about the work that goes into the way I speak when I'm at the mike? The tone, the emphasis? "Jack Bonehead comes up on the Brand X label with a very very lovely melody and gets great support from Buddy Muffin and the Surgical Bandages –" Did you hear it? That bromide lilt? As if I was rustling a herd of wildebeeste and didn't want to sound as if I was doing it? Well, you don't think I talk to my *friends* like that, do you, let me tell you that takes practice.

'No, no, fair's fair. Call it low cunning if you like, but it's not everyone who can sound as if he's trying to brighten your life when he's actually trying to flog you noises that sound like a stomach in peristalsis.'

I left Ron stepping lithely into his tailors to bespeak an opalescent suit, arm in arm with J. Fred Muggs the song-plugger who, it is popularly rumoured, has settled on his protégé a lifetime's supply of fibre needles.

Low Notes on a High Level

THE headline 'Cockroaches at the Dorchester' read like an invitation to a party: 'Cockroaches, 6.30 to 8', sort of thing – 'Caviar or cockroach, sir?', 'My dear, does anyone do a cockroach better than the Dorchester – could you manage another?' 'Mmm, divine!'

The news item quoted the Cockroach Operative as saying the Dorchester was 'a haven for cockroaches', and the report went on to note there were 280 rooms. You got the impression of 280 cockroaches enjoying a Weekend Break, each with a room of his own, lolling on the bed and ringing for room service. Touch of Kafka crossed with Lewis Carroll.

The pleasing element in the report was the unexpected mingling of high with low, as when my teenage daughter, working Saturday afternoons in a garden-centre, tailed the Duke of Edinburgh from plant to plant, taking him to be a smartly-dressed shop-lifter intent on nicking the buddleia. As the Duke peered at the rubber-plants, other customers were staring at *him*, which made my daughter think she'd got a conspiracy on her hands. She was just about to feel the Duke's collar when the manager interposed his body.

A school my son once attended was giving its annual treat to the less well-off members of the parish, and the boys had been detailed off to serve the sandwiches and make themselves agreeable. My son got a fairly frail, threadbare old pair in his sights and proceeded to colonize them in approved fashion. He was exceedingly polite, and forced cake on them thinking to himself that perhaps it was all they would have to eat all day, when the Headmaster came up to him and said Ah, Robinson, I don't think you've been introduced – these are my parents.

Tap-dancing Days and Ways

TAP-DANCING is something I associate with suburbs long buried under ring-roads and hypermarkets, in whose leafy heyday small girls were taught tap by not-quite-so-young ladies in leotards, while boys with sex permanently on their minds peeped through the keyholes of church halls hoping to catch a glimpse of the lady in tights. How imperiously she would snatch open the door and cry 'Cheek!' as they ran away.

I'd have said tap-dancing was as dead as the spoons and bones if I hadn't come across a newly-published handbook teaching you the steps – I hadn't thought of tap-dancing as something anyone wrote about, so perhaps there's a whole literature I've missed: *My Life in Tap by Old Stager*; *Tap-Dancing – the History of an Obsession*; *Theory and Practice of Tap-Dancing by a Member of the Aristocracy* ; *Tap-Dancing Through Upper Burma* ; and the great First World War classic, *Memoirs of a Tap-Dancing Man*. The new book suggests there's a lot of tap about, if you know where to look, but the idea of dancing in order to make a clicking noise always struck me as odd. Not the Spanish stuff, of course, because that doesn't tap, it goes off bang.

You may say that Fred Astaire was a tap-dancer, and of course he was, but you didn't notice it. Astaire was so good at dancing that all you noticed was the movement he seemed to have vanished into (with Gene Kelly who did the same sort of thing you could never keep your eyes off his arms – his arms seemed to get in the way, whereas you only noticed Astaire's arms when he got round to acting: the acting consisted of thrusting his hands into his pockets and wagging his elbows.)

But what use was all this tap-dancing to the little tots who learned it? Those who had lino or parquet at home might be able to get the clicking going, but how could they entertain an audience on the carpet in the front room? And what use was the accomplishment in later life? You can't get up at a party and tap-dance at everyone. Perhaps it was just thought to be good for them, like cod-liver oil.

You never found ordinary people doing it. In those days dance-halls were crowded, but though you had all manner of waltzes and foxtrots,

Latin American and jive and bop, tap-dancing never had a vogue. People lined up and Hokey Cokey-ed dismally across the sprung floor of the Lyceum, but it never occurred to them to liven up the cortège with a bit of tap-dancing.

Too technical, perhaps. All very well for Donald O'Connor to tap-dance up a wall in one of those bring-on-the-clowns movies, but it was like conjuring: everything had to stop for it. Max Miller used to emphasize the expertise that was called for by declining it – he'd come on in his star-spangled plus-fours and make a feint of doing two or three steps before launching into the monologue, as though he could have danced a whole routine but didn't want to bore anyone; a review in *The Times* said 'Mr Miller enters tap-dancing, with remarkable economy of effort.'

You can imagine some people doing it, not others. The Duke of Edinburgh certainly, spinning round one of those empty ballrooms in Buckingham Palace after the footmen have gone to bed. And I seem to remember Bernard Shaw saying he'd tried it late one night after the theatre, in Fitzroy Square, with a policeman. But though he offered the most intricate guidance when it came to the Cha-Cha-Cha, Victor Sylvester classed tap-dancing as a sort of affliction. 'You might as well get a band to play while you shake dog-shit off your shoes,' he once remarked to Ivy Compton Burnett.

Clochemerle-in-Borrowdale

In Borrowdale the hills wheel in the sky like continents torn loose, pressed from the unfurnished landscape to sail like space-ships behind the clouds, nudging the world. The land is silent as though the noise of the cataclysm had yet to reach us.

From sky to middle-earth a casual turbulence hints that there is no limit to size, that size has no standard, that things grow bigger without let, monstrously expanding in the agoraphil universe. Right in the middle, slap in the centre, man is about to assert himself by putting up a public – actually, in view of the locale, perhaps a cosmic – lavatory.

Man in the shape of the Cockermouth Rural District Council wants to found it at the south end of a little patch of ground close to the Bowder Stone; the Bowder Stone being an enormous boulder (bowder) weighing about two thousand tons, balancing on a knife edge, a sort of crumb fallen from the act of Creation, and a natural object of pilgrimage.

Man in the shape of the Lake District Planning Board wants to found it at the north end of the same pleasaunce, tucking it beneath the fall of the land so that only its roof is seen.

Man in the shape of the National Trust (man's best friend) wants it at neither end, but opposite. Man in the shape of Mr Pepper who is the only human being actually quartered on the spot – in a slate cottage surrounded by begonias of his own growing – doesn't give a goddam where they put it so long as they put it somewhere and stop people knocking at his door and asking to use his.

Cockermouth Man wants the thing to be seen – wants it to be seen for what it is, set up boldly at the southern end, a jakes, a shambles, not Buckingham Palace but a consolation to all who pass. Planning Man is not against lavs on principle (though there is rumoured to be a splinter group who feel that science may yet uncover something more genteel) but feels that if it is exhibited at the southern rather than hidden at the northern end, *it might attract people off the road.*

Man in the shape of Mr Pepper thinks it's bloody ridiculous and doesn't care for a lavatory that isn't a beacon to all. Man's Best Friend (the National Trust) thinks that if we're all going to feel insecure unless we can rely on never being more than four hundred yards from a public lavatory, then this isn't the spirit which conquered Everest – but in any event let the lavatory be put at the other side of the road, along with the car park, and pretend it isn't there.

In the course of discussions both official and unofficial the following locutions have been heard and there is no guarantee that they will not be added to: viz., call of nature, nature must have its way, the natural function, spending a penny, relieving anxiety, the bodily requirements, the little boy's place, and of course, toilet.

Cockermouth Man is critical of the site recommended by Man's Best Friend on the grounds that there is no satisfaction to be had from letting nature have its way if you are going to be troubled by the thought of rocks crashing through the roof from the quarry above.

Planning Man thinks that, if it's put where Cockermouth wants it, it will spoil people's picnics. Cockermouth says that if it's hidden away where Planning wants it you'll have to smother the place in noticeboards so that people won't have their picnics spoilt by *not* knowing where it is. Man's Best Friend – with the blandest of smiles – feels that the preservation of natural beauty should come before the convenience of conveniences.

Cockermouth says if the thing's put on the opposite side of the road you'd have to drill pipes through solid rock. Man's Best Friend says no, lay the pipes on the surface and cover them with loose slate, well pressed down. Cockermouth wonders if Man's Best Friend has any notion what this would cost.

Sometimes Cockermouth must feel like slipping into something loose and having a good cry because after it's got this one fixed (and the argument's been going on for a couple of years) it's got to try to get another one put up on a piece of land owned jointly by twelve men, of whom eleven say they don't mind and one won't agree at any price.

At this late stage no one knows who first thought of having a public lavatory at the Bowder Stone, but it must have been someone rendered uneasy by the tenuous grip exercised by humanity upon this frightening landscape. In a gale of wind the trees race hysterically down the side of the hills, roots start like veins from the earth, and the terrible sky sucks up the geography and bowls it off into the infinite. Someone must have said 'What we need here is an anchor.'

Try a Grasshopper

LEISURE is work you volunteer for. I know this because I decided to take up fishing again, and the minute I framed the thought I experienced a sense of fatigue similar to what I imagine the man felt when he said to his wife, 'Wake me early tomorrow, I'm going to start building the Forth Bridge.' I'd still got the rods, but I couldn't find the tackle, so I set off for the angler's heartland which is Earlsfield and said briskly, 'I want a reel, a line and a few flies.' 'Ah,' said the bloke behind the counter, 'how heavy's the rod? Six, six and a half?' I groaned and said to him, 'I somehow knew I wasn't going to be able to come into your shop and say what I want and walk out with it. I'll come back tomorrow after I've been to the library.'

But in the fifteen years I haven't been fishing, the books on the subject have come to rest on as many ambiguities as you'd find in a piece on economics in the *Guardian*, and after leafing through one or two I knew enough not to know what to ask for. One particularly maddening commentator on the sport multiplied the entities by saying, 'If you're not having much luck, try a grasshopper.' It wasn't enough you had to find the fish, you had to find a grasshopper as well. That left you wondering whether it was all right to use your hat to catch the grasshopper or whether a true sportsman always lured the insect with a Tupp's Indispensable and a number eight line.

Garden Centre of Eden

WHAT shall we do on Bank Holiday? Why, huddle like orphans in garden centres. Maunder through the groves of plastic tubs, and peer through the hanging baskets of lobelia, like children who have lost their parents and are trying to find them in the trellised vistas of the ideal garden.

If I'm lost before I go in, I'm loster yet once I get inside. Did I come for a pound of grass seed, a few geraniums, some African marigolds? Then why this paralysis of the will, this inability to *act*? Hypnotized by wellingtons, shining unused rakes, the endless varieties of sacks of peat, I turn and turn in a fog of indecision. Why is it the plants don't look like their names sound, why is it that grey-haired women in anoraks can walk directly up to the anonymous shrub and know him for Jackmanii, shaking him by the hand while I carry off The President in mistake for the Nelly Moser of my heart's desire? In garden centres, helplessness grows over me, semper florens, and if I fail to fall backwards into a display of trugs I may yet collapse into the trolley carrying the alyssum saxatile, to be wheeled off like a Victorian heroine, consumed with languor.

And when, one time, I did get round to serving myself with grass seed, scooping it out of the sack with the measuring-cup very carefully in case I gave myself too much, the boss came chortling up and cried 'Go on – take *lots*!' and grabbing the cup from me piled extra dollops in as though encouraging a child. He wouldn't have done that to a *real* gardener, he wouldn't have given away his grass seed to anyone he respected. I knew what he thought of me, because when I asked where the aubrieta was he said, with something between a chuckle and a sneer, 'I ought to be prosecuted for selling that – it grows like weed.' I could tell he thought I ought to have propagated my own, that the cockney appetite for instant gardening kept him in business, but couldn't be taken seriously.

But it's always the same – anyone else in a garden centre knows more about gardening than I do, especially the females. They are the expert women shoppers in Sainsbury's who buy the serious nourishing foods while I'm tantalized by the coloured pictures on the boxes of sorbet: and here in the garden centre they search out pairs of workmanlike leather gloves while I fantasize over the picture of Albertine climbing luxuriously across a pergola. I buy my trellis and though they're invisible to anyone else the roses are already growing up it.

Of course the indecision of the garden centre is an acute version of the wasting disease all gardening suffers from: it is *always too late*! If you were to sow the grass, you should have done it the month before; if you were to prune the Ville de Lyon – see the tell-tale new buds on the old wood – you should have done it last year; everything you'd half-way like to do in the garden is subverted by all that you haven't done, and a constant state of being too late means that at any given moment you can't bring yourself to start.

That moment is never more apparent than when, with the garden centre behind you, and the climbers and the chaenomeles and the alpines and the ericas dug out of the boot of the car and ranged across the lawn you stare at them and realize they've all got to be planted. *This* is the moment when you are visited with such a lassitude you might wonder whether you hadn't been receiving the attentions of a vampire. Where's the electronic chip that should be sold with all plants, so that when you've lined them up you simply cry 'Bricklebrit' and they all hop into place?

I sometimes think the Garden of Eden must have been a garden centre – the ping of the till, the spray of the hoses, the smell of the creosote, signalling the endless, the eternal Bank Holiday. How relieved Adam and Eve must have been when they were chucked out.

Away from it all

BASIL wears a dicky and a wing collar and has the gift of apocalyptic utterance. About one third of what he says is intelligible, but it's always the apocalyptic third. He rises to his feet, removes his bowler hat, turns it sideways, puts it back on his head so that he looks like Napoleon, and says, 'Time's creeping on, squire.'

The first time I heard it I thought it was one of those prefabricated idiosyncrasies that some people use when they leave you – 'Chiz', 'Tarar'. But I couldn't get it out of my mind. The banality seemed to dissolve into an enormous simplicity, and I was left with a sense of revelation.

I run into Basil in the cemetery round the corner – Basil sits among the urns and the broken columns like a bailiff in a drawing-room, and blows his cheeks out fiercely as if earlier in life he'd been one of those cherubs on a map and can't shake off the habit. Our favourite spot is a snug little seat near a water-tap which is lagged by a creeping-plant, and close to a great tomb where the inscription refers to 'the certain hope of Salvation' – I once asked Basil what he thought hope was doing among so much certainty, but Basil's scanner is tuned-in at the galactic level and he doesn't hear small-scale queries.

'I went visiting this afternoon to a niece of the wife's down at Purley,' Basil told me one pleasant evening when the graves seemed to be floating in the long grass, 'for tea.' The other place I run into Basil is a pub, so I said, 'Tea's not much in your line is it?' '*Gin*,' he corrected me, in a reproachful fury. 'You mean gin's not in your line?' 'I'm off gin,' he said, 'but it would hardly have been polite to have asked for tea when gin was the drink, would it?' 'Let me get this straight. They were drinking gin and so you drank it too?' 'Well, after all, it was tea-time,' said Basil, as if I'd failed him again.

He seems to be in touch at a runic level. Nothing he says comes within a thousand miles of being apt, yet all he says – I mean the intelligible fraction of it – sounds like cosmic ore from which lesser men might manufacture aptness.

I know when summer has come, for the long grass gives off a sweet mashed smell, and Basil exchanges his bowler for something close to a stetson.

'There are some cow-sons travelling first on third-class tickets,' Basil once gloomily observed, but he can't have been referring to Julius Johnson. Julius Johnson's sepulchre is stuck with quartz and reaches to the sky. Once I heard boots creaking inside it and wondered whether Julius was eternally breaking in the new pair he was wearing at the time. Julius went in 1860, but is the only one in his enormous catacomb – did the rest of the family subvert the mechanism of life and death – did they find out the join in the continuum, work their fingers into the seam, and hold the whole thing up?

'I'll have bread pudding,' Basil once said, out of an enormous silence. And continued, in a voice that rumbled like an avalanche, 'The present generation is a load of twerps.' I once drew his attention to a tombstone which carried an address as well as a name as though it were a parcel, and Heaven a sorting-office. But Basil blew his cheeks out harder and said, 'Some of these fellers in cars.'

Yet once upon a time he *did* come back aptly, and it gave me goose-pimples. I was reading the saddest inscription of all – *Euphemia, wife of the above, who departed this life on Wandsworth Common, aged 24* – and Basil said, 'It's all this childless painbirth.' My hair stood on end when he spoke – I didn't know whether he'd actually said it or my ears had wanted to hear it. But getting him to go back on his tracks is impossible: there is no track, he pulls it up as he goes along.

Basil sits in the cemetery, stands in the pub – always stands in the pub. This dates from the age of fifteen when he was taken to a public house by an aunt who lived in Swanage. He drank what she drank and when she said it was time for lunch he got off his stool and fell down. 'Never accepted a seat in a pub again,' says Basil, winking horribly, rather like the late Eric Blore, 'and never suffered from the blackouts since.'

My feeling about the inscriptions in the cemetery, indeed about all the furniture of memorial, is that they say rather more about life and death than the inscribers either knew or felt. Yet Basil's mystical transfusions seem to be made from the very centre, the very sun, of experience. A notion which he himself might describe – in a phrase he reserves for his darkest vein – as 'a very Mancoonian idea'.

Ha Ha Among the Trumpets

I n the Breznev era the Moscow Philharmonic Orchestra came to London and gave a concert which was broadcast on Radio 3. After the music started, part of the audience began to rail bitterly against the treatment of Jews in the USSR. As I listened to the strange sounds invading the harmonies I was aware of a faint feeling of excitement, as though, yes, I regretted the dissonance but, at the same time, no, I didn't. It wasn't as though these feelings were mixed, they seemed separate and distinct; one was saying no, the other was saying yes.

I'm as able to reduce this kind of public disruption to its basic moral geometry as instantly as anyone else – the exercise of your freedom to shout protests infringes my freedom to listen to the music, and is thus a denial of freedom, at least to me; even time won't tell which of the freedoms in collision at that particular moment was the innocent party, since *post hoc propter hoc* is no argument.

Something of the same sort had once happened on the programme *Any Questions*, brought to a halt by the mindless howling of bully boys in the audience, and I remember then feeling nothing but anger – the sound was ugly, threatening, tyrannous. But I felt scarcely a twinge of resentment as the voices came through the music; they were rough and discordant but curiously helpless, as though through the complex patterns of the music they hadn't a hope of prevailing: at the same time, the music seemed to dignify what they were at, seemed to bestow a measure of abstraction on what was happening, as though the voices were a deliberate counterpoint. The music rendered the protest almost impersonal, and in so doing did it, involuntarily, a favour – the naked aggression which is always more in evidence at demonstrations than the disinterested love of humanity on which they are supposed to be based – was by virtue of the music, absent.

There is no argument to any of this – I have no argument to deploy, and would assuredly have lost my marbles if I implied we should all go round shouting protests at concerts. I was simply intrigued by the dual nature of the event and my own responses to it, not to mention those of the audience at the Festival Hall who curiously applauded between every movement; was the applause saying keep politics out of music, get politics *in* to music, was it simply music-lovers closing ranks against the philistine, or was it no more than boasting that we can make as much noise as you can?

And how did the musicians feel? I couldn't help thinking that their experience of what it was like to give concerts in a free, or freeish, society was being somewhat uncomfortably broadened. And the announcer? He had to say *something*, and what he said was er-hem why couldn't they confine the protests to the interval, and thus keep the sympathy of music-lovers? A sensible, Solomon-like adjudication, except that announcements in intervals are always ignored.

No way of knowing, of course, but as a listener I had no sense that the protesters were being selfish. These things are very subjective, but the combination of the music and the desperate shouts suggested a group who were more interested in getting people out of prison than spoiling a concert. It even crossed my mind, though faintly, that in being momentarily deprived of my pleasures, I was deprived of a fraction of the freedom that the prisoners had none of.

I make a record of this because of a certain strangeness about it all. The patterns of the music prescribed a fixed course, a trajectory the sounds must inevitably move through, to a destined close; to find it happening slightly otherwise, to hear someone crying Ha Ha among the trumpets, was to smell the battle.

Not All Rembrandts

S OMEONE had said that the forger's standards were in decline, but this charge was later denied.

'We're not all Rembrandts,' said a spokesman, interviewed in his front room on the south side of the river, 'and for every artist who knows enough about fine oils and astringents to brush in a water-mark with Chinese White, well, you've got hundreds who'd trace a signature and wouldn't even bother to ink in the carbon.

'Is it fair to judge a whole trade by the few who get tumbled?'

The spokesman had square waxy hands and on the under side of his wrists the tendons protruded.

'Would you ask a bricklayer to design St Paul's Cathedral? A post-office book is one thing but there aren't six men in the world – excluding Soviet Russia – who could get away with an English fiver. Look at the shading, the overlaying of the blue, the line-work of the surrounds. Look at the screening of the portrait – you've only to misplace one of those little dots to alter the whole expression of the face.

'The old white fiver,' said the spokesman, 'was a different thing. Once you'd fluffed there was an indent on the reverse side of the dot over the "i" of "O'Brien" you were laughing.

'Of course you had to know your papers, silk, fibre, or flax – mostly flax or linen these days. But now the white fivers are gone you've got the fluorescence to contend with. A good man can get his paper to give off some sort of fluorescence when its tested under a quartz light, but unless it's a bluish glow it won't do. That blue tint comes from the river water which flows through the premises of the people who make the real thing.'

The spokesman opened and closed his hands, then grasped each finger in turn and pulled it.

'Signatures are a subject in themselves. You can do them double-pen or use a light box – a piece of frosted glass with a bulb underneath, put your cheque on the glass, put the paper with the signature over it, and simply trace. But –' the spokesman shook his head impatiently, 'freehand every time for the artist. That way you don't get variations in pressure and line.'

He coughed. 'I knew a man who specialized in wills. He didn't *copy* the signature, he wasn't a duplicating machine, he'd find out what type of man the testator was, how he sat, what he thought of his relatives, how he dressed, what sort of mood he might have been in when he was writing the will, then he'd say to himself I *am* the man and dash the signature off.

'Now that was an artist. Like someone else I know,' he coughed again, almost modestly, 'who didn't duplicate the geometric lathe work in the currency, he simply *suggested* it – used a camel-hair brush and gave you an *impression* of seeing the real thing. Those notes were worth more than their face value as works of art, which is what he told the police who came to arrest him after one of them had got a bit damp on a bar-counter.'

The spokesman paused, flexing his fingers. 'I can crush an apple in one hand,' he said absently. Then he said, 'No, really, if a young fellow was starting today I'd tell him to leave currency alone and stick to rare stamps. Well, they're not legal tender so it's not a crime, is it? And if a dealer buys a fake for a high price and finds out it's a fake he's not going to let on and lose his investment, is he? He's going to sell the stamp to someone else.

'It's a lovely line,' said the spokesman, 'you get hold of low-value stamps of the period you're interested in, wash out the ink, and start forging in the confident knowledge that your paper is one hundred per cent genuine.'

The spokesman smiled.

'There was a foreigner did sovereigns. He put more gold in them than the Mint did in theirs. Of course he sold them at a premium. He reckoned he was entitled to twenty per cent over the market price of what he regarded as the Mint's inferior product. They tried to make a case of it but it wouldn't work because sovereigns aren't legal tender. This fellow proved they weren't, he got his lawyers to come over to England and try to spend them. Eyetie, I think he was.'

The spokesman intertwined his fingers and said, 'I can write simultaneously with both hands, forwards or backwards *or* forwards *and* backwards at the same time.'

Then he said, 'They used to ask for it with Savings Stamps. No watermarks. Dollar bills are easy – tens, twenties, and fifties. French 100 franc notes are difficult. Strange that, when it's the currency with the least behind it.

'But when it comes to forging a death warrant of Charles II all on sheepskin, then you do well to go to the top.' The spokesman coughed again, very slightly. 'I knew someone who did it. He went along to Carisbrooke Castle with a con man who kept the attendants talking while he photographed the thing and took its measurements. He sold the finished article inside a week to an American who'd come over for the tennis. But that man,' said the spokesman, holding his chin very high, 'that man *was* Rembrandt.'

The Gormless Telephone

I NATURALLY didn't expect the British Telecom Gallup Poll survey of what's fashionable these days to come right out with it and admit that cordless telephones are sold exclusively to men in Ilford with gold medallions in their chest hair and who sleep each night with airline tickets to Marbella under their pillows. But I give BT marks for effrontery in suggesting that if you haven't got one of these tawdry electronic gewgaws people are going to cross the street when they see you coming.

It became clear what sort of people the pollsters had canvassed when the list of things that were socially inadmissible these days included 'writing letters'. Well, if you're a member of the upwardly mobile scrap-metal crowd you know just how hard holding a pen can be with all those gold rings on every finger. And anyway, who do you know who can read?

I was just warming up, and was about to tell the assembled company about a man who'd pawned his answering machine because no one left him any messages, and how Uncle had offered him a cut-price cordless telephone left behind by a distinguished Ilfordian who'd just gone into receivership, when a respectable man stirred uneasily and said he not only possessed such an item but couldn't contemplate life without it.

Bit of a shock, since the fellow did live in Weybridge. He's a doctor,

so I felt his pulse and realized what his trouble was – he's a big shambling
fellow who makes his own trousers, and he believes his cordless telephone
is going to turn him from Clark Kent into Superman. But I discovered
it went much deeper. As I was writing out his prescription he told me
the great boon of his gormless telephone was that it allowed him to
take calls by his swimming pool.

The tableau conjured up was too much for me. My friend the doctor
sitting by his pool with the rain lashing Weybridge, his legs getting
bluer by the minute, waiting bravely for his hand-held telephone to prove
its worth by ringing! No, the pathos was too much, and I fell forward
into a saucerful of Friar's Balsam, crying like a child.

Colour supplement junk, electronic kapok. Once only – just once –
I joined the Ilford mob as a country member by sending away for a tiny
electronic alarm clock with a light you pressed so when you were travelling
you could see it in the dark. There I was in some Holiday Inn wondering
how much longer there was to sleep, pressing the button of my gormless
alarm, but unable to read the dial since it was powered by a single one-watt
glowworm who seemed more deeply asleep than ever I was. So next morning I packed it up and sent it back, since when any impulse to purchase
a self-assembly exercise bicycle has been sternly repressed.

What Ilford insiders tend to forget is that when you get your gormless
telephone the first thing you will do is mislay it beneath a pile of newspapers and you won't even hear the little fellow ring. Some distant echo
– is that a phone? – no, no, you're imagining it. And how many would
you need to make sure that when you were in the drawing-room your
gormless wasn't down in the basement? On this point I am at one with
the *gratin* of Ilford who are clear that a collection of the things is indispensable, one to match the decor of each room. But then, having equipped
oneself with half a dozen of these irreproachable chunks of shiny crap,
how to be certain, carting them about, that they aren't left in the wrong
rooms? Unbearable if the tartan motif intended for the fumed oak table
under the stuffed moose in the front parlour were to find itself hideously
clashing with the flock wallpaper in the rumpus room.

But the idea of holding a telephone in one hand while punching at
it with the fingers of the other has an uncomfortable wobbly element
built in. Telephones were intended to be stationary objects which could
be guaranteed not to move while you stabbed away at them. To carry
one around with you is like stuffing a parrot in your pocket: too big,
too alive, too talkative.

Of course, I do speak as one whose telephone is screwed to the wall
in the corridor next to the hallstand, and all I have to do when I want

to make a call is turn a little handle and an old gentleman wearing an eye-shade and played by Donald Meek answers and says the lines are all down because there's a werewolf on the loose. But if BT is right, I'm going to have to buy a gormless or resign my clubs.

Who Am I?

I SPOTTED him – he had a red, unamused face. I thought with mounting excitement He's – Roper? Bowles? Rowley? But that wasn't the important thing.

I shouted, 'Excuse me, we were in the Army together.'

But he didn't hear that time and the actual person I'd been having the conversation with registered my rudeness by stopping talking very slowly. Then I saw the red-faced man cutting his way through the party towards me and towards the door. It was years and years ago but I knew him instantly. It thrilled me.

'Excuse me, we were in the Army together.'

He said, 'No we weren't.'

Wouldn't the normal response have been, 'Really? Wait a minute –' or 'Was it Aldershot?'

I proved we were in the Army together. 'I know where you were at school. Mell's. Right? I just happen to remember. You told me.'

But he seemed only more irritable.

'Well that's right,' he said.

'Do you remember Pillar Barracks?' I said.

'Mmm.'

'I was there. You were there.'

How could he not remember? Why wasn't he curious?

'You remember Catchpole? The platoon officer. Kind of an intellectual. Then they tore off our white tapes on the passing-out night. A man called – Someone drank a pint of beer in four seconds.'

'Walters?' he asked.

'Who Walters?'

'You Walters.'

'No, you've got the name wrong,' I said, 'but you do remember me.'

You don't meet someone from years and years ago every day. I didn't want him to join a club or anything. But it was like time-travel, a bit magic.

'Don't you remember me?'

'I can't honestly say I do.'

I did a sort of dance. Waved at my hair – 'I'm bald now, I had a lot of hair then.'

'You remember Souter?'

'Yes.'

'*Well I slept in a bed between you and Souter.*'

He'd worked his way round to the door side of me. He said, 'Did you.'

I'd been the man's acquaintance. Not his close friend, but his acquaintance. For instance, we went and ate cakes at a café when we should have been marching. I knew – I remembered – he had a mother, a kind of a smart mother with antique furniture, etc. The unlikelihood of our paths ever crossing again was immense – it was like discovering the lost City of the Incas. And to reject it!

'I knew it was you. I knew your walk.'

'I've got a spinal thing,' he said.

No malice, no interest, no remembrance. Was I a ghost at Pillar Barracks?

'Souter came from – Frome.'

'Frome.'

'And there was a locker between his bed and mine and then there was me. I was the fellow who –'

Who was I the fellow? Perhaps I haunted the place. Perhaps nobody wanted to walk past it after dark.

'I can remember the smell of the floor polish. When we polished it we called it bumping.' But how could I prove it?

'There was a big glass where we all put our officers' uniforms on and looked at ourselves in, the night we passed out.' But he had his hand on the door-handle. 'Catchpole came round to the barrack-room in his blues,' I said eagerly. 'He looked like a bus-conductor. Pretended he had a bell-punch and went ting-a-ling.'

Then there was quite a long pause, and the third party – the person I had interrupted in the excitement of rediscovering this old acquaintance – felt there was no reason why the conversation should not be resumed. 'I say,' he said, 'that anybody who tries to make any sort of communication is trying to convince himself of his own existence. If he really knew that what he was saying was true, why should he bother to say it?'

'Where did you go after Pillar?' I asked the alumnus.

'Kenya.'

'I went to West Africa.'

He glanced about him, perhaps hoping he could leave before I touched him for a fiver, got him to write a reference, importuned him for a card of introduction to a wholesale warehouse.

'Such a person,' continued the third party, 'seeks ratification of himself—'

I thought of men who walk down corridors tapping the walls to remind themselves that they are physically present, of others who rise up and down on the balls of their feet in lifts hissing between their teeth, thus advertising a preoccupation with important matters within which (they seem to suggest) their identity is secure.

To drop out of someone's memory: a sort of death.

Then the alumnus said, 'Did you – wasn't there – were you the chap who did the –'

Relief started to flow in from a great distance. I nodded in anticipation.

'– imitation of Sergeant Cramer?'

'No,' I said, 'that was Bean.'

The third party said, 'The adequate man requires no reassurance –'

My man pushed open the door then said – scraping up a civil inquiry from wherever he kept them – 'What are you doing here?' I looked across the heads and saw our host. I said, but the phrase had no meaning, 'I *know* him.'

Clever as Paint

WHEN the late Marquis of Salisbury said Iain McCleod was 'too clever by half' he meant something else as well. He meant the man was getting above himself. (That particular Marquis of Salisbury was a dreadful snob, and said of another MP who had a very genteel accent that 'he makes me feel so common'.) What the grandee was letting everyone know was that to come on as strong as McCleod you needed rather more than straight 'A's in your exams; being good at Scrabble didn't get you an invite to dine at Hatfield.

Not very nice. But when you run into fathers at parties who say of their own offspring 'They're frighteningly bright', the fact that you find your mouth is having to fight its way through fifteen milligrams of novo-caine in order to go on smiling, tells you you have rather more in common with the appalling aristo than your grammar school upbringing would have led you to suspect.

Once upon a time being clever was something real nobs kept dark; if the second son got a First they treated it like a shameful secret – after all, they didn't *need* to be clever. They dissembled, even apologized; couldn't think where he'd picked up such middle-class habits. But this was when they actually ran things and were supplying the country with Prime Ministers. Latterly, they've become rather warier and sometimes pretend that their estates are a penitential anachronism which has forced the whole family to take evening classes in accountancy and live in the stable block. They never bother to make any of this sound convincing, since although the natives get cleverer and cleverer they still buy the beads.

So when the man tells you the headmaster thinks his son is scholarship material, and you feel he is telling you what he paid for his furniture, does this mean you are making a bid to inherit the mantle of the Marquis of Salisbury – nicer, of course, more fastidious, more rational, easy fre-quenter of the humblest parties, unaffected, no side?

But of course! How else do you think marquises become marquises? Still, just because your impulses are impure doesn't mean you're wrong.

The bloody man who parades the cleverness of his son, parades himself, and although the marquis may have felt parade itself was the exclusive property of *his* tribe, and he was seeing off a trespasser, your own irritation comes from feeling it's disagreeable anyway.

'Prig!' cry those in opposition to the popular movement in favour of making you a marquis. But when clever people do clever things you only know they are clever afterwards, when they have identified gravity or the double helix. *Seeming* to be clever is showbusiness, but clever people never attract the adjective; did you ever hear T.S.Eliot, Isaac Newton, Schopenhauer, Leonardo, Mozart, so described?

Perhaps clever isn't the right word when it comes to people like that, since using it as though it were straightforwardly descriptive makes you feel uneasy. Commoners as well as marquises view 'clever' as derogatory: 'too clever for his own good', 'clever clogs', 'clever dick', 'clever as paint' – the last encapsulating a general perception of the quality, since paint is shallow and meretricious, in that it thinly covers all manner of defects.

There's something temporary about cleverness that a phrase like 'bright as a button' seems to sum up: *flashes* of cleverness, as when someone spots the flaw in the argument, points out the mistake in the bill, knows a short-cut, corrects the quotation – flashes, as though the supply weren't constant, and couldn't be relied on. Clever stuff, we cry, as though applauding a trick or knack. But if there is more to it, the word is avoided, and when a man whose skill, perception, insight, is seen to be rooted in sound good sense and an ability to get to grips with an idea or a situation, he is not clever, he is able.

In Vienna or Budapest, at cafés where groups still have their regular tables and conversation is a theatre of cleverness, bravura displays are admired, respected, rejoiced in. But here in Britain where there is no such arena, cleverness on show is edged away from, and being put next to someone who goes in for conversational fireworks is thought to be worse luck than getting the dullest man in the room.

There may be something in this. Whewell, Master of Trinity College, Cambridge, annoyed the Fellows by being able to talk with authority on any topic that came up at High Table. Some of the dons, driven mad by these wanton exhibitions of cleverness, trawled through all sorts of works of reference to find a subject they could down the Master with. This, they decided, was Chinese musical instruments, and for some days they mugged it up. Then at dinner they launched the discussion, to the bewilderment of colleagues who weren't in the conspiracy. Whewell was silent awhile, then turned to one of the conspirators and said, 'I see you have been reading the encyclopedia article on Chinese musical instruments which I wrote some years ago.'

Families, when a child is born
Want it to be intelligent.
I, through intelligence,
Having wrecked my whole life,
Only hope the baby will prove
Ignorant and stupid.
Then he will crown a tranquil life
By becoming a Cabinet Minister.

from the Chinese of Su Tung-P'O
(1036–1101) translated by
Arthur Waley.

My Leg in His Mouth

I WAS walking across a footbridge over the Kingston By-pass and, as
I went down the steps on the other side, I saw a lady and a boy and
a big black dog coming up towards me. The dog seemed to spot me
and crossed over to the side of the steps I was going down. As he got
nearer, I thought maybe I'd better move over. Then I thought, 'No,
dammit, he's only a dog, let him move over.' The next thing I knew
he'd got my leg in his mouth.

I said, 'My goodness. Goodness me. Crumbs.' Then, the three of us
– and the dog, of course – stood looking at each other, none of us
quite knowing what the appropriate response might be. Then the lady,
as though she'd suddenly had a good idea – and I must say I applauded
it – turned round and welted the dog round the mush for about a minute
and a half. But that was OK by the dog, he'd had his bite and, as I
looked at it pretending to hang its head, I knew it knew I knew you
couldn't get a dog to unbite you.

I felt awfully angry but, since the dog couldn't understand English,
there wasn't any point in telling it anything and I couldn't say much

to the woman since after all *she* hadn't bitten me. But I felt I was entitled
to some sort of complaint and I looked at the hole in my trousers and
cried aloud, 'Well, you can buy me another pair.' And the woman said,
her voice rising to match mine, 'Have I said I won't?' And for a second
or two it was touch and go whether I wasn't going to apologize to
her: I even started to try to soothe her. Then I thought, Here, hold
on. It's you the dog bit. And the next thing I said was, 'Waist 38, inside
leg 29, the next time you're in Marks and Spencers you can buy me
some.' And she said anxiously, 'Are you sure they're navy blue?'

At this, for reasons I can't quite fathom, but probably because I felt
he wasn't playing his part, I rounded on the small boy and shouted,
'You can remember the measurements.' 'Yes, yes,' he shouted back, 'I
will.' 'All right,' I said threateningly, 'what are they?' 'Waist 38, inside
leg 29,' he responded – and I suddenly thought, 'What on earth am
I doing getting a perfect stranger to shout out my inside leg measurements
in the wilderness of the Kingston By-pass? '

All very unsatisfactory, and I can only say that the faintly surreal air
that the whole event carried was endorsed when I took my purple
mumbled leg into St Stephen's Hospital to have an anti-tetanus injection
and found myself thinking that the doctor who supervised this delicate
operation looked exactly like a schoolgirl on the television programme
Ask the Family, only to have her tell me that that was where I'd met
her, ten years before.

Bookburgers

SOME book shops are open all hours like take-aways, so that passersby who suddenly feel hungry can nip in and buy a bookburger and eat it in the street. The fast-book side of things keeps the place open, so if you want something else its going to be pretty hard work.

I edged through the queues waiting for barbecue-sauce to pour over their Jackie Collinses and finally located what I was after in a corner where the sell-by rejects were awaiting collection by the Salvation Army. Then I went to the man behind the counter who took the book from me, handed me a ticket to take to the cash-desk where they'd give me a receipt after I'd paid, and when I brought the receipt back to him he'd surrender the book.

This ritual suggested the management couldn't believe an individual book, as opposed to a meat patty, was something anyone would willingly pay for; that in this Macdonald's of the printed word they'd lost sight of the book as unduplicatable experience in re-marketing it as an *entirely* duplicatable experience to be sold to masses of people who have generalized expectations of what the printed page can deliver; and that each time some anarchist came in asking for *Religio Medici* he had to be contained by a security system as tight as the one you pass your hand-luggage through at airports.

But even to arrive at the process whereby you're allowed to take the book and leave the shop calls for effort. All sorts of *cordons sanitaires* are thrown round you in the shape of categories. Categories used to be a way of getting you to the book quickly, but now they seem to want to do the opposite, beckoning you down false trails into a wilderness men are seen to enter but not to come out of, lost between Theosophy and the History of Art, doomed never to guess that the book they're looking for is under Cookery because the author called it *Eating People Is Wrong*. A passion to classify is a fear of the singular.

Waiting my turn while the staff were microwaving copies of books by the woman who looks as though she's wearing a dog on her head, I was thinking that the junk-book addict always tells you he takes something *light* to read on holiday, leaving you with the impression he spends the rest of the year slogging away at Gibbon and Wittgenstein. Yet the only time I ever think of dipping into the heavy stuff *is* on holiday, when, of course, it lies by my bed unopened.

Scott and Richardson and Carlyle and all the writers we respect but don't read, live on in second-hand bookshops, to be picked up and put down by people whose real interest is in the soft ice-cream they're planning to buy next door. Sometimes I think of shelves of old books stretching out to the crack of doom, a chorus of the unlistened-to screaming silently for attention, each book the coded face of someone still burning to tell the world who he is centuries after his bones have crumbled in the grave.

I suppose there are so many books (I went on daydreaming, as assistants slipped the Jeffrey Archers into grease proof bags) because you don't need qualifications to write one, only obsessions: think of the motivation required to compose a book of two hundred and fifty pages, think of the effort needed to *type* two hundred and fifty pages. Yet the book I was waiting to pay for – an anthology of strange but perfectly genuine book titles* – was a monument to the intensity of people's need to get it down on paper: *The History and Romance of Elastic Webbing Since the Dawn of Time* (Clifton A. Richmond, Easthampton, Massachussetts): *How to Shave Yourself* (J. Litchfield, 1912): *Rubbing Along in Burmese* (Directorate of Welfare and Education, Adjutant-General's Branch, GHQ, 1944): *Goodbye to the Flush Toilet* (Carol Hupping Stoner, Pasadena, 1984): *Who's Who in Cocker Spaniels* (Edward Vaughan Bevan and Bernard Trevelyan Rees, Chapman & Hall, 1937): *Do Snakes Have Legs?* (Bert Cunningham, Scientific Monthly, 1934).

An Irishman's Difficulties with the Dutch Language (The Revd Dr John Irwin Brown, 1908) might have been ironed out in less time than it had taken me to reach the point of sale. The chap at the till, propped up on his elbows, scrutinized my ticket and gave me permission to pay the girl who actually works the machine. He then turned the scrutinizing apparatus – his pebble lenses – on to me, and from a distance of eighteen inches, chin on hands, he appeared to commit a detailed inventory of my face to memory ready for the police when they arrived. Somewhat put out, I finished writing the cheque, stared levelly back at him and cried 'Boo!' He nodded. 'I'll tell them you don't want ketchup,' he said.

* *Bizarre Books* by Russell Ash and Brian Lake (Macmillan)

Jorrocks in Ewell

I HIRED a horse in Ewell. I had a vaguish feeling that a distant suburb might take the unpredictability out of the enterprise, though it didn't seem right to be looking a horse up in the Yellow Pages. I thought a horse based in Ewell might not have the red insane eyes that I think of as natural in horses, and I felt the balmy airs of Ewell might have had a calming, even a debilitating effect on the beast they hired out to me, and what I'd get would have all the reliability of a Volvo, but with four legs.

As we left the stables, the ancient party in charge of the yard said to me, 'If he tries to roll over, just give him a flick with your crop on the tip of his right ear.' I laughed heartily, not wanting to seem unfamiliar with what was obviously an old joke among horse-lovers. As we moved slowly down Fruitwood Crescent, I was torn between thinking I cut a pretty figure and hoping this didn't encourage the young woman in charge of the group to think she was boring me by going too slowly – while the horses are walking you can't tell the difference between me and Nimrod: it's when they start going a bit faster that the fraudulence of my boots and breeches becomes apparent.

I was gravely acknowledging the respectful greetings of the peasantry as they leant out of their primitive bungalows crying, 'Get off and milk it,' when all of a sudden we clopped off the nice safe asphalt and found ourselves in a ploughed field and the ugly beast I'd been trundling along on started throwing its head about as though now we were coming to the bit *he* liked.

One by one the others took off down the path that ran through the middle of the field, and then it was my turn, or more accurately the horse's turn, and he shot away like a high-speed goods train and then after a bit he slowed down as though he were approaching a station. He veered off the path and into the field and the others shouted something, but the horse was now doing an old-fashioned waltz, going sideways and backwards across the furrows, and suddenly I realized what the man at the yard had said was no joke but an actual piece of advice but it was too late.

We were going down like the *Titanic*, and solemnly, gracefully, the horse and I landed on our backs, he with his legs in the air, me with mine. I'd like to know how you aim at the tip of *anyone's* right ear when you're falling from what seems an eight-storey building; but as I went home with the mud of Ewell plastered all over me, I had a curiously contented feeling, as though for all my efforts to exclude the unpredictable, I was glad I hadn't succeeded.

A Little Embroidery

THE day the tree fell on our house a reporter came round to get a couple of pars for the *Evening Standard*. It was six o'clock in the morning and we were all standing in the street in our dressing-gowns. Canon de Zuluetta came across from the Rectory to give him the full strength. 'Maurice Baring lived in this house,' said Zu, looking up at my shattered windows, 'and Belloc would come over from Cheyne Walk with Chesterton. They'd all meet here –' and Zu's face took on the distant look I'd first noticed when he told me he had a parishioner who collected photos of the Archbishop of Canterbury and stuck pins in them– 'every Friday, regular as clockwork.'

I knew he'd made the last bit up, and I knew exactly why he'd made it up. When the man from the News arrived, Zu went through it again, and then added, not quite catching my eye, 'And they'd end the evening with a sing-song.' By this time the chap from the *Daily Mirror* was on the scene and Zu went over to the other side of the road with him. The giant ailanthus was lying across the street with its branches through my casements and its roots sticking out of the tarmac. 'The seed for that particular tree was brought from Shanghai in the middle of the nineteenth century,' Zu told the man from the *Daily Mirror*, 'where they call them Trees of Heaven' – he glanced over at Carlyle's house, a couple of doors down, and his face went out of focus again – 'and Carlyle planted it with his own hands.' When the scribes had gone, Zu said anxiously, 'I hope they got all they wanted.' 'I'm sure they did,' I said, 'you're not the man to send them away empty-handed.'

As I say, I know exactly why he added the extra bits, he was obeying the impulse that lies behind all embroidery – it's a compulsion to make things complete, people embroider because they can't see a loose end without wanting to tat it up into something decorative. Once upon a time we were setting up a programme about Thomas Hardy and doing some research in a Dorset pub. Chap behind the bar, polishing the glasses, said, 'He was often in here when my dad was alive, you know. Oh yes,' he went on, polishing ruminatively, as he selected the colours that seemed suitable for a spontaneous piece of tapestry, 'he'd have a few pints, nip out and bang a village maiden against a five-barred gate, then back in for a few more before closing-time.'

That stitched up Hardy in much the same way the students at the local university in the town of Normal, Illinois managed to weave Dr Johnson and Shakespeare into the one seamless garment. Primarily an engineering college, they laid aside their micrometers to welcome a group of strolling players from Oxford University who were to perform *King Lear* and *The Alchemist*. 'Dr Johnson and Shakespeare would often meet in The Mermaid tavern,' wrote an inspired metallurgist, enthusing about the event in the college magazine, 'where Boswell recorded their friendly wrangles for posterity.' Well, I remember thinking, they'd got it to within a tolerance of a couple of thou, which is more than I could have done, if I was machining copper.

The Munchausen effect is really a form of courtesy, a desire to pass on nothing that is asymmetrical. But I should like to meet someone who was actually in the BBC van at Aldershot when they recorded RSM Brittain's voice at a distance of five miles. Or any member of those four squads he would drill simultaneously by ear alone, while lying on his bed, shaving. And would anyone who was in the warrant-officer's mess that time Brittain marched himself up to the long mirror and confined himself to barracks for parading with an idle bootlace please be in touch with me? I'd appreciate it.

Symmetry is all. As in the tale of my housemaster and his newly-married wife who went off to a pub in Wales for a fishing trip. That being the style in Wales in those days, the landlady asked to see their marriage lines. My housemaster blithely handed over the fishing permit, and the two love birds retired. An hour or so later, there was a tap at the door. 'If you have not,' whispered the landlady, 'do not. This is not for it.'

Who's Whomanship

THE raw material of *Who's Who* is swank, and swank calls for the greatest possible restraint. Your recreations may be needlework and early Renaissance keyboard music, but spare the readers – who are understandably irritated that they are reading about you, instead of you about them – the full force of your charm, and if the impulse to enter *something* under this heading cannot be resisted there is no substitute for 'Walking, music and the theatre'.

But alas, how often the impulse to entertain will overcome the best of us: I note that my friend Ann (for I shall identify her only by her first name) when making her debut offered, under Recreations, 'Motherhood and photography'. Oh, as the months rolled on and that tiny pirouette remained frozen in mid-air, how she must have longed for the next edition and the chance to alter it! For like many another she missed the point: all reference to personal habits is a chance to mitigate, rather than to inflame, the annoyance of those who are not included. The entry that perfectly met this rule was that of Christopher Isherwood: 'Recreations: usual'.

But Ann was a fledgling. What excuse can there be for the friend I shall call Laurence? Under recreations he enters the words 'Restless socializing'. The picture conjured up is of a tall curly-headed minstrel moving from pub to pub with a harp, some latter-day Blondel or Cavan O'Connor, a vagabond with a heart of gold and a way with the girls – no, impossible to continue. Such advertisements belong in *Spotlight* where people quite properly pay for inclusion.

And who is this telling us his recreation is 'Loitering with and without intent'? Why, Michael. But if he is willing to lift the veil so far, on what grounds does he make no mention of the even more interesting fact that he owns a pair of yellow trousers? But before it is supposed that as a small boy I made my mother a solemn vow only to make friends with people who appeared in *Who's Who* I must end this section with Harry who gets away with the tail and ears. He permits us to understand that *his* recreation is 'Popping round to the post'. For sheer winsomeness, that beats Shirley Temple.

But Harry isn't simply Harry Keating. We have *Who's Who* to thank for the revelation that behind the unassuming initials HRF emblazoned on the spines of his admirable novels there stands a Technicolor figure whose forenames are Henry Reymond Fitzwalter! I see him riding into some great Hall on a shire horse to offer the Queen's enemies the best of three falls. But the book is replete with such felicities. Where else could you stumble across the information that Mr Michael Barrett's parents are called Wallace and Doris, leaving you to wonder how often they had been addressed as Warris and Dollis?

Has anyone listed in *Who's Who* ever risen to the heights of snootiness achieved by one Dennis Skinner MP? The man refuses to name his parents (dost think tha was born under a gooseberry bush, our Dennis?) and fills up the space with the words 'Good working class mining stock'. As far as ancestor worship goes, this puts Sir Walter Eliot wholly in the shade. It is scarcely possible to emulate the canting Skinner, but there *are* those who appear to have been born by parthenogenesis: put forth by one parent, usually a father, they hint, by the obvious omission, at a Sophoclean sense of shame. Others list their in-laws *if* they have titles, and some, in the section which asks after Education, rather oddly name a university: did they first learn to read and write at the age of 18, and is it Eton or Harrow they don't care to list? Such delicious little snobberies are much relished by the connoisseur.

After all, you aren't composing a testimonial for yourself, and attempts to try and get the book to do more for you in conferring status than it already has done by letting you in at all is a solecism. One allowable vaunt, I think, is 'First Class Honours, School of So and So'. The only teeth this is going to put on edge will belong to your fellow biographees.

One must not *parade* one's privacy (if the paradox be allowed). But there is a charmlessness about those entries from people who are willing to publicize their curriculum vitae yet when it comes to saying where they live coldly substitute an agent or an office. Unless this is to indicate they are of no fixed address and are living rough, the suggestion is that readers can only approach, or hope to approach, via an intermediary. The man is making it clear that he doesn't mind you knowing *him*, but in concealing his address, makes it even clearer that he doesn't want to know *you*.

The book is a wonderful way of wasting time, an invitation to stroll in an architectural folly consisting entirely of the statues of people you've never heard of. Reading of chairmen, accountants, town-hall functionaries, their wives and offspring, taking note of the names of their houses and the clubs they belong to, you dwell on how the conventional nature of their entries might compare with the wild disorder of their real lives. What a very public place to hide.

The Diva

INCIDENTAL pleasures at Covent Garden – not on the stage, but in the Grand Tier. It was *The Marriage of Figaro* and every time the soprano swam up to a top note or thereabouts, a great fat dame in raspberry bombasine who was sitting behind me went off like a phrase-book with the cork half out. '*Oh, ça alors!*' she sneered venomously. '*Incroyable!*' '*Ah, non – ma foi – ça, c'est trop!*' Evidently a superannuated diva who'd sung the role herself and wasn't too keen on anyone else having a crack. In the first interval they fetched the big man in the mulberry livery to tell her she had to shut up or get out. Well, she was rather noisy, but I had such a pain down the side of my neck from turning sharp left to look at the stage that I suppose I was in the mood for a little dissent. The seats had cost twenty-five quid a head, meaning you got a perfect view of the man's head who was getting a perfect view of the man's head who was getting a perfect view of the man's head, in front. I wouldn't have minded this so much if the rest of the audience hadn't given the impression of being people for whom no night at the opera was complete *unless* they went home with a pain in the neck. I mean, there was a good deal of free-floating worship going on: they not only looked to a man as though they didn't mind missing their dinner (which they were certainly going to do, since the performance had a touch of the slow bicycle race about it), they looked as though they would miss it joyfully. So it's possible that the carambas of the *diva* were more acceptable to me than to the rest.

After the second interval she quietened down (I offered a burst of silent applause for her marvellously stoical nephew, a lad of about eighteen who sat beside her and never by so much as a look or a blush let on about how awful he thought his aunty was), though she still simmered, and I found myself increasingly taken up with what didn't matter, like whether or not the Count was wearing a jockstrap and counting the mouldings in the outer architrave of the proscenium arch (not easy – I should be glad to have confirmation that there are, looking stage right, twenty precisely, to the red velvet on the ledge of the third tier). I wasn't exactly turning against Mozart, but what I had suspected for a long time was becoming a certainty: that Mozart is too refined for opera, that there isn't any Mozart opera that wouldn't sound better re-scored as a sequence of symphonies or *concerti*, and that while he does his best to get down on all fours with those who came after him, he never convinces you that he's anywhere near as robust as Verdi, Rossini, Donizetti, who were to turn opera into the vulgar treat it really is.

When the curtain came down the *diva* gave a loud and derisive sigh – 'Pfuiiiiii' – and waltzed out. If ever I saw a non-religious member of an opera audience, she was it. Her awful lack of loyalty was, I have to admit, like a warm poultice to my aching neck.

Basingstoke Studios

ONCE again I was trying to force my way into Basingstoke, a town which lies within its concrete and tarmacadam forest like a virgin under the spell of an Enchanter; and once again I was thwarted by the ring-roads which ensure that whatever route the Prince takes he always finds himself up the back of Sainsbury's again (is it as hard to get out of Basingstoke as it is to get in? Is there a coming-of-age ceremony at which Basingstoke lads are shown the network of tunnels which leads to the outside world and freedom?)

But I received a sign that the Enchanter's victories are not final. Backing out of the umpteenth cul-de-sac I swung the car about, and as I turned I saw a small red-brick house confronting the flow of traffic that thundered endlessly by on the raised carriageway. The house had been separated from the diesels and the juggernauts by a grim Berlin Wall topped with steel railings and iron mesh, an indication (if one was needed) that to the 'plan' which had resulted in this cruel nowhere, people were an afterthought. A foolish error. For above the front door of this house which had been ignored was its name. It read: Sea View. Such jokes bode ill for the tyrant – let the Enchanter beware.

But until Basingstoke is returned to its decent dull humanity the verse which has often invoked it must be considered to be suspended –

> *Of Basingstoke in Hampshire*
> *The claims to fame are small;*
> *A derelict canal,*
> *And a cream and green Town Hall.*
> *At each weekend the locals*
> *Line the Market Square,*
> *And as the traffic passes,*
> *They stand, and stand, and stare.*

Were Basingstoke its old self – a real place that made smart people smile – it might form part of a special A-level course (French, Music, and Basingstoke) which would lead to a degree in Basingstoke Studies, the culmination of a diligent research into the question, why is it certain place-names invite derision?

Post-graduates, led by the Senior Basingstoke Wrangler, would then address themselves in their doctoral theses to the matter of why Baldock and Biggleswade not only made you smile but also made you thoughtful, since no one driving North ever saw anyone turn off to either of these places: they were names on signposts only, and now with motorways by-passing the route where the names were seen, even the signposts are forgotten, and you wonder if Baldock and Biggleswade lie under the light Bedfordshire tilth, lost cities whose bells children put their ears to the ground in the hope of hearing.

One member of a group of television folk I was working with lived in Pinner, and the others thought this was uproarious. They spoke as though in evolutionary terms Pinner had just about reached Tudor times, and there were ox-carts parked in lay-bys while people drank beer from leather mugs crying Here's a health unto Bluff King Hal as they watched the beheadings in Pinner High Street. Penge has been so mythologized that nobody believes it's a real place any more and even the inhabitants call it *Ponge* as though inverted commas were obligatory; and there are those who run Croydon and Penge together to produce Croynge, distilling the essence of something they find exquisite.

Then there's Ilford, essentially the Great Terminus, saturated in sodium lighting and covered in buses. An occasional tall elm mixed in with the concrete lampstandards reminds you of the time it was the Eel Ford, and drovers would water their flocks where Rymans now sell tartan biros. But perhaps it only exists as one of those places shopkeepers offer as an excuse for not having something in stock; as, We're waiting for it from Ilford, or Ilford says it'll be next Tuesday, or (a great favourite) I don't know what Ilford's playing at! I think of the pubs in Ilford as places where a man with a sawn-off shotgun sometimes rushes in and shoots an old friend.

Wimbledon sounds as though it ought to be funny, but what makes people go a bit serious about places they might otherwise think were comical is the feeling they're rather expensive – nothing like high prices for wiping the smile off the face of someone who doesn't live there. Surbiton is still good for a laugh because it sounds like a proper name derived from the actual noun 'suburb' – SubURBiton. *Queen* of the suburbs, the estate agents once called it. Unbelievably, there was Surbiton Lagoon, but when I was a boy I never thought this was a contradiction in terms, I simply felt that because it was an open-air swimming pool where you stayed all day, lagoons had at last succeeded in being taken seriously. But I was rather a straight-faced child, and it's only recently that I've recognized that Effingham, which was the last station on our local line, could have come out of a Benny Hill sitcom.

It's clear enough the joke lies in feeling one-up. But that's only because you might otherwise feel one-down – Noel Coward wouldn't have found Clapham funny, if he hadn't been born in Teddington. When you smile at Basingstoke it may start an epidemic of instability and uneasiness among the inhabitants. But never forget that the smile itself is the first symptom.

B. Traven: A Mystery Solved

THE aim of the investigation was to crack a literary conundrum that had foxed everyone who'd ever tried their hand at it – to the world of letters it was the equivalent of the Colonel Fawcett mystery, and many a grizzled critic and many a saddleworn don had set off up this particular Amazon to find their man, and all had returned from a jungle of misdirection, false trails, Indian signs and tiger traps to explain that they hadn't actually *found* anyone but they'd heard rumours: that the man was an American millionaire, that he was Jack London, that he was a German prince, a Negro slave, and even the last President of Mexico but three. Our own expedition, fully provisioned with the previous literature, and armed to the teeth with the man's actual work, set forth with modest expectations, but we got lucky. Three quarters of the way through impenetrable savannahs of identity, we picked up a spoor. Breaking into a trot, next into a run, we burst into a clearing – and found him. But I was there first . . .

It all began one evening in a bookshop. Wandering round the shelves with a friend I picked up a paperback. It was called *The Bridge in the Jungle*, and the author's name was one that had always sounded a note that was strange: B. Traven. I said, 'Traven. Let's find him.' My companion said, 'Who's Traven?' and I said, 'That's the point – no one knows.' I went to the cash desk and I bought the book. I hadn't read a line of the man's works, but there are certain books you haven't read that exercise a stronger grip on your imagination than many you know by heart.

Whoever B. Traven was, he manufactured his anonymity so carefully that he might have been as fictional as the novels he produced. His books sell in their millions, particularly in America and in Eastern Europe, but no actual physical presence, no single individual, had ever claimed to have written them. There wasn't a publisher who had ever met Traven, no agent came forward willing to introduce his client. The name Traven was on the books, but the man Traven never signed his name, he typed it. The letters arriving in publishers' offices and purporting to come from

Traven, were inflexible in their prohibition of biographical details: dust-jackets were to be left blank, and the writer would have preferred it if his name had been left off the title-page. Nobody knew in what language the stories had originally been composed, nobody knew in what country the author had been born, indeed nobody knew if Traven was one man or several. But what's clear is that in absenting himself in this curiously complete way, Traven became more real rather than less. In the absence of humdrum flesh and blood, he became legendary, and it was even said that those who went in search of him were mysteriously destroyed, like men in fairy-tales.

We decided to risk it. My companion in the bookshop was Will Wyatt, a television producer with whom I had often worked. Like mendicant friars we shuffled the corridors of the BBC begging money for the expedition, advertised for seasoned researchers who had no fear of the telephone, and embarked for Mexico. This romantic destination was the one fixed element in the Traven story, for though nothing else was known about the provenance of the manuscripts, Mexico was the country from which someone had posted them.

By this time the zest I felt for the chase had been underpinned by something more substantial, my reading of the books themselves. Traven had written a dozen novels as well as many short stories, awkwardly expressed fables that have an imaginative grip that rivals 'The Ancient Mariner'. Indeed, his first published novel is a tale of the sea that exudes a paranoia reminiscent of Coleridge's poem – placelessness and anomie dog the hero of *The Death Ship*, another Flying Dutchman who is doomed to wander the world stoking the boilers of a hulk, without papers, without identity. The world affronts Traven in its treatment of the individual, as his stories of the Mexican Indian clearly show.

On our arrival in Mexico our first witness, living in the seaside resort of Puerto Viarta, was John Huston, whose film *The Treasure of the Sierra Madre* had been based on Traven's novel of the same name: a classic study of the corrosive effect of greed. Huston spoke of Traven's quality as a writer in the following words:

'He was a very passionate and eloquent writer, a defender of the victims of society. He hated injustice, and God knows he found a great battlefield here in Mexico. The vision was so great … and that's what Traven had – a great vision. The books are all marvellous affirmations of his faith in the beaten man.'

No one had ever spoken of meeting Traven, but one night in Mexico City, while Huston was preparing the shooting-script of the *Sierra Madre*, he heard a sound in his hotel room in the early hours of the morning:

'I woke up and someone was standing at the foot of my bed. I sat up in bed and said, "Hello." He took out a card and gave it to me – just shortly after daylight this was. I read the card. It said "Hal Croves – translator, Acapulco and San Antonio". After I'd read the card, he gave me a letter, and the letter was signed "B. Traven". The letter said that he, Traven, was ill, and that in his stead he was sending his intimate friend, Hal Croves. And that anything that I could have got from himself, Croves could furnish me.'

Croves is just about as strange a name as Traven: it has an anagrammatic quality that suggests the absence of anyone real. Why would Traven have so intimate a confidant? Croves knew so much he might well have been Traven himself:

'Croves expressed the same thoughts that Traven had, and the thought crossed my mind, could this possibly *be* Traven? I told Traven – I told Croves – of certain changes that I intended to make, and he listened and nodded. He was obviously an old Mexico hand.'

When the film got under way, Croves was a constant bystander. He came each day and watched intently. It was noticed that he avoided the stills photographer, but he was snapped once, unawares. When the film was finished, Croves disappeared. Huston said that this was the last he saw of the man, he went away, and they never corresponded. But Huston had relinquished his early suspicion that Croves might have been Traven. To Huston, the man Croves – diminutive, socially maladroit, in his baggy shorts almost a figure of fun – could surely not be Traven, a writer whose obsessive self-assurance was his hallmark. But who was Croves?

In his way he was as elusive as Traven, as one of his friends who is still living in Mexico City discovered. This was the distinguished cine-matographer Gabriel Figueroa. Figueroa's sister-in-law, Esperanza Lopez Mateos, had become Traven's agent, though of course she had never met Traven himself, only the man who explained that he was Traven's translator – Hal Croves. On one occasion she had arranged to meet Croves in a café in Mexico City. But Miss Lopez Mateos was ill and Gabriel Figueroa went in her place:

'So I went over to the café, and there was Mr Croves sitting with his cup of coffee, waiting, and a few customers around. So I get close and say, "Are you Mr Croves?" He turns, looks at me and says, "No." So what can I do? No telephone in the café, so I had to go out to find a telephone and tell Esperanza that probably I was mistaken or some-thing. She says, "no, no, he is the man you are describing." So I go back and he was not there any more.'

This was some time in the Forties, and a little while later Croves was gone. He had left Mexico City. But now for the first time someone was planning an assault on Traven, someone had decided that he would hunt B. Traven down and give him a face. It was a Mexican journalist called Luis Spota. These days Spota is a great whiz on Mexican television, but at the time Croves disappeared from Mexico City Spota was a callow 22-year-old reporter and, as he himself is the first to say, none too scrupulous. Spota had a chum who worked in a bank, and it was a casual word from this man that started things off. The friend said there was an account in the bank under the name B. Traven Torsvan. This added a further name to a growing list, but Spota's friend thought it might be a clue. Spota was delighted:

'I went to the bank, made some moves, not always legal – but we are reporters anyway – and I get a small short-cut to this box. And in this box I found some interesting material, especially a letter in the name of M. L. Martinez, a very common name in Mexico, with an address – Post Office 49 – in Acapulco.'

Getting leave of his editor, Spota took off for Acapulco and homed in on the post office:

'So one day a lady, dark lady, Mexican lady, young, went to the post office, take the letters. I follow her. I know exactly the address of her house – Cashew Park – something like a big beer garden. In that place, Maria de la Luz Martinez was living with an American – we supposed he was an American – named Berick Torsvan. He was a very small man, thin man, blond man, shy man.'

Straight away Spota was convinced that this man Torsvan, who was the owner of a roadside café and small-holding, was B. Traven. Posing as a tourist, Spota began to make a habit of dropping in at the café:

'This man – who has, by the way, twenty-five dogs always with him when he comes and when he leaves the place – came spontaneously to my table to drink the same lemonade, and he start with me a nice friendship. He told me he was living in Mexico since long time ago, and he told me the first thing that convinced me I was in the good direction. He told me a story of two men in the south of Mexico who fought with machetes until one of them killed the other and the other dies, too. It was one of the stories in one of Traven's books.'

Spota returned to Mexico City and started a search in government offices for the immigration card he was confident he would find in Torsvan's name, and sure enough there it was. The name was on record as Traven Torsvan, and the birthplace was down as Chicago. Returning to the poste-restante number at the post office in Acapulco, Spota bribed one of the clerks and with his assistance laid hands on a letter addressed to Torsvan from Gabriel Figueroa.

'I make a friend in the post office, and I am a little indiscreet, and we have a great curiosity – and we open the letter from Gabriel Figueroa. We make a copy, a photostatic copy. Well, when I think I have enough proof against him, I tell him, "I think you are B. Traven." And his reaction was, he was very upset. And then later he got very quickly angry. He put his hand very violently on the table and told me, "You are a son of a bitch." And he left the table with his twenty-five dogs.'

But the next day Spota turned up again at the tea-garden and the man called Torsvan denied the charge in elaborate and contradictory detail:

'And he said, "You are wrong because I am not B. Traven, I am his cousin." He told me, "Well, Mr Traven is dead. He dies many years ago." Later he told me Traven is sick of tuberculosis. The other day he told me that he was able to pay me, to give me some money in order to keep me silent, and I tell him, "I don't care about money. I don't want your money because *you* are my goal. B. Traven is my goal, my challenge. I want to be a very good reporter." I was then twenty-two years old. And he say – I don't remember when, this day or this night – "You are going to be responsible for the death of a man if you publish your story in your magazine *Mañana*. I am going to kill myself and you are going to have over your conscience my death." Then I said, "Well, that's your choice, that's your problem, not mine." I was very cynical then. And I published the story and by good fortune for the literature in the world and for humanity, he did not kill himself.'

No doubt about it, Spota had worked like a beaver, and all this foot-in-door stuff earned him a prize for investigative reporting. But a month after his articles had appeared in *Mañana*, the editor received a letter from Traven. It came from England, where Traven claimed to be living. Spota was dubious:

'I took the paper to the Technological Institute of Mexico. And we discovered this: the paper was Mexican, the ink of the typewriter was Mexican, the glue of the envelope was Mexican.'

As the reader might expect, Torsvan disappeared from Acapulco. And as the reader might also guess, Croves re-emerged in Mexico City. It is plain from the photographs that exist that Croves and Torsvan were the same man. And all Croves's documents were in the name of Traven Torsvan. But to show that Torsvan was Croves is not the same as showing that either of them was Traven.

As Huston recollects, people who assumed Croves was Traven, and used the name Traven in his presence, were mercilessly snubbed:

'Occasionally, someone would come up, some brash person, and ask him directly and rudely, "Are you B. Traven?" And when that happened in my presence I'd flinch. I never asked him that question, by the way.'

Sanora Babb Howe, widow of the famous Hollywood cameraman James Wong Howe, and a friend of Croves, committed the same solecism:

'One day, when we were talking about one of Traven's books, I made the mistake of referring to him as Traven. And he didn't say just then, but he left soon after that – not in any anger – and came back and put a note under my door. The note was a personal note about that I must understand that he was absolutely not Traven, and I mustn't address him in this way. And it seemed to me if he weren't, he really wouldn't have to give that elaborate excuse. The next day he came again and asked me if I had got the note. And I said yes. And he asked if he could have it, and he tore it up.'

Figueroa was a great friend, and Croves had the use of a room in Figueroa's house. But then Figueroa did not allow himself to question his friend's identity, punctiliously avoiding the name Traven. To Figueroa the man was always Hal or even Mr Croves. Lawrence Hill, who published some of Traven's Mexican stories, thought he might well be meeting Traven, but Croves always held out his hand and announced, 'Croves'. Perhaps Croves's refusal to agree that he was Traven is explained in the simplest way – that he wasn't.

For the last sixteen years of his life, the man who was known as Hal Croves lived in Mexico City. His initial address was 353 Calle Durango, and his second and final home was at number 61 Calle Rio Mississippi, right in the centre of the town. His companion throughout was Rosa Elena Lujan, his agent and translator and the wife he married in 1957. Croves called the room he worked in The Bridge, and thought of the house as a ship. His wife was First Mate and his two stepdaughters Second and Third Officers. Croves died in 1969, and a fragment of home movie is the only living record of the man. He is wearing glasses and seems small and old and meek, a character much at odds with the hectoring, even bullying personality of the writer who typed the name B. Traven at the end of his lengthy letters.

But one thing Traven and Croves had in common. They were secretive. Croves could not bear questions even from his wife, and when they stayed at hotels he encouraged her always to give a false name (returning to the hotel on one occasion, she couldn't remember what name it was she'd invented, and wasn't able to get back into her room). Croves's nationality was a matter for speculation. His passport said he was Mexican but he became Mexican as late as 1951, and before then – as the journalist

Spota had discovered – his papers gave his birthplace as Chicago. The way he spoke English ought to have offered some clue to his origins, but there again the evidence was conflicting. One of Croves's friends told me she thought the accent was German, another said Scandinavian. One morning in Mexico City while I was talking to Señora Lujan (Mrs Croves), she remembered there was a tape-recording in the house. Her daughter had idly turned on the machine one evening as her stepfather had been talking. Mrs Croves fitted the tape on the spool and the voice of Croves who might be Traven filled the room. But there was a distance and indistinctness about the sound, as though the man knew that a day would come even after his death when he must be specially careful to deceive. It was a 'foreign' accent, that was all. His widow believed he was American but then he was typing in German one day and she looked over his shoulder and said, 'But darling, you told me you didn't know any German,' and he simply looked up, stared at her and said, 'I don't ...'

What about the language in which the Traven stories were composed? Bernard Smith was an editor at the American publishing firm of Alfred Knopf and remembers the day the English manuscript of *The Death Ship* found its way on to his desk:

'It was written, I surmise, as a direct word-for-word literal translation from the German language, because the sentence structure, the paragraph structure and so on was really German. Whereupon I rewrote the first twenty or twenty-five pages of *The Death Ship* and sent them to him. And back came a letter from him saying he was enormously enthusiastic and I had a free hand to do the whole book. I don't want anyone to misunderstand what the nature of the rewrite was. It was not any literary contribution from me – that is to say, I didn't add anything to his narrative or to his characterizations, I merely put his literal translation from the German into acceptable English.'

The Death Ship had originally been published in Germany in 1926, and this and other Traven manuscripts (*The Bridge in the Jungle, The Treasure of the Sierra Madre*) arrived at the Büchergilde Gutenberg – the left-wing publishing house which first brought out the Traven books – written in German. But the German used by Traven is something of an oddity. A student of both Traven and the German language reported that he had taken a passage of forty pages and found over two hundred barbarisms of style – once every second page, on average, there was a glaring error in simple German grammar.

Odd English, odd German. As our final unmasking was to show, there was an uncomplicated, even technical explanation for this ...

The man who called himself Torsvan and later called himself Croves first emerges in Mexico in 1925. The following year he was a member of an archaeological expedition to the jungle region of southern Mexico, the Chiapas. The language and culture of the Indians were Torsvan's passion, and this was the first of many journeys he made to the Mexican jungles. Now it happens that many of the B. Traven stories are set in these same jungles and tell of the Indians in terms that suggest a reworking of their own folk myths. Does this mean that Torsvan, who was later to become Croves, actually wrote the books of B. Traven? If he did, then a further mystery has to be solved.

If Croves was the author of the work of B. Traven, why did production of the Traven books all but dry up round about 1939? For Croves, who turns up under this name in the early forties, was alive and well and lived for another thirty years. New editions of old Traven material continued to appear during the Croves era, but the texts had been tampered with, German names and references were expunged in what looked like a determined attempt to blur the past. A trickle of new short stories came out in cheap magazines, and there was one long novel called *Aslan Norval*. This book was submitted to several publishers, all of whom turned it down on the grounds that it was unrecognizable as the work of B. Traven. In Germany there were those who took it to be a forgery, and as the Traven scholar Robert Goss has said: if Croves *was* B. Traven, why couldn't he write like B. Traven?

Perhaps the gift had deserted him, perhaps he was written out, perhaps age had diluted the talent. But it must be remembered that Croves invariably denied that he *was* Traven, even going so far as to put it about that Traven as a separate individual didn't exist, that his work was the joint product of two men. This notion sponsored by Croves himself is specially enticing to all who, loving a mystery, love to give it a further twist: what if the work of Traven was actually experienced by one man and written down by another? And if the writing half of that literary duo disappeared in 1939, it would explain why the other partner produced so little.

But if the story of Traven contains two men, it now has to make room for a third. He bears an equally strange name but is a real, even an historical, figure. Ret Marut was a German anarchist, a member of the Revolutionary Workers' Soviet in Munich which had been put down by the authorities in 1919. The day after Croves died in 1969, his widow announced that her husband Hal Croves had also been Marut.

What do we know about Marut? He is first heard of as an actor in Germany in 1907: we find his name as a player of bit-parts on playbills that have survived. But later in Munich he emerges as editor and publisher of an anarchist newsletter, *Der Ziegelbrenner* – literally translated, *The Brick-burner* or *The Brick-maker*. The bricks were for the building of a new society, and the magazine which came out during the First World War was the size, shape and colour of a brick, a fact that later in our researches, and to our great surprise, was to prove the determining factor in our discovery of who B. Traven actually was ...

One aspect of temperament that Marut certainly shared with Traven and with Croves was secrecy. *Der Ziegelbrenner* carried the words 'No visiting allowed. There is never anyone at home', and all correspondence was via a PO box number. And though Marut would address revolutionary meetings in Munich, he would only speak to audiences in the dark, when the lights had been turned out.

So Croves, who had been Torsvan, was also Ret Marut. Why therefore had Croves's widow waited until Croves's death to make this disclosure, and why, when he was alive, had both Croves and his wife flatly asserted the contrary? Explaining the contradiction when we visited her in Mexico City, Señora Lujan (Mrs Croves) simply said that she was following her husband's instruction. On his deathbed he had said she might now tell the truth, he was no longer in any danger from his past.

As collateral for her claim that Marut and Croves were one and the same, Señora Lujan showed us a copy of a novel Marut had written, *An das Fräulein von S ...*, published in Munich in 1916 and a very rare book indeed. She had a parcel which she unwrapped: it was a collection of original *Der Ziegelbrenners*, their red covers slightly faded. All were souvenirs of a previous life, given into her keeping by her husband. Upstairs in the room Croves used as a study – The Bridge – hangs a picture. It is a picture of Croves but it is also a picture of Marut, for when Croves died the German newspapers canvassed the possibility that he had been the old anarchist, and Marut's secretary, who was still alive, had unearthed the picture and sent it to Señora Lujan in Mexico City.

When the Munich Soviet had been dispersed, Marut had been taken prisoner by the authorities and condemned to death. But he had escaped and disappeared. Towards the end of 1922 a postcard arrived at an address in Germany, postmarked Rotterdam: 'In a few hours I shall board a ship to take me across the Atlantic and thereby I cease to exist.' That was the latest information on Ret Marut until our own researches revealed more. Thanks to the US Freedom of Information Act, we discovered in documents unearthed from the CIA, the FBI and the State Department that Ret Marut was in London in 1923 and 1924. At the Home Office, following up the references found in the American files, we brought to light two hitherto unpublished photographs of Ret Marut taken by the British Police. And that clinched it: the man who was living in London in 1924, on the run from the German authorities, was Croves, was Torsvan and was Ret Marut. He had been arrested for failing to register as an alien, and spent two months in Brixton Prison before being deported early in 1924 on the steamship *Hegre*, a Norwegian vessel bound for Tenerife via Brixham. And that gets us back to B. Traven . . .

We know from a document in the American consul's office that Marut worked his passage on the *Hegre* and the job he was given was that of fireman. The hero of *The Death Ship* by B. Traven was also a fireman, and the parallel is hard to avoid. But if Marut *was* Traven, the problem is this: Marut could not have arrived in Mexico until the middle of 1924, yet the manuscript of *The Cotton Pickers*, an account of adventures among the poorly paid Mexican Indians, arrived at Traven's German publishers early in 1925. How could Marut have absorbed so much of a strange milieu that he was able to write an amazingly convincing book about it, *and* earn a living, all in the few months available?

At least two Traven scholars, Michael Baumann and Robert Goss, believe it was impossible. Baumann said:

'There is sufficient evidence, not only in the novels, but also in the one non-fiction work that has been published so far, that the man who wrote in the first person had lived in Mexico for at least ten, perhaps fifteen or twenty years before Ret Marut could have got to Mexico.'

And Robert Goss adds:

'I don't believe it would have been possible for a newcomer to gain the trust and get the inside knowledge that the B. Traven books show.'

Of course, if the Mexican work of B. Traven were the product of two men – one who had already experienced what the other then wrote down – the difficulty would be resolved. Baumann feels there's something in it:

'A Swiss Traven reader had suggested already in 1964 that an American had been what he called the *Erlebnisträger*, which means the carrier of the experience or experiences. He thought it was this American who wrote the original manuscripts of the early Traven novels and stories in English, and that Ret Marut met this man. If there was another man, he was probably an American "wobbly", a member of the Industrial Workers of the World group of labour unions. The first German version of *The Cotton Pickers*, Traven's second published novel in Germany, was called *Der Wobbly*.'

Well, the possibility of this other man haunts the Traven mystery. The idea seizes the imagination. But facts have to be faced. There is no scrap of evidence that such a second man ever existed. And if it is simply a matter of puzzling out how a writer of the first rank might instantly convert a place and a people he had never before seen into high imaginative fiction, then the words 'imaginative' and 'fiction' are the key: the possibility of the experience is already in the imagination of such an artist, the facts simply supply the opportunity. And fiction is not a process of finding out, it is a process of guessing or divination. Señora Lujan has never doubted that her husband was Traven, and she showed us the diaries he kept while in the jungle, which closely parallel the incidents in Traven's books. Marut was Torsvan was Croves was Traven. But who was the man behind the names?

What is it, to find out who someone is? Traven hoped to vanish into his work, to become, as he put it, 'the word'. And of course the work of writers of his calibre tells us more than ever their names and addresses could. But in a purely scientific sense, to find out who someone is to find out who his parents were. Marut's identity card gave his place of birth as San Francisco, but to claim San Francisco as your birthplace is to ensure that no one can check it – all the records were destroyed in the fire and earthquake of 1906. When applying for an American passport, Marut gave his father's name as William, and from a letter in State Department files we see that the American consul in London carefully studied a photograph of Marut and, perhaps because Marut had come from Germany, was struck by what he took to be a distinct resemblance to a very famous William – the Kaiser.

Was Wilhelm II the father of Ret Marut? Anyone who compares a picture of Marut/Croves/Torsvan with one of the Kaiser's sons, the Crown Prince, will see there is an undeniable similarity. As editor of *Der Ziegelbrenner*, a subversive tract, Marut was never hounded, which might be thought to be curious, and another curious consideration was where the money to keep the magazine going came from. The third oddity was that Marut, a revolutionary, on occasion wrote almost kindly of the Kaiser. Did he have the protection of a great man – Kaiser Wilhelm II who was doing it all for his natural son?

Even at the time of *Der Ziegelbrenner* there were rumours that its editor had friends in high places. Many years later Croves spoke ambiguously to a journalist: 'Forget the man. What does it matter if he's the son of a Hohenzollern prince?' His widow agreed that Croves looked very much like the late Kaiser's family, and told me that her husband often talked about Wilhelm II. But Croves was full of tales. At times he told his wife that he was the son of a poor fisherman in Norway who had died before he was born.

I don't believe that either Wyatt as the producer or I as writer of the film and instigator of the project ever really thought we would find out who B. Traven was. We hoped to make a careful record of what was known with the object of turning it into a coherent narrative. And the witnesses we spoke to made it clear that in their view Traven had not so much blurred his tracks as pulled them up behind him as he went along. Lawrence Hill, one of Traven's American publishers, said:

'The problem of writing the biography of Traven has stumped already four or five writers. They keep running into road blocks and stone walls and blanks in the flow of information.'

And the Traven scholar Michael Baumann simply concluded, 'In my opinion we do not know who B. Traven was.' Traveners felt that their avatar had died with his secret intact, and as Bernard Smith, who had edited *The Death Ship* for Knopf, put it, 'I think we know all we are likely to find out, but I am quite certain that we do not know all that ought to be known.'

How strange that having done no more than stray into the competition, we should have won the prize!

We sorted through all the aliases. As Wyatt and I roamed the world interviewing witnesses, the *équipe* at base camp were seldom off the telephone. Names were the man's obsession. He had been Ret Marut, he had been Fred Maruth, he had been Rex Marut, he had been Richard Maurhut, and of course Croves and Torsvan and Traven Torsvan and B.T.Torsvan, as well as B.Traven. Every alias was tracked down and in each case there was no collateral. There was no such address or there were no such parents or no such name or no such record. The man passed out names like dud cheques. The police, the authorities, asked him for names and he gave them names. The more he gave them the safer he felt.

With a sigh, we were about to close the file. We had one last name, one last place, to check. It was a name and a place that Marut had given the police in London in 1923. We assumed that like all the others it would be a false trail. As with all the other names, there would be no real person hiding behind it. We sent off a telegram yet again to a place he had claimed to be the town of his birth. Back with unnerving swiftness came a copy of his birth certificate.

We couldn't believe it. From the little town of Swiebodzin on the Polish–German border came the typewritten evidence: Hermann Albert Otto Maximilian Feige had been a real live human being who had been born in that town on 23 February 1882.

Caution asserted itself. Feige was real, but that didn't mean he was

Marut. Marut might have borrowed the identity. We looked again at the birth certificate. Marut had told the police the occupation of his father and his mother: his mother had been a mill-hand, his father a potter – and the certificate confirmed it. Would an impostor have known the occupation of the father and mother of someone else, forty years before? We looked again. The mother's maiden name had been Weinecke. On the list of aliases used by Marut, preserved in the police files of 1923, the same name appears – Weinecke. Would an impostor have known so much?

But when we went to Swiebodzin, we found the parallel was finer. In his deposition to the police in London, the man had said his mother was a 'mill-hand'. But in the birth record-book in the town hall at Swiebodzin, her occupation is listed more generally as 'factory worker'. We made enquiries. There was only one place a factory worker could gain employment at the time of his birth: there were no factories in Swiebodzin, there were only cloth mills. Could an impostor have been so precise?

But the deepest chime, the truly pregnant echo, was one that my own ear was the first to register. We knew the man's father had been a potter. Back in Warsaw, we were drinking coffee and I was chatting idly to our Polish assistant, asking about the word *'Cupfe'* – the town hall records for the 1880s were all in German, for all that time Swiebodzin had been Schweibus and a part of Germany. Yes, she said, *'Cupfe'* would be the German word for potter. I said I thought of a potter as a man who made cups and bowls. Yes, she said, but *'Cupfe'* suggested he made other things – tiles, perhaps.

I let out an unholy roar. 'He made tiles. Tiles are bricks. He made bricks. He was a brick-burner. And since the town was German, he was *Der Ziegelbrenner!*'

That, as far as I am concerned, was the moment I knew I had found my Colonel Fawcett, and the assonance I had heard was given its physical location by an elderly citizen of Swiebodzin who told us where the pottery had stood. It was not an ordinary pottery, he said, it had been part of a brickworks where they had also made tiles and earthenware. I said to the man, 'Would a man who made tiles in such a place be thought of as a brickmaker?' The old chap nodded. 'Would he have been called a *Ziegelbrenner?*' The old chap nodded again. 'Yes,' he said, 'he would.'

For me the search was over. Feige was Marut was Torsvan was Croves was Traven. All of us on the expedition had sailed into the heart of the mystery, but the beat of that heart was something I was first to hear, and I claim the moment as my own.

But more was to come. The town hall at Swiebodzin yielded the names of other members of the Feige family. Feige had brothers and sisters and two of them had moved to Germany – Ernst and Margarethe. They would now be very old, eighty-three and eight-six. But they would be the only two people in the world able directly to confirm what we had discovered. Even if we managed to trace their last addresses, it was a very long shot that either of them would still be alive. But they were. In a tiny village in Lower Saxony they talked to us about the elder brother they had always called Otto.

> MARGARETHE HENZE: He was a very self-willed, intelligent boy.
> ERNST FEIGE: He was a strange, peculiar boy. He lived in his own world – no one else had room in his world. He never even played with anyone. He was a loner. He would browse through our books – we had quite a few books – he studied them all.
> MARGARETHE HENZE: He was very good at school and so he was going to become a priest. The town of Swiebodzin was going to pay for his studies, but our parents would have to pay for his board and lodging. At that my parents said, 'We can't afford it. There are seven children and we cannot afford that.' And so he had to become a locksmith instead. He was an apprentice for four years, and then he joined the army. And after his time in the army – that was when he disappeared. We never heard from him again.
> He was a stubborn boy. That stems partly from the fact that he didn't live with us until he was six – he lived with my grandparents.

And yes, Otto had been a political activist since his earliest days. Margarethe recalled that he planned to rally the village to the socialist cause, and his room was stacked with placards and leaflets.

> MARGARETHE HENZE: And he also planned to make political speeches in the village, and that made my mother furious. That is when he went away, angry. Well, I mean, you can see why – he had invested a lot of work in this project, and then he doesn't have a chance to get it actually off the ground. So he was mad at them.

After Otto vanished, Ernst recalled his mother had received one letter. It was to tell that he was in London, and about to be deported.

> ERNST FEIGE: He wrote to us once – I think to my mother. That is how we knew that he was in England. And then he wrote again saying that he was no longer in England, that the authorities had kicked him out.

Then Margarethe remembered a later occasion when the police called at the house to discover whether it was the home of Hermann Albert Otto Maximilian Feige.

MARGARETHE HENZE: One Sunday afternoon about 1922, they came to the house. And afterwards I found my mother in the loo, crying, and I said, 'Mother, why are you crying? What happened?' She said, 'The police were here, they were looking for Otto; he must have done something wrong. And so we said to them: no, he was not our son.' You see, they were afraid that they might get into trouble over him. And since then we've heard absolutely nothing from him.

They then produced two photographs. One had a face that had been stuck on afterwards. The picture had been taken at his mother's silver wedding anniversary, and since Otto had already disappeared, his face had to be cut from another photograph. And the second was an earlier picture of Otto, taken at the time of his confirmation, when he was about fifteen years old. These photographs were of one man. He was Marut, he was Torsvan, he was Croves, he was Traven. Finally, we showed the two old people our photographs of the brother they had not seen for over seventy years. Their recognition was the final endorsement. We had found B. Traven.

MARGARETHE HENZE: What a funny face he's pulling. Yes, that's him.

What Traven always said turns out to be true. He had no personal claim on anyone's attention. He wasn't after all a president or a millionaire or a prince. He wasn't even born in wedlock, since his parents married a year after his birth. He was the son of a humble brick-burner, and no wonder his German (let alone his English) wasn't very good, since the town of his birth was neither Polish nor German but a mixture of both. All that matters about him at last is his work: he hid behind it, vanished into it, and achieved his wish. He became the word.

Noodleburger's Misnomer

FROM the Boondock and Maxwelton Life Enhancement Laboratories
– or some such – in downtown Wichita comes a survey of the ways
people waste time. Did you know you spend nineteen years of your
life doing household chores? Four years queuing up at supermarket tills?
Six months waiting at traffic lights, and three years returning telephone
calls?

The madness of this method of computing lies in the dizzying change
of perspective – what has the business of sitting at traffic lights to do
with *months*? Where's the relevance of *years* to household chores? At
this very moment people are polishing fenders or trying to find safety-
pins, activities so tiny they don't even know they're doing them, and
suddenly they're being stared at through a cosmic telescope held by Professor Ted Noodleburger who switches into galactic mode to study a
man who is trying to refill a stapler. Is this a lost episode of *Gulliver's
Travels*?

And what does he mean, waste of time? Doesn't he know that holding
the moulded sole of a shoe under the hot tap while you prod the dog
dirt out with a meat skewer, or trying to work the water out of a flat
wind-up hose, are ways of *experiencing* time, of getting close up to it,
of feeling the day pass, second by second? Only the man who has been
held up at four red lights in succession can savour in anticipation another
day when he will speed through the same four traffic lights because
they are green. Waste of time: when you think about it, there's no such
thing.

The fatuity of this sort of survey lies in the implication that if you
weren't sitting at the traffic lights you'd already be back at home painting
The Last Supper; if it weren't for the traffic lights, you'd be Vermeer.
Or at least, according to the document under review, instead of declining
into the sear, the yellow leaf, while waiting for the traffic lights to change,
you could be talking to your wife and children. Flipping the switch,
Noodleburger makes an instant change of time-scale to tell you that while
willing enough to hang around traffic lights year in year out, the average

male spends only thirty seconds each day talking to his children and four minutes talking to his wife. The Noodleburger theory is that if he gave up returning telephone calls the average man could spend three years trailing round the house inflicting monologues on his family. But think of the enormous capital expenditure this would entail in constructing extensions to existing lunatic asylums.

As for the four years spent queuing at supermarket tills, how can such an exercise in self-control be called a waste of time? Wasting Time: the label is Noodleburger's Misnomer, what the whole human race is engaged in is *passing* time. To be *aware* that time is passing is to be conscious of being alive, and viewed in this light nothing is a waste of time since all activities have the same value to the people engaged in them. A man burrowing through cupboards in search of the finial of a Viennese long-case clock, discarded many years before, with which he hopes to enhance the pediment of his Admiral Fitzroy barometer, or in a chronic state of deferring a decision to begin marleytiling his downstairs cloakroom, is as wholly occupied as the man composing a monograph on Schiller. Occupation is the filigree on time's ribbon, which allows us to feel it passing through our fingers.

You can only *waste* time by deliberately setting out to do so. Buying a single stamp at a post office is as good a way as any. But all these matters must be viewed in the light of the proposition that life is an accidental phenomenon entirely devoid of meaning. By a random conjunction of particles, life appears in the universe, and ultimately we are all sitting in the kitchen solving a puzzle that may win us a holiday for two in Bermuda. Meaning is something we invent, we chalk out patterns, and no one device is superior to another. Chaos is the given condition. Within it, we play hopscotch.

Weekend in Prague

ALTHOUGH, on looking back, I realize the jacket I was wearing in Prague had something indefinably *long* about it, reminiscent of the dust-coats worn by old men in hardware shops, I hadn't thought it was the sort of thing that would get you turned out of the opera-house. For a fleeting moment, as the woman tearing the tickets at the top of the aisle pressed her hand against my chest and stared at it, it did flash across my mind she might think I had recently been painting the scenery. But after studying the coat she inspected the trousers and then, bending down to get a better look, she examined the shoes as though expecting the worst, which I suppose would be wellingtons.

Straightening up, she saw the tie and nodded (I think the Regiment earned her approval) but now, with an expression of genuine amusement on her face, she began actually to finger the garments, and plucking at my Pringle as though working out a price for the lot, she said 'This is better' (mulling it over now, I can see how the coat with its cavalier touch had puzzled her, but surely she should have disallowed the woolly? What was I doing in knitwear at the opera? All I can say is there's a nimbus of strangeness everyone carries about with them, and in certain circumstances abroad seems to make it condense).

Struck by the possibility that she might start to look behind my brasses, I bowed sharply from the hips like Eric von Stroheim and turning to my wife barked, 'Forward!' I followed her down the aisle, the hairs on the back of my neck bristling as I anticipated being brought low by a flying tackle.

We had to leave at the first interval since it was so bad you felt sorry for the singers. As we approached the *vestiaire* my wife hissed, 'We mustn't offend them, I shall feign a headache', and clasping her brow wildly as though she were playing the lead in the opera herself, dragged me through the swing doors and led me blindly into the Ladies under the impression it was the exit. Driven back by a solid phalanx of women in bootees, I reversed into the arms of the female who had criticized my clothing, and she seized this opportunity to sell me a small crimson badge as a memento.

Back at the hotel, enormous Edwardian pictures on each landing featured what looked like the same man. Always in full evening dress, he is either haunted by the spirit of absinthe in the form of a green see-through lady, or is staring out through French windows on some dream sequence of battling soldiers, while surrounded at the dinner-table by a family who plainly cannot see what Father sees or they would be taking more notice of the large undraped female corpse which for some reason (felled by the dinner, perhaps) is sprawled next to him.

This theme is not entirely abandoned in the dining-room where a life-size silver statue of a lady with her arms raised ambiguously above her head presides. She is naked, but in a fully-clothed sort of way. 'The spirit of what?' I wondered aloud. 'Indigestion,' said my wife sombrely. Impetuously I drew my wife on to the tiny dance-floor and whirled her round in an old-fashioned waltz, thinking a little action might dispel such dark thoughts.

She seemed alarmed as we cannoned into fraternal delegates from the GDR, but the respectable middle-aged man who was playing several instruments and who by my computation made up four-fifths of the band to the pianist's one, was going good-oh. Moving easily from fiddle to xylophone, then flinging down the sticks and taking up the trumpet, he gave every one of them the College try, and when all else failed, he sang.

As we all applauded and began to leave the dance-floor, one of the men from the GDR shook me warmly by the hand and I felt pleased that my natural sense of rhythm had been noted and approved (my wife's inability to fathom which foot I was going to lead off with seemed now, more than ever, something of an affliction). But he was effusive. 'It is good to see our special friends from the West,' said this amiable man, with just the slightest emphasis on the word 'special'. We all bowed to each other, and my wife and I made our way out. At the door I clapped my hand to my lapel. The tiny red badge sold to me by the lady at the theatre was in my button-hole. He had taken it for the Order of Lenin.

Refraining

I WAS working in the Reading Room of the British Museum and nipped out to the loo, and while I was in there saw a notice telling you not to write on the walls. This seemed a bit out of the way in those lofty purlieus, but the only concession to the politeness of the surroundings was the curious verb the notice used.

It didn't say 'Don't write on the walls', it said 'Please *refrain* from writing on the walls'. I went back to my books but couldn't get under way for about ten minutes, trying as I did to plumb the significance of the word 'refrain'. After all, I imagine your average wall-writer either does it or doesn't do it, I don't see him struggling *not* to, an effort the word 'refrain' seems to enjoin: I don't see him returning home to his housekeeper to tell her he had an all but overmastering impulse to write on the wall of the lavatory at the British Museum Reading Room during the afternoon, but managed to 'refrain'.

Or was it that there had been an outbreak, a rash of the stuff? Oh, not the usual run-of-the-mill graffiti, but epigrams, *vers de societé*, much of it in the original Old High German, Classical Greek, Sanskrit? And this had been all scrubbed off, not because it was felt the wall had been defaced but because the material just wasn't good enough?

I found myself thinking I was glad I hadn't volunteered a line or two. It had never before occurred to me to write something on a wall, but now that the prohibition made it clear that unnamed persons had taken it upon themselves to publish without anyone's leave, and had had their unsolicited offerings savagely reviewed in that they had been expunged, I felt I'd been saved from what I'd never been tempted by. How dreadful if I'd slapped up the words that have stayed with me ever since I read them on the wall of a fish-and-chip shop long ago —

> *Oh Mother, isn't it ripping?*
> *Yes, dear, they fry in dripping.*

and —

– only to find the next day that they had been bleached off by cleansing staff, all of whom had D. Phils. Would they have appreciated 'Monty's Spanish Removals' or 'Mogg's Elected Bacon', both of which I thought by no means disgraced the sides of the vans on which I'd seen them inscribed? Surely they wouldn't have obliterated 'Ramsey Macdonald is as useless as a chocolate tea pot'?

When I went out I was feeling defensive, as though already awaiting a rejection slip from an editor to whom I had refrained from sending a contribution.

Big Game Hunting in Somerset

'I DARE say you know the sort,' said the other customer in the gun shop. 'Blazes away at low-flying pheasants. Dammit, if you're going to call that sport, you might as well stay at home and take pot-shots at the Rhode Island Reds on the home farm.'

A salesman, who looked a bit like Arthur Treacher, placed himself at a sporting distance from me, clasped his hands behind his back and rocked gently up and down on his heels. What I'd heard made me feel I was in deeper water than I'd been banking on, because up till then it wasn't low-flying pheasants I'd aimed at so much as ones that had actually landed – birds going for strolls on the A30 – and my weapon had been the motorcar. Several times I'd had my wheels up a grassy bank, trying to down one of the succulent creatures with a left and right from the near-side hub-caps. I felt my face getting red, and the other customers looked at me narrowly.

'I – er – hear that guns from Czechoslovakia aren't bad –' There was a crash as the other customer dropped his matched Purdeys. He shied as he hurried out of the door, scenting a parvenu.

Arthur Treacher smiled. 'Well –' He fetched a gun out of the rack, hefting it in one hand like a butcher wondering whether to give you the scraps for nothing or charge you fourpence. 'Hear that?' he said as he opened and closed the action with a flourish. 'Just like a dustbin-lid going back. Look at the carving on the grip. Probably done with a knife and fork by an old lady living in the Carpathian Hills. They do it like my granny does her knitting, watching the telly at the same time. I wouldn't use that gun,' Arthur Treacher said, bringing to a close this lightning tour of his similes and his prejudices, 'for anything but spreading ready-mixed cement.'

I dashed off to Scotland Yard to expedite the licence, scooped up the gun from Arthur who condescended to receive payment for it, and bore it off to the country feeling dreadfully potent.

'Is that what you take when you go out *killing*, Dad?' my small daughter asked, profoundly approving. With some unction I explained that I wasn't going to kill anything I didn't mean to eat, a red herring which suitably obscured the more basic question whether my standard of marksmanship would not forever protect me from such a moral dilemma: obscured it, I should say, from all save my son, a boy with a touch of the sphinx about him, who offered to consume uncooked anything I hit, up to and including water buffalo.

Actually, I wasn't terribly interested in bringing anything down, only in the possibility. I don't like going for walks in the country because it is so easy to turn round and go home again that you can't help wondering whether it's worthwhile setting out in the first place. There are no *limits* in the business of going for walks – rather like golf: you hit the ball, and if it doesn't go far enough you just hit it again, and if that doesn't work you hit it again, and so on, with nothing to make you feel that fewer strokes, rather than many, really matter (whereas with tennis, hit the ball wrong, and the mistake comes back at you over the net). I thought a gun might lend consequence to a walk, it might be an object round which a walk could accumulate, and you'd find yourself doing uncomfortable things like climbing through hedges and getting brambles in your eyes without it ever occurring to you – as it always does when you're just out for a stroll – that you don't have to.

I had this vague idea that it was pigeons I was going to slaughter – the only pheasant in our neck of the woods being an ancient bird who each night marched bad-temperedly into the hen-house at Lower Farm, pushed a hen off its perch and roosted asthmatically in its place till dawn. But in the light of me having to eat everything I shot, I wasn't too happy about it being pigeon: when did you last choose pigeon at a restaurant? Answer, never, on the grounds that you know it's going to chew like elastic bands. And I had a premonition that if I did manage to down one, it would turn out to be not a wood pigeon, but one of those unshaven meths-drinking Trafalgar Square birds drying out in the country for the weekend.

But I was committed to shooting at something edible, and I set off with my special country hat (wrested from the head of a man I met driving a yoke of oxen down Bond Street), slid unhandily over the wall at the end of the garden and started across the meadow to the copse below. The buttercups had barely stained the tops of my wellies when I heard a sound I knew – a derisive rasp, a tinny trumpeting – and there in the lane at the side of the field I saw the hideous moustachioed face of the man they call The Pill blowing rudely into one of those tiny cigars which make a noise like a comb and paper.

I'd been wrong-footed by the chap from the moment I'd had the bad luck to run across him relieving himself against my wall as though he were doing the flints a favour. Indeed, he had so much of the air of conferring ducal status that I found myself sneaking through my own garden gate as though my credentials wouldn't bear inspection. Just A Minute, Just A Minute, he roared, buttoning up and approaching me like a gamekeeper who'd copped a poacher. He let me off with a caution that time, and withdrew playing Colonel Bogey on his lousy gazooka. But a couple of nights after, his face floated up in the twilight outside the kitchen door, and swaying slightly he invited me to drive him home. When I said how far and he said a mile and I started to get the car keys, my wife looked at me as if I'd taken leave of my senses. I can only say that although I had this dim sensation of being the sort of punter con men like him dream about, his very presence seemed to cast me into a light trance.

He announced (as though he'd been doing care work) that he'd passed the day at Taunton Races, and trying to rid myself of the 'fluence I said I hope you won. I Have Never Put A Shilling On A Horse In My Life, he said severely. He made Taunton Races sound like Taunton Assizes at which he had presided as Lord Chief Justice, and all I could come back lamely with was, 'Why do you go, then?' He answered, as though my question had led us into a world far beyond tomfools like me, To See Some Men. Going down the garden path, he was full of the conditions under which he would accept what he had importuned, *viz*. How Fast Do You Drive, I Am Not Sure Your Wife Is Happy About This – even making a feint of going back into the house for reassurance. He offered me a fag, and when, in another weightless attempt to get my identity back into phase in the face of the man's appalling command of any ridiculous situation he might prescribe, I said, 'No,

I don't want to get cancer,' he said, I Will Introduce You To A Doctor.

So when I heard the gazooka, I made a rude gesture and crashed into the copse to kill the pigeons. No luck, of course, and I didn't really mind. I bore them no animus, indeed if the eating business hadn't been paramount, I'd sooner have been banging away at the sort of birds who make facetious noises when a man is working in his garden. To someone sweating with exasperation as pieces of rock keep rolling out of the dry stone wall he is trying to repair, it quickly becomes apparent that the wise thrush doesn't sing each song twice over lest you should think he never could recapture the first fine careless rapture, he sings it twice because he is a dumb thrush and didn't get it right the first time.

Paranoia in the ascendant, I went deeper into the wood. And suddenly I froze. In our part of the country, there are deer. There was a rustle in the boscage ahead of me – a crackling noise – a distant brown shape. My heart beat faster – if I could bring down a stag! I raised the gun, then lowered it. I wanted to be sure; supposing it was a cow? Looking slightly to one side, I saw there was an open ride: if I snook out on to the path, then chucked a stone, the deer would break cover too – and I'd have him. I moved as in a dream, found a piece of rock, and heaved it.

There was a fearful noise, like the word 'Aaaaaargh!' when you see it coming out of the mouth of someone in a cartoon, and up from the undergrowth galloped The Pill. Whether he had been snuffling for truffles I know not, but as he dashed out crying 'Don't shoot!' I was about to lower the gun when I realized (rather like Mr Winkle who saw the reflection of his own cowardice in the eye of Mr Dowler) how things stood, and I put up the weapon again. With a howl, The Pill disappeared into the canebrake, and as I walked home I thought to myself I shouldn't care to eat him, casseroled or otherwise, but if that's the last we see of him, the gun's paid for itself already.

Paymaster General

Is any officer of the Crown more invisible than the Paymaster General?
On a clear day a Minister for Sport can be dimly discerned, but a Paymaster General is *transcendingly* invisible and in vain do people go up
to men in pin-stripe trousers and cry You are the Paymaster General
and I claim the *News Chronicle* prize; search-parties comb Whitehall,
snatching open cupboard doors and shouting Come on out, I know you're
in there; beefeaters have their hats whipped off with shouts of Gotcha!,
and well-spoken children point at horse-guards, screaming Mummy, it
must be he!

Once Sherlock Holmes thought he had him cornered, but it turned
out to be Moriarty, and once the conductor of a 49 bus, handing a
ticket to a man dressed as Napoleon, said Excuse me, sir, are you the
Paymaster General? only it was just someone on his way to a fancy-dress
ball in Putney. Yes, they seek him here, they seek him there, that damned
elusive Paymast-air. Then Mrs Thatcher said Abracadabra and for a brief
moment he was manifest in the shape of Mr Peter Brooke, only to disappear again in a hail of adjectives insinuating that Mr Brooke was as
invisible as his office.

I think there ought to be a nationwide competition to design a costume
for the Paymaster General, and he could be flown in on a wire every
year at the Royal Tournament. Or what a subject for a new opera –
Der Fliegende Geltmeister, a legendary figure doomed to go round and
round Whitehall asking people if they can tell him who he is.

As titles go, it sounds rather menacing, a grim figure played by Oliver
Cromwell, but of course it's simply a euphemism for Cloakroom Attendant, Second Class. I challenge anyone to give me a list of the great
Paymaster Generals, though on reflection you could make up the names
and no one would know any better – rise solemnly to your feet at a
City banquet – 'No list of the great Paymaster Generals could omit the
names of Karl Marx, Stanley Mathews, Al Jolson, men who in their
very different ways adorned an office respected by all.'

High time the Paymaster General, whoever he is, adopted a higher profile. Let him march into Parliament with his carpet-bag full of money and bellow 'None of yous layabouts is paid until I get a bicycle with nine gears and a personalized parking-space.' That should stop them sending him out to fetch their sandwiches.

Opinions : Some Opinions

OPINIONS can seriously impair your contact with reality, though this has never been known to put anyone off. The reverse, in fact, since an opinion protects you from the unpredictability of what's going on outside it, and a selection of opinions can replace whole landscapes. Habitual users find that rolling up the world into opinions ultimately makes it disappear, and they are left in a state of nirvana, at ease in the contemplation of their own reflections.

No given opinion can ever be proved wrong. This alone would account for widespread addiction to the things. And since opinions are to thought what jokes are to humour, *viz.*, second-hand, you never hear a new one : the addict feels secure in the knowledge that what he thinks he thinks came to him via someone who thought he thought it too. Opinions guarantee sanctuary with the like-minded, where singularity is willingly surrendered to assent.

Opinions being ends in themselves, they have no practical application : where action is required, an opinion can only mislead, since an opinion is a reaction that has degenerated into a reflex – actual response on the other hand is always conditioned by the circumstances that prevail. If, therefore, on the subject of famine in Ethiopia, the problem of AIDS, the difficulties of Northern Ireland, you find you hold an opinion, you are speaking from behind a parapet.

Opinion edges up over the horizon of conversation, rising gently beyond the distant foothills, bringing a blush of colour to the give and take. But once opinion is at the zenith, blazing overhead, the conversation turns into a forest fire. A tissue of speculation, a skein of possibility, is burned away under the hammering intensity of opinion, which insists on capitulation. Casual invitations people extend to each other – 'What if –', 'Have you ever wondered –', 'Just imagine –', 'Just suppose –' – are abandoned, and the possibilities of exchange are reduced to the dull clang of clodpole meeting numbskull.

For while opinions will protect against most things, they can't remove the threat of other opinions. You climb into an opinion because you're frightened of some real condition which otherwise has to be *lived* with; your opinion makes it go away. But what happens when you meet someone who has avoided the same condition by climbing into a different opinion? The poisonous clamour that is generated when two such armoured-cars meet bespeaks agitation and terror. Nothing less than unconditional surrender will do.

Disagreement, of course, is another matter. Disagreement takes place between those who are willing to live in the tension of the unresolved. People who disagree can try each other out. They remain vulnerable. But disagreement is what those who are addicted to opinions are seeking to avoid. They are interested only in victory or defeat. For finally they do not hold their opinions, their opinions hold them.

Or, anyway, that's how I see it. But I feel I ought to point out that someone once said I was the apostle of the not-very-strongly-held opinion. With his permission, it's going on my tombstone.

Being Rude

WHEN someone's deliberately rude to you, you can hardly believe it. As when a complete stranger at a party joined the group I was in and after a bit, baring his teeth in a smile that anticipated the pleasure he was going to give himself, said to me in a high clear voice, 'How *unctuous* you are,' turned his back, and walked away. I nearly burst into tears. Then there was a waiter in a restaurant long ago who when I asked for the manager simply stared at me stonily and said, 'He wouldn't come.'

For a second the whole world crackles with malice, is lit up by a sinister glow that is not without a dangerous warmth. But there is another sort of rudeness that turns life down so that it is a fraction of a degree colder, and people are helped to stay away from each other in a climate of endless mutual disregard. I'm thinking of daily encounters where the negative possibilities are the only possibilities the two parties are interested in. You're looking for an inner tube, a sheet of plate glass, a music-centre, a place to park, an evening paper, floor tiles, a typewriter ribbon, and the really awful thing isn't that the man stares through you, it's the way you've come along prepared to stare through *him* – long before he refuses to acknowledge *you*, you have been ready not to acknowledge him simply because this is the response you expected. And when he shakes his head but doesn't say anything, and just because you're determined to give him even less than he gives you, you force yourself not to say 'Thank you'. Walking away from the bleak moonscape of one of these encounters – was it a doormat I wanted, planning permission, change for the telephone? – I realized it wasn't him I was damaging, it was me. I'd let his coldness prescribe my own, and in turning up with my refrigerator already on, had done my little bit to ensure that his would be in perfect working order. The icecap of anomie is spreading, so I make a vow to smile and say 'Please' and 'Thank you' and 'Goodbye', irrespective of what anyone else does, and it is a self-interested decision, for I know that the ritual of the smile will protect me, not from his resentment, but from my own.

At the same time, I wish there was the slightest chance of my ever plucking up courage to use a foreign language phrase-book I have on my shelves, which is written in the traditional stilted idiom of such guides, the only difference being that every single phrase is abusive – indeed, the book's sub-title is *How to be Abusive in Five Languages*. At the laundry, for example, you are advised to open rhetorically with the disobliging inquiry 'Don't you use soap?' and follow up this thrust with the words 'I suspect your dirty staff have been wearing my shirts.' At the beach you may endear yourself to your neighbour by saying 'Move your fat carcase so I can get some sun' (*'Eh, gros! Enleve-toi de mon soleil.'*) remarking cordially to the beach attendant, 'These deck-chairs look as though they are covered in dog muck.' Swinish at the beach, you pick quarrels in bars by saying to the barman, 'When you've sobered up, perhaps you'll bring me a drink', and when it comes you ask him, 'Is it your general practice to water the beer?' On arrival at the theatre you find someone in your seat and you cry threateningly, 'Move your fat arse', and once you have settled in you enquire in a loud voice, 'Is this supposed to be an amateur performance?'

At a restaurant afterwards you maintain your reputation for wit by asking genially, 'Do you keep pigs in here between meals?' or possibly, 'Are indigestion tablets served with every course?' Blundering back to your hotel, you observe pleasantly to the desk clerk, 'I suppose you have been letting my room by the hour while I've been out', and having called for the bill and read it you ask, 'Are you sure you haven't added in the date?' Picking up your bags you leave, turning at the door to say, 'Congratulations, your hotel has the biggest fleas in Europe.'

Simple abuse can be very refreshing, but most of us don't have the courage and mask hostility by straining after subtlety. We go in for pale imitations of the odious Mr Bennet in *Pride and Prejudice* ('Thank you, my dear' to his daughter at the piano, 'you have delighted us long enough'), when what we'd really like to be able to do is clap someone on the back and cry, 'Talking of sewers, how's your father?'

Nicknames

I MET a man at a party, and he was introduced to me as Chunky Cartwright. Why Chunky Cartwright is called Chunky Cartwright I don't know, and I hope no one tries to tell me because a little mystery is an exercise-yard for the imagination. I myself was known in Africa for a brief period as Mungo, but that was simply because I'd been seen haggling with a bushman over the price he wanted for his spear, and so Mungo explains itself. But my son has two friends, one called Mucker Metcalf and the other called Masher Merrick, and even the two people themselves seem bewildered when asked *why* they're called thus, as though their nicknames were as absolute as their own existence. Even more elemental are two figures out of a family past known only to my elders – Doodle Dick and Dippy Day. Nobody has ever been able to tell me much about either, since from early childhood every time I've asked them they've tried to tell me but the very thought of Doodle Dick and Dippy Day has made them collapse laughing, and they've never got very much further than saying they were pals of your Uncle Bill and Hooky Walker. They were probably sober-sided men in quiet offices off Upper Mersey

Street, but the nicknames turned them into demiurges, like clowns in Shakespeare. Other figures looming out of the mists off time are Bluey Barlow, Cherry Johnson and a boy called Krish whose first name was Justin but was always referred to as Whiffy – Whiffy Krish. Nobody ever makes up nicknames, a nickname is your real identity, jumping out from behind you like an afreet.

The Scouse Admiral

SAUSAGES have been tamed – *Which?* says they are all loyal, hard-working, decent little fellows – and meat pies are going to be standardized until they can be relied on to vote Tory, so what is there left that retains its mystery? The haggis? Invented for tourists. Savoury-duck? Too local. Lamb's pluck? No real identity. But scouse – ah!

It doesn't *taste* very special, it's only a sort of stew, but it is curiously regenerative. Nobody in Liverpool, to which it is indigenous, can hear it talked about without grinning rather slyly as people used to grin when drink was mentioned. As if they knew something secret about scouse, something faintly scandalous which, if it were made public, would cause the authorities to impose sanctions on its manufacture and license the hours in which it might be consumed.

Strange, really, because the actual stuff is rather bland. When it's got meat in it it's called lob scouse and when it hasn't it's called blind scouse. But the natives talk about it as if the very thought of it energized them, as if there were something enormously potent about the idea of scouse, as though in essence its substance were uncontrollable and if a pan of scouse were left unattended it might go critical and you would need special clothing to come within two miles of it.

The longer it matures, the more interesting it becomes, the more flavour it acquires – it decays gently like the city itself, it is a loose, homely, unstable dish, symbolic of a place which has seen better days, whose melancholy gantries, sad Liver birds, and mournful Ballroom, loom up out of the mist at the mouth of the Mersey like emblems of a civilization which has perished. The dish won't travel – if you got it as far as Birmingham the odds are it would be rechristened estifado, and the further south you went the more certainly would it dwindle into ragout, and get served with rice, plus candles.

But as plain scouse it is mysteriously grateful, creating its own lore, and producing its own *magus*. This last was a figure like Robin Hood or the Lord of Misrule who leapt fully grown from the heart of the scouse myth, always seeming to have been there, from the start of time. He was called the Admiral of the Scouse Boats and some say he still haunts Scotland Road, though he was last seen in the flesh in Paddy's Market, before they pulled it down.

Lascars (whatever they were) would come off boats and ask the way to Paddy's Market, and there they would haggle for miscellanea, *pots de chambre*, lorgnettes, one-string fiddles, while the stall-people shouted, 'Shirt buttons, shirt buttons, any mugs', and the tram-cars whistled along outside, tipping up and down like ships in a choppy sea.

'Ninepence, John.'

'A shilling.'

'No shilly, John – ninepence, and chance it.'

Then they would trot away in single file, buttoning old sturdy corsets round their reefers while the shawl-women cried to one another, 'If I couldn't do you a good turn I wouldn't do you a bad, but the next time you come past our house I'll cut the eye out of yous with the fender.'

This was the Scouse Admiral's stage. About midday an air of tension spread through the market, the stallholders grew restless, craned their necks anxiously, took out pocket-watches and consulted them, leaned sideways to scan the long aisles leading down to the entrance of the market. And the cry would go up –

'He's here!'

'He's off the port!'

Down that long vista, refulgent in the dusty sunbeams, the Scouse Admiral appeared, his hands steady on the tiller of the Scouse Boats – two great bins, swinging gently on either side of a four-wheeled handcart, each bin full to the brim with steaming scouse. He served it with a ladle like Excalibur. Sometimes there was meat in it and sometimes there was not.

'Blind as a new-born kitten!'

'More trickery, be Jasus.'

No one remembers his face, he was simply a sort of presence. In the evening he made scouse for hot-pot suppers which took place in Assembly Rooms, and sometimes even attended these suppers as a guest, accompanied by his mother. It was on one such occasion that he spoke the line which – of all the unwritten lines of Liverpool folk-poetry – is perhaps the most memorable.

Some say this particular supper was held in Walton, others that it was Garston, some place it as far afield as Tuebrook. There was very often a good deal of excited speculation at these affairs as to whether the scouse served would turn out to be blind or otherwise, but naturally this time, with the Scouse Admiral present, not to mention his mother, they canvassed matters of a more general nature, and were delighted to find when they had served themselves that it was lob of the very highest order. The eating had got beautifully into its stride, enjoyment was at the height, when the Scouse Admiral leant forward at the end of the table and said, with simple dignity: 'If anyone doesn't want their fat, me and me mother'll eat it.'

Some took the short view and felt the tone of the whole occasion had been lowered, but others recognized the durability of the line and wrote it down in their commonplace books.

When Paddy's Market went, the Scouse Admiral went with it. Some say he retired to New Brighton, that he sold pills to the men on the Dock Road, that he ran the last of the cocoa-rooms near the Gorree Piazzas. He thrived on scouse and embodied its mystery. One day he will be the subject of an opera.

Oh, Moses, Moses, You Stubborn, Splendid, Adorable Fool

I WONDER what it is that everyone enjoys about really bad films? It doesn't make sense, since good ones are what you're paying to see, but when a film is *exactly* bad, the pleasure is intense.

Perhaps my all-time favourite is the one where at HQ CMDF (Combined Miniature Deterrent Forces) they are briefing Stephen Boyd. He is to be shrunk to microbe size and injected (along with a submarine and a crew of four) into the circulatory system of a master-scientist who lies unconscious from a head injury.

Boyd's orders are to navigate upstream to the brain, and there dissolve a blood-clot that is short-circuiting the injured man's capacity to pass on a new idea that will save mankind. 'Well,' chuckles Boyd, as if he didn't want anyone to think he hadn't had his leg pulled before, 'that's a wild one!' But having paused for sober reflection – about three seconds – he decides his suspicions are provincial.

'Prepare for miniaturization!' The sub gets smaller and smaller and is sucked up into a syringe. Crew member Donald Pleasance, overcome by a touch of claustrophobia, dashes spiritedly for the conning tower. 'You'll feel better once we're under way,' nods the senior surgeon, played by Arthur Kennedy. Red and white blobs hang around the pulmonary conduit as the craft slides easily downstream.

'What are they?' enquires Boyd. 'Corpuscles,' replies the surgeon, with a hint of asperity. Physicist and paramour, Raquel Welch dotes on the scenery. 'I never dreamed it could be like this,' she breathes. But Donald Pleasance is knitting his brow. 'We're in the carotid artery,' he mutters thoughtfully, 'dammit, we should be in the jugular vein.'

Back at HQ two generals are contributing to the enterprise by pacing the control-room with mugs of coffee in their hands. 'How long can we stop the heart for?' rumbles one. His companion whips out a slide-rule, consults it shrewdly and replies, 'As short a time as possible.' Meanwhile, the sub's propellors are tangled up in lymphatic sea-weed and the craft has run aground in the inner ear. 'What about turbulence?' Aye, what indeed. As to flatulence, Surgeon Kennedy is supplying us with all we need – 'The meedeeval philosophers were right,' he say, staring with visionary eyes at Disneyland outside, 'man *is* the centre of the universe . . .'

I suppose a really bad film offers a holiday from the responsibilities imposed by the authentic. Our sensitivities are not put to the test, and we know we are looking at something we shall easily feel better than. The dialogue in particular operates like valium, dissolving anxiety. For instance, in the epic *Solomon And Sheba* the Temple has fallen in on Gina Lollobrigida, she's been stoned by disaffected extras dressed in tablecloths, and a dreadful thunderstorm is augmented by the voice of God handing down six months without the option for everybody. Whereupon the High Priest, played by Raymond Massey, raises his eyes to the heavens and mumbles 'Its been a hard day for all of us.'

The bathos is reassuring. A bad film – a precisely bad film – lets us off. A bad film is not good for the character because it turns experience into foolishness and we are freed of all obligation. *Africa – Texas Style* was essentially an earnest travelogue into which a little genteel Pinewood romance had been decanted. What gave pleasure was the way neither element had been absorbed into any sort of whole, and the script's efforts to stay conversational while dropping lumps of zoology into the storyline was specially enjoyable.

'Yes, you can see them now,' says John Mills, squinting down at the bush from his light aircraft, 'moving in their typical wedge-shaped formation. We'll hear more about them later.' Ronald Howard plays the pipe-smoking cold-fish scientist. 'The contents of that eland's stomach,' he volunteers, 'will yield valuable information.' Valuable information is being yielded all over the place. 'What are those?' enquires a visitor to John Mills's game-farm. 'Flamingoes,' his host replies, indulgently.

The film switches to romantic mode. 'There's a balance of nature out here,' cries tempestuous Adrienne Corri, clasping the chest of Hugh O'Brian as though it were the north face of the Eiger, 'and you're upsetting the whole thing!' The girl is troubled – she is affianced to the cold fish. 'All you ever think about,' she taunts him, 'is your old microscope.' 'Pass me another slide, Fay,' the swot rebukes her. 'Slides!' exclaims the girl, defiant in her khaki-drill, 'I couldn't *look* at another slide.'

A rascally cattle-farmer releases all the wild animals that have been carefully rounded up for scientific study, but has not reckoned with the beasts' natural devotion to John Mills. Twice, they're let out, twice they come back under their own steam. 'Jim, they're coming home,' yelps

Fay, then adds (as in all decency she is bound to) 'I still don't believe it.'

Sometimes a genre accommodates absurdities, and must take the blame for the Bad Films its conventions inspire. *Dracula, Prince of Darkness* was but one film of many in which a sinister butler fags up umpteen flights of stone stairs to bang on the door of the guest-room. Since it's the middle of the night and no one has summoned him, what's he doing glowering at the man who opens the door, asking in sepulchral tones, 'Is there anything more you require, sir?' Students of the genre will immediately reply, 'He is announcing that he is a vampire', and if you should ask them what the guest's response is likely to be they will tell you, quite accurately, that he shakes his head cannily and says to his wife, 'Queer fellow, that.'

The guest appears in all such films, but seldom to such pure effect as in this one. Offered a lift by riderless horses, locked in a deserted castle by an unseen agency, and confronted by a table mysteriously set for four, he might have been expected by the uninstructed to say something on the order of 'What the bloody hell's going on'? In fact, he rubs his hands, looks at the table, and says 'Dinner sounds like a good idea.'

As ever, the crucifix is used as an early form of six-gun, but the special brand of the prosaic that this sort of film deals in is raised to its apogee when the butler picks up the box containing Dracula's ashes, sprinkles them inside his empty tomb, then pours on blood to reconstitute him like packet-soup. The butler's name is Klove, but the director didn't take the hint.

Occasionally, the witheringly serious film can be more grotesque than the commercial turkey. When I reviewed a Japanese offering called *The Pornographer* none of the hacks present was left in any doubt as to the film's high purpose, since famed sexologists Phyllis and Eberhard Kronhausen did the pre-screen warm-up, and we settled back in our seats reassured that what we were about to see would not breach the high standards of the Cinephone, Oxford Street.

The hero of the story was a Mr Ogata who in addition to being a big importer of rhino horn from Hong Kong, runs a blue film and dirty book business, while enterprisingly slipping tape-recorders into the bedrooms of his neighbours. He is not one of your nine-to-five men, for on his return home he is regularly dragged into his landlady's bed and obliged to make love to her under the gloomy eye of a pet carp in a glass tank on the sideboard. Every time Mr Ogata gives his landlady an extra hard squeeze the fish turns a moody somersault, thus confirming the landlady's suspicion that it is the reincarnated spirit of her dead husband.

What with the fish and the flesh, Mr Ogata's nerves are under siege. Dashing a volume of his own merchandise from the hands of his daughter, he exhorts the girl to bone up on the works of Dr Schweitzer. The landlady is carted off to hospital with a heart-attack, where she offends the other inmates by sitting up in bed and singing indelicate songs. Already worried by the police, the protection rackets, and the expense of buying a new enlarger, Mr Ogata doesn't know which way to turn. The landlady goes mad, and the fish does double-Axells all round the tank.

We fade into the final sequence. Mr Ogata has retired from the hurly burly of retail sex and spends his time on a small houseboat, working diligently at his masterpiece. This is to be a rubber landlady complete with central-heating. As we watch, the houseboat sheers its moorings and in a shot that must be included in any list of the great non-sequiturs, floats out into the Pacific, with Mr Ogata crooning heedlessly as (a stickler for detail) he stitches the last of the hairs into the armpit of the inflatable chatelaine.

Yes, you're right, you couldn't make it up. Phyllis and Eberhard loved it, but I seem to remember I took a gloomier view and predicted a split week at Scunthorpe.

Peter Pan in Red Square

CAN'T you picture the plane landing in Red Square, bumping over the cobbles outside St Basil's while the teenage pilot leans out and says, 'Am I right for the Bolshoi, or is it a couple of streets further on?' And the solitary copper on point-duty outside Lenin's Tomb lounging over to ask the lad if he'd come far, and could he take a photo for the wife. The great thing about the *hugely* unexpected is that everyone automatically believes it must have been allowed for, only somebody forgot to tell them. 'Publicity stunt, is it?' says the copper, 'Haven't got Joan Collins in there, have you?'

Then having got the plane *into* Red Square, the next bit is getting it out. I see the copper scratching his head like Ernest the Policeman and leading the little plane off by the propellor to where his brother-in-law runs a garage in Gorki Prospekt. 'Just over the weekend, Volodya, while we sort things out.' 'Where do I find the room? I've got eight MOTs booked in – couldn't they find a space in the Kremlin car-park?'

Pure fantasy – yet it happened. Practical jokes are usually unimpressive, but pulling Mother Russia's leg is in a class of its own; the rest of the young man's life is going to be one long anti-climax. At first, I was rather surprised Mr Gorbachev didn't get someone to write a comic piece for *Pravda* just to show he'd seen the funny side of it, but then I realized how the whole thing had been master-minded.

First of all, its patently absurd that a little aeroplane could fly all those hundreds of miles from somewhere in Germany, undetected. I particularly scout the Gulliverian theory that it flew *under* the radar; what's the good of radar that everyone knows you can fly *under*? Wouldn't any hostile force plan its assault with just this in mind, if any country was mad enough to instal radar that only worked if you flew *over* it?

So right. The next assumption that won't wash is the idea that the lad could have done all this intrepid flying over vast tracts of nowhere-in-particular and be sure of arriving at a destination as tiny as Red Square just in time for tea. If you believe that, you'll believe anything. What actually happened was on a smaller scale altogether, but infinitely more cunning.

In fact, the youth had flown into Red Square from the Moscow suburbs, taking off at the Moscow Dynamo's new football-ground, just a dozen miles away, and following the tram-lines into town. Mr Gorbachev never puts a foot wrong, and in devising this apparent own-goal he was enabled to get rid of as many Generals and Ministers as he chose to accuse of incompetence, leaving an even larger number shaking in their shoes. That's as neat a theory as anyone could wish for, it fits the facts precisely, and there isn't a single loose end. And to anyone who says its far-fetched, think how far-fetched an aeroplane landing in Red Square is anyway.

When everything had quietened down the lad was given the Star of the Order of Lenin, with safety-pin and beige accessories, and his parents spent Easter with the Gorbachevs in a *cottage ornée* on the Black Sea.

An Ounce of Civet

My house is old. When I walked for the first time into the tall square rooms I smelt the oldness. What luxurious wax had tanned the wood where the panels lay beyond the windows? No wax, but time. The wood yielded its aromatic heart and I turned by the window and faced the empty room.

Afterwards I sat in my dining-room at morning and wondered who sat with me. Those whose house it had been, those who had trodden the creaks into the staircase, who had shivered in the draught that is not excluded by the shutters over the long, end window in my drawing-room, who had died in beds in the rooms where my child's voice rings like a bell – none of them laid a soft hand on mine. I paused with the toast and marmalade between my fingers and knew that the action was lost for ever.

The house is bright and smells of the musk drawn from material by the slow curing of nearly three centuries. 'Hush, darling, mamma's coming.' How many children have been soothed in this house in how many night-times? I walk past a half-open door listening for the murmur of many voices.

The first man to live in my house was Maddox Westerband and Maddox Westerband was an apothecary. He inherited the house from his uncle Oliver who built it in 1708. Maddox lived in the house from 1709 until 1738, and his name stays with me like an old tune. If Maddox wore a fine cinnamon cloth suit with plate buttons, were his breeches knitted or velvet? He was an apothecary – was he an average apothecary? Did he wear a tye-wig to look learned, or did he wear a great full-bottomed one so heavily powdered as to look like a gooseberry bush under snow? Did he wear pulvil against the smells of his profession, did he regard himself as entitled to red heels and a hat of the Monmouth cock? When he rode abroad, did he do it in gambadoes or spatterdashes?

But he stared out of my windows at morning. He wore an Indian nightgown and a morning cap over his shaven head and where the milk-man comes with yoghurt there came a running-footman with a message in a cloven stick. Who roared in this house before me? Who whispered in the night? Who stood at a bend in the stairs? Maddox walked in my corridors and heard the wind lift the latches of the inner doors while he went to bed with a candle.

Maddox sold the house to a fishmonger – 'ffishmonger' to be precise – called Thomas Broughton and after ten years Thomas Broughton sold the house to William Giles who was a gentleman and William Giles sold it to Dame Elizabeth Hare who lived in it a quarter of a century. When she died she willed it to her daughter (in a will fraught with conditions favouring a bankrupt son) and later this daughter married a confectioner and *her* daughter came into the house, having made an excellent match with Clement Smith who was a Doctor of Music.

But before the Doctor and after Dame Elizabeth, there was 'the Widow Coates'. She took the house on a short lease about 1780 and she may have seen them plant the Tree of Heaven which bursts out of the asphalt opposite my windows and hangs its long arms over the house like an afreet. *Was* the Widow an elderly party in weeds or was she a fashionable piece of five-and-thirty, unencumbered and jolly, who went to Assemblies in ostrich feathers, a spray of sunflowers, and a cork rump?

The space within my rooms has not expanded or contracted, it is the same space. In this parcel of the universe, cut up and delineated by these walls and these ceilings, the Doctor played to his wife upon the flute, Dame Elizabeth pondered the extravagances of her bankrupt son, Thomas Broughton told the guests he hadn't come into contact with the actual *ffish* for well over a decade. Yet, though I wind clocks which tell the same hours which chimed for them, I have no device to make their hours chime again. I raise my eyes and though the room is crowded, nobody is there.

The staircase is wide. My hand falls on the banister rail which runs from top to bottom of the house. It is smooth beyond smoothness, beneath its hard surface a light glows, burning in the wood, lit by the fingers of all who have ever used it. My hand rests on it in the dark, my imagination is sweetened by Maddox Westerband the apothecary, and across three centuries my fingertips touch his.

Our Betters

IN 1950, royal asides at public functions were printed in newspapers with the verbal elisions carefully subbed out. No royal person was allowed to say 'that's' or 'it's', they were always heard to speak the words in full. So that when – during his visit to the South Bank Exhibition – the King was handed a weather report which rather unnecessarily pointed out that it was raining, the *News Chronicle* got him down as saying, 'That Is Certainly Accurate.' On the same occasion, the Queen ('fascinated immediately by the 74-inch telescope') was heard – at least by the *Chronicle* man – to remark, 'What A Pity It Is Not Working.'

The words are recorded as though they aren't examples of speech so much as plucky imitations of it. Royalty has to talk (so the *Chronicle*'s message seems to go) because that's the primitive way you and I do it: left to themselves, they'd probably communicate by osmosis (an extension of the myth, rife among schoolboys, that the King and Queen never engaged in sexual congress, but produced children by methods that were very much more polite). But just because, by a wild act of graciousness, not to mention ventriloquial skill, they managed to adapt to our style, this was no excuse for listening too closely and overhearing those touches of the vernacular which might make a decent person feel he had startled his father by coming across him too suddenly in the lavatory.

The obligation felt by sub-editors to preserve this kind of distance, while at the same time pretending it was all going down verbatim, led to the concoction of royal ad libs that sounded as if they were being delivered over the public address system at a railway station. When Queen Elizabeth copped a deserter who had had the bad luck to stray into her bathroom at Windsor Castle, the *Sunday Pictorial* told its 1950 readers that she said, 'What Are You Doing Here?' and in case they missed the point, added that she said it 'without losing the natural poise and dignity associated with her' (an MVO, one might have thought, for the amanuensis hiding behind the door). Having got him nicely in her sights, the Queen (according to the *Pic*) then sent the following impromptu ringing round the white tile: 'And now I will press this bell and have you turned over to the Castle guard. I advise you to serve your punishment like a man – and then serve your country like one.' A clear case (if you took the *Pic*'s account literally) of a malefactor being cornered by a Speak-Your-Weight machine.

Perhaps the style was set by the royal speech writers. In 1950, it was still mandatory on royal persons to make statements that could be guaranteed to yield no meaning. 'When you leave school,' Princess Margaret was heard to say at a 1950 Speech Day, 'you will all go your different ways. But I know that each one of you will give something towards upholding and cherishing the great traditions which you have inherited.' It was a strange runic idiom, bearing little relation to human speech. Indeed, it was anti-speech, since its object was to insulate the speaker against the possibility of communication. 'Free men everywhere,' Princess Elizabeth discovered to President Truman on arrival at Idlewild, 'look towards the United States with affection and with hope. The message which has gone out from this great capital has brought help and courage to a troubled world.' But on this occasion the distinction between royal rhubarb and ordinary words was splendidly highlighted by the President's reply: 'I thank you, dear.'

There was no hint of discrimination in the reporting of royal 'news'. In 1950, the *Daily Mail* found space to tell its readers that Prince Charles had changed his parting ('from left to right'), and the *News Chronicle* revealed that the King owned two tartan dinner-jackets. 'For some time he has kept them a close secret,' the *Chronicle* added importantly, in case you hadn't realized it was a scoop. Pressed to say more, the tailor who had made these interesting garments was alleged to have replied, 'My lips are sealed.' A solemn aldermanic note was maintained, no doubt because the subs sensed that if the obligation to keep his face straight wasn't placed squarely on the reader, he might make a rude noise. 'News of a carefully kept secret was given at a distinguished gathering at London's Savoy Hotel last night. Princess Anne has been enrolled by the Automobile Association as its millionth member.' By making it perfectly clear that this information was not being offered to the infidel, the *Mail* was hoping to distract the reader from any suspicion that – since Princess Anne was only two months old – the Automobile Association may have slipped a few of its cogs.

No discrimination, no irony. When Queen Juliana and Prince Bernhard gave a dinner for the King and Queen at Claridge's, fifty boxes of gold plate were sent on from Holland, along with seven chefs, one Master of the Royal Household, two silver-room staff, two under-florists and a wardrobe man – an advance party later reinforced by thirty-one Dutch waiters, a clutch of footmen, and the royal florist. Three thousand freshly cut flowers were flown in, and the meal began with pâté de fois gras, turtle soup, went on to sole and capon, and ended with iced meringue and fruit. To drink, there were four several wines. At the time these events were being placed on record, a number of papers were carrying an advertisement for a dish called Brown Betty, a sinister compound conjured (in those days of austerity) from Weetabix and marmalade, and this ad could sometimes be seen flanked by another urging you to lay hands on a bottle of Rajah pickle 'and pep up your cheese sandwiches'.

Even so, the *News Chronicle* – culturally the most progressive of the popular dailies – made obeisance to the vulgarity of the Dutch state visit as though it had been Mr Pecksniff himself. The paper went so far as to print (with every sign of endorsing its premises) a hand-out prepared for the occasion by Claridge's Hotel: 'Reporters meet very polite but very complete barriers between them and people they want to see, and after wasting some time generally go quietly away, infected by the spirit of quiet good manners that abounds at Claridge's.' Purified by his contact with the hotel staff, the *Chronicle* man went down to Victoria where amid the loyal huzzas of the taxpayers, one royal family met the other. 'This moment,' reported the *Chronicle* man, still reeling from the cleansing influence of Claridge's, 'had all the warmth of delighted friends saying: "It's lovely to see you." And manfully banishing from his recollection the fifty cases of gold plate and the thirty-one waiters, the reporter – a credit to hotel diplomacy, if ever there was one – added: 'The Queen and her Prince are such a homely couple.'

Having it both ways was a feature of royal reporting in 1950. The *Mirror* wanted to make it clear, or clearish, that although Princess Margaret had been known to buy a new dress, 'ball gowns are retrimmed and renovated, and so are hats'. Just in case you thought royalty was mostly engaged in the exhausting business of having a damn good time, the papers liked to draw your attention to homely economies. For instance, the Yeomen of the Guard: 'As the Yeomen retired,' reported the *Mail*, 'the king simply could not afford to replace them. There should be 100 Yeomen – now there are only 76.' Dashing a suspicious moisture from his eye, the 1950 reader was only too pleased to learn that 'the £40,000 the Yeomen and the Gentlemen-at-Arms cost will be met by the government'.

In case, from time to time, a subscriber was besieged by the thought that the business of waiting on royalty was anything other than an enviable pastime, magazines like *Woman* were alert to disabuse him: 'I often think', wrote a correspondent in 1950, 'what fun it must be to be on the staff of Buckingham Palace. How proud you'd be to think if it wasn't for you, Princess Margaret wouldn't have had that boiled egg.' And the task of convincing the readership that royalty was having a hard time of it was intimately associated with that other branch of double-think, the proposition that if they hadn't devoted themselves to opening bazaars, they might well have soared to the top of any profession you cared to name. The *Chronicle* man's line on the Queen's visit to the South Bank – 'She was instantly fascinated by the 74-inch telescope' – is a little classic in this vein. Here, the reporter hints at a natural aptitude for astronomy that would have left Galileo standing at the gate.

In 1950, any indication that royalty wasn't wound up like clock-work was greeted by Fleet Street with open-mouthed incredulity. This was due both to a natural commercial disinclination to let an easy source of copy evaporate too quickly, and to a dull conviction that the readers shared the social prejudices of their scribes. The *News Chronicle*, in attendance at the birth of Prince Charles, swore public fealty to what the subs secretly believed in, when it announced that 'a ghillie carried the good news to the King'. And borrowing a hazel-twig from the news editor, the *Chronicle* man divined that to the crowd outside Clarence House 'the birth of a royal baby is a needed symbol of national stability in an uncertain world'. This left the *Times* leader-writer free to strike a note of arcane bonhomie in allowing that 'as a future sovereign, Prince Charles may now look forward to exercising himself in the art of government at the head of his own nursery'. It was as though the newspaper-and-radio age of 1950 thought communications was a picture you looked at, instead of a window you looked through. How else account for the fact that when the *Mail* reported that Princess Margaret had been ticked off by Queen Mary for wearing a head-scarf and the old Queen had said, 'You look like a housemaid,' the *Mail* seemed to accept her premise, without at all convincing you it had noticed the implication.

The Suburbs of Arcadia

I KNOW I shouldn't laugh, but the middle-aged Japanese dressed in boy-scout uniform, and with ten million pounds worth of heroin tucked up his baggy shorts, knocking on the door of a respectable scout-master in East Grinstead and asking to join the local pack, is surely a comedian.

If you read the news-item you'll have noted that the man's name was Mr Mariwana –

Oh my name is Mariwana,
I would love to join the band –

and apparently he kept on protesting his loyalty to Lord Baden Powell in such fulsome terms he rather embarrassed them in East Grinstead, where displays of emotion aren't welcomed in respectable circles.

And that's the nub of the thing. East Grinstead is the world capital of respectability, and respectability is what this chap affronted. When I was in my teens and wearing woolly red ties and holding myself in readiness as Second-in-Command to any pirate whose 12-gun frigate might sail up the Kingston By-Pass to loot and pillage the Sir Joseph Hood Memorial Playing Field, respectability seemed to be the enemy: all those cul-de-sacs with flowering cherry, all that nine-to-five. What I held against respectability was the way everything had to be allowed for, the way its function was to protect subscribers from the unforeseen.

Those front-gardens with army haircuts were the emblem of a self-imposed solitary confinement, and the standard-rose trees stood to attention all the way up the path like prisoners' escorts. Respectability meant constraint, and nothing was more sharply, more absolutely defined than the limits. Chucking a handful of earth at a girl-friend's window one sweet-scented suburban midnight, I missed my aim and the romantic missile flew through the diamond panes of her parents' room. 'This isn't Peabody Buildings' her father bellowed, sticking his head out like Dr Bartolo, 'This is a respectable neighbourhood!' I skipped away into the dark avenues, charmed and gleeful. Such a perfect epiphany could hardly have been hoped for by a grammar school buccaneer who was sometimes worried by the enemy's refusal to fly his colours.

But now – well, well. Now. Now, I'm not quite the old bold mate of Henry Morgan. Once I felt I'd been marooned among the privet hedges, now I can see they were also a harbour. I see a dimension I couldn't see when I thought, *oppugno*, I take by storm. 'Respectability' was the target, but what I missed was the core of the word: 'respect'. Which could mean that people who did seem respectable, were. That their lives would bear inspection, that they might turn out to be what they seemed to be; that being respectable was a function of decency.

The notion of respectability attached itself to many a false standard: keeping up appearances must often, at its callowest, have meant just that – putting a face on things, keeping up with the Joneses. And there was a retentive impulse which went with cold unentered 'best' rooms where as the years slipped away carpets faded without ever having been walked on. But if keeping up appearances was pretending, something must have been perceived as worth pretending about. 'Respect' as an ideal must have exercised a powerful compulsion, for pretence is a genuine tribute.

But maybe the wooden cutlass I was whirling round my head in the hope of terrorizing the ratepayers had edges on it after all, for the impulse of recent years has been towards a dissolving of limits, and 'permission' is now a word that isn't usable outside inverted commas – 'permission' is no longer given or received. And jolly good I say, for the complex condition of existence can't be governed by rules and conventions suitable to a game of ludo. However, the price imposed scarcely suggests anyone got a bargain: when the conventions and constraints hampering the free spirit are exchanged for freedom itself, everyone is called upon to be a hero, all the time.

Which is why I sometimes hope that Mr Attlee and his hat and his moustache are alive and well and living in East Grinstead, that men who have overstayed at the buffet at Waterloo still carry bunches of flowers as peace offerings to their wives, and that when the Japanese smuggler saw the error of his ways and was received into the 1st East Grinstead pack, he joined with them in the centuries-old East Grinstead Carol which celebrates unchangingness, as it is experienced in the suburbs of Arcadia –

> *I drive a yellow Volvo*
> *And wear a new tweed hat –*
> *Green wellies on the doorstep,*
> *A spaniel on the mat.*

Show Business

I HAD sometimes thought that if there were a single human being able to resist an invitation to appear on a chat show it might turn out to be the Archbishop of Canterbury. But there he was on *Parkinson*. I suppose Cantuar thought he might as well contribute a Christian presence to the thing, but he reckoned without the power this sort of show has to fictionalize everyone who goes on it. Instead of the Christian presence dominating the worship of idols, the Christian presence was converted into one of its active ingredients: instead of the mantle of Augustine covering the show, the show covered it, in the mantle of Narcissus. Here is another funny old gentleman (the picture, the idiom, the style, the arrangements seemed to be saying) willing to entertain us.

I think the Archbishop might have tumbled to all this as soon as he heard he was to be teamed with Norman St John-Stevas. Norman is a work of fiction long before he ever arrives at a television studio, and when the Archbishop heard who was to be his partner he should have realized that what they were really after was a couple of adagio-dancers. Once the Archbishop is available for this sort of gig, it means that show business extends in a seamless integument, right from *Parkinson* to Canterbury, round the Cathedral, and back again.

A Little Palace

ALL week I'd been muttering 'Its a little palace', and walking round the garden one more time for another look at my new shed.

'I've got a new shed,' I shouted to a neighbour, walking past in the lane. 'Oh yes?' She stopped and nodded. 'I've never had a real shed before,' I said, 'its a little palace.' 'Fancy,' she nodded again. 'And my outside loo,' I went on, 'my outside loo's a little palace as well, although it wasn't always.'

'Is it?' she said, 'well, I'd best be getting on if I'm going to catch the post,' and I realized my enthusiasm might have sounded a little peculiar because she rushed off before I had a chance to tell her that whereas before you had to climb over bags of peat and the edging shears to get to the pedestal – and even then, you had to sit sideways, because of the lawn-mower – all the rakes and spades and so on had been taken out of the loo and installed in the new shed.

Installed, by golly, that's the word! I put screws in the wall of the shed and hung them all up. 'Not only a little palace but a bloody work of art,' I said to myself, adding a phrase of my mother's, 'It might have been done by *a practical man!*'

Dragging the garden chair to a spot where I could admire both the shed and the loo – shed door shut, nice and neat, but the loo door ajar so the spartan simplicity of the interior, beautifully empty but humanized by spiders, could be fully appreciated – my feelings ran deeper than these humble amenities might seem to account for.

Memories rose up of childhood dens and camps, burrowed out of hedgerows or the banks of streams, little houses made of the curved sheets of corrugated iron left behind on building sites, or the tiny cave you could creep into within a mountain of rusty girders, where you listened to the rain, fizzing with excitement at being so close to the elements, and yet so safe from them.

I suppose the shed and the loo touched the nerve of this fantasy, by serving all its purposes; a personal secret place, whose secrecy would be forever guaranteed by its humdrum outward appearance. Outside loos, in particular, aren't just physically adapted to the dream of the private cave – small and makeshift, and the rain blowing in under the door – they are emotionally right, being the location ·of early fictions where the mindless story running through your head while you perched in such places as a child turned the space into a personal universe.

Such miniature environments wouldn't have been exciting if they hadn't been extemporized out of material intended for other purposes; as soon as the fantasy is allowed for, it disappears. There was a wendy-house in the garden of a little girl who lived across the road when I was a child, and the wendy-house rotted away because it was entirely neglected; nobody wanted a secret place that had been supplied complete. And while the toyhouse decayed, the crook of an old apple-tree in the same garden was polished smooth by the behinds of the children who turned it into the real, imagined thing.

The two afternoons I spent creosoting the shed (and creosote's one of the magic smells that return you to long-gone summers; creosoting happened at the same season, every year, like haymaking) reminded me of the making of dens. The great feature of a den was the way you never ever completed it before some other preoccupation like cricket or table-tennis took over, and the slight resentment I felt on realizing that having painted one side of the shed I'd still got three to go, brought back those days when you simply walked out of one fantasy into the next, with no sense of obligation at all.

Small ad hoc spaces make you feel all of a piece. There you are inside your own head, with all your particles racing outward like the Big Bang, and the small spaces help you to feel contained. I should think this is why children like them, as they retreat from flying apart by crawling under sofas and beds, hiding in cupboards and cardboard boxes. Why else would you have all this children's fiction about rabbits living in burrows? I can't believe there's anyone who hasn't once in his life felt that living down a rabbit burrow was the height of felicity.

But a functional place, somewhere you don't volunteer for but are obliged to be is, however tiny, quite different. I was working in my small study when the man came to measure up for the carpet. He said, 'There's a wonderful atmosphere in that study of your's – I feel it's a place I could get away from everything.' Did he hear me grind my teeth? ·My little study is the opposite of *away*, it's the centre of a maelstrom

only I encounter, it's the place I am anywhere but hidden. The shed
and the outside loo are little palaces. But my study is a shithouse.

Feast of St Salesman

I WANDERED lonely as a cloud into Selfridge's toiletry department and
found people buying things agitatedly, as though the act of purchase
was sovereign against the scurvy. I only wanted a packet of razor blades,
but it didn't seem right to be there on such mundane business when
you were among people buying *superstitiously*. The place was crowded,
and I wondered for a moment if flying pickets had been bussed in to
ensure punters exceeded their norms – you could tell buying wasn't much
fun, just compulsory.

It was the buying time of the year, Feast of St Salesman and All the
Consumers, and in the queue at the cash desk everyone's nerves twanged
like silent tuning forks, and when the woman behind me clucked impatiently because the cashier was slow I weighed up my chances of getting
out alive if I paid by cheque.

Doesn't matter what you buy – bath salts and talcum powder, after-
shave and foot lotion, items that remain unopened throughout the year,
bought to save the face of the donor, bought in the same spirit a child
says Sorry, i.e. Shut up, don't bother me – it's the thought that counts,
and it's all too clear what the thought is. I fought my way through
the angry toiletry buyers and braving the murderous odours of the Per-
fume Department, a hail of assegais, heard a girl who was selling the
scent talking to a big American as though he were a baby. 'I'm sure
she'll like it,' she fatuously observed, and the enormous American looked
at her with an infant's large and trusting eyes. I knew exactly what I
wanted, and said so, receiving the faintest of impressions that perhaps
I'd overstepped some mark. A chance to regress gracefully was offered
when she said sweetly 'Is it for your wife?' Sidestepping the temptation
to say it was for an old nightwatchman, I replied 'That would be telling!',
exactly like a child spilling his milk to show nurse who's boss. And still

she cooed – 'Oh – for your girlfriend!', adding the clincher, 'I'm sure she'll like it'. Stumbling out, I fingered my nose to adjust the piece of whalebone that had betrayed my rural origins.

When I got home I found the mat knee-deep in brochures telling me to buy wine, exercise machines, monogrammed wallets; tracts that urged me to repent while yet there was time, and not leave unbought all those things I ought to have bought. One was from an outfit trying to sell me a special sort of fruit-cake 'as eaten by Enrico Caruso' – alarming, since Caruso choked to death on a high note, perhaps after a little nibble in the prompt corner.

Topside, the cake was 'crunchy with native pecans' with a base that was 'plump with glacé cherries', the latter effect not lacking a touch of the haemorrhoidal. But I liked the idea that 'every detail of your order is supervised by old-time mail order specialists'. It made the front-office sound like a barber's shop quartet, with the young Caruso an apprentice, crooning over the invoices under the benevolent eye of the old-time mail order specialists, until the day when he was presented with the farewell cake that was to accompany him on his journey to Milan, nobody foreseeing the fatal role his loyalty to the brand was destined to play.

Another brochure suggested 'giving a *book* as a present' which was like urging you to donate half a dozen eggs or a pound of bacon to someone unable to lay hands on such necessities for themselves. Buying a book for someone is like buying a child a piece of clothing – they expect to get that *and* a present. But the book as gift reminded me of one of those rare disobedient souls who are caustic unbelievers when it comes to the Church of St Salesman.

This was a lady who was given a novel for Christmas and having read it, decided she didn't like it, so took it back. And the man at Harrods said But we don't take books back – you've probably read it. Of course I've read it said this member of the unawed, how would I know I didn't like it unless I'd read it? The man struggled to make a point he'd never expected to have to make, that once you'd read a book it had, so to speak, been *consumed*. But it hasn't been consumed, said the lady brusquely, it's here. He tried to say they only took back defective books, but she said It *is* defective, and he said No, he meant books that had pages missing, and she said There isn't a single page missing, more's the pity.

I have to say she was in the world class when it came to bending salesmen to her will. She once took a tin of paté back to the Food Halls and the chap looked at it and said, You couldn't have bought it here, madam, we don't stock this brand. But his triumphant tone was no match for her own when she said, It doesn't matter whether I bought it here or not – this is Harrods, you take *anything* back.

As the Feast of St Salesman approaches, tension crackles over Oxford Street like summer lightning, and decent burghers grow nowty and bad-tempered. Be assured that you are not imagining it when you say to yourself, 'People are bumping into each other more often.'

The Place of the Volvo in Old Norse Mythology

I'VE always felt it was the car which went down to the showroom to choose the man, not the other way round, and Volvos like to pick a dentist who is going to send his son to a not quite first-rate public school. Never forget that Volvos come from the far north, and as each one rolls off the assembly-line it is ritually danced round by Lapland witches. Possibly this is why the front of a Volvo comes to look like the back of any other car, so that it appears to be travelling in a permanent state of reverse. And as you know, every Volvo driver takes a great oath, sworn before a notary public, never to turn his sidelights off – they are to be kept meaninglessly, mindlessly on at all times, in order to induce fury in other road-users. The lights, of course, don't radiate actual light, they radiate self-satisfaction, as though the driver is taking extra special care about some mysterious hazard – possibly reindeer or elk – that the rest of us are too thoughtless to bother about.

I'm a liberal in all this, of course, and I'd never supposed that Volvo owners were actually insane until I spoke to an expectant one – he was waiting for his new model, due to be flown in on a flight of broomsticks from Uppsala. 'Look,' he said, his eyes burning like sidelights, 'look – it's got a double brake-line and a treble oil-line, so you could take an axe' – he mimed this bit with an early edition of the *Evening Standard* – 'you could take an axe and actually sever' – saying 'sever', he drew back with his rolled-up paper and tipped three toilet-rolls out of the string-bag he was carrying over the same arm – 'you could sever one of the brake-lines or two of the oil-lines, and you'd still be laughing.' I said, 'What axe?' He said, 'What do you mean, what axe?' I said, 'The one you were talking about.' He said, 'No, no, I was just asking you to imagine.' Then he drew a deep breath as though he realized I wasn't up to this sort of intellectual rigour, and he said, 'There's even a little door on the headlights.' I said, 'Is that where the dwarf lives who works the windscreen-wipers?' 'Yes,' he said, 'and you only have to change his oil every 10,000 miles.'

Losing Marx

WHEN they held the Karl Marx Festival I went about like a man haunted by a guilty secret and terrified that a political scientist would leave off dancing in the streets long enough to question me about the Sage. We all know its perfectly OK not to have read *Finnegan's Wake*, but with the London School of Economics dressed overall in fairy lights, and *Playboy* issuing a centre-fold of the Prophet complete with facial hair, it wasn't a good time to be confronting the certainty that all you knew about Karl was the bit about him being plagued with boils, inventing a patent medicine called Opium of the People (sold only in asbestos casks) and sitting in Highgate Cemetery, half man, half paving-stone. But I bought my souvenir mug from one of the stalls outside William Rust House, and turned to my copy of *Marxism Today*.

A daunting title for the uninstructed, since it implies that what needs to be known about Marxism Yesterday has already been absorbed. A strap-line on the front cover hit what I took to be a characteristically severe note. 'What does Marx mean to *you*?' it asked ominously, a question very much in the strict fundamentalist tradition of those cold red brick little churches which display threatening quotes from the Bible outside. But the evangelizing thread was to be expected, and runs throughout.

It is seen very clearly in a four-handed discussion that is reminiscent of those moralizing 'Chats with the Padre' which were an obligatory feature of early boys' magazines. There are three junior members of the *causerie* – I imagine them sitting cross-legged on the floor – and the Padre. None of the four bother to define what they mean by Marxism, and each uses the word without referring it to anything save his own feelings. It is the very spirit of religious zealotry, in which the speaker assumes God's sensibilities and His thought-processes to be identical to his own.

Among interesting questions that do not get answered in the course of this colloquy is 'the problem of elites, oligarchy, bureaucracy, and the reproduction of privilege and repression in the ruins of the old economic and social order'. Allowing that 'the challenge … is very great, but need not be paralyzing,' the speaker could hardly have guessed that this Gordian knot was due to be cut. 'We are faced with two difficult problems which Marxists have not come to terms with. How is it possible to organize a complex society in a non-bureaucratic way? And how is it possible to maintain centralized institutions while preserving their democratic character?' To which the Padre answers 'I think we have to establish a new starting point,' as though this was something he might get round to thinking about – as things turn out, he seems to have been dilatory.

Throughout the chat the speakers refer unselfconsciously though perhaps a bit wistfully to 'the proletariat' – even to 'the traditional proletariat' – as though this was a bunch of chaps they used to know very well. I wonder when they met them did they chat them up as the proletariat? And when they chucked the proletariat under the chin and asked What does Marx mean to you, child, did the proletariat drop curtseys and mumble Thank you, kind sir? The Padre and his little circle speak of 'the disappearance of the industrial proletariat' as though mourning the evaporation of a constituency essential to their trade. But this always happens when there's a buy-out: in purchasing the equity direct, the workforce elbows out the priesthood which thought to use superstition to bring about the same ends, and thus avoids having its own property sold back to it in the form of holy wafers, retail. It begins to look as though Brecht was right when he said it wasn't possible to sit on people hard enough.

But how did you come to *miss* it? asked a friend of mine, making Marx and Marxism sound like a stop on the Underground. All I can say is that during the formative years Marx and his works seemed about as relevant to my own position as Baden-Powell's *Scouting for Boys*. I had to sit out the time when people went round saying 'Is he a Marxist?' as the undergraduate Betjeman once asked 'Is he High?', the question always put with a sort of awe, as of one viewing from the distance of his own mediocrity a being whose purity and commitment were of an altogether mystical order.

Apart from some dim notion that Marx had once lived in Manchester, or it might have been Walsall, my ignorance was complete. I'm not at all proud of it, and still feel I would like to know all about Marx in the same way I would like to be able to speak Dutch, namely, without having to try.

Wonderful old Ladies

You knew Gladys Cooper was a Wonderful Old Lady because when she made her first entrance everyone clapped like mad before she started doing anything. And you knew Ethel Barrymore was another Wonderful Old Lady because she used to appear in films as Cary Grant's mother, and while the rest of the cast were just listed by name in the credits, Ethel Barrymore appeared as *Miss* Ethel Barrymore, which indicated that she was to be judged by sacred not profane standards.

The point about Wonderful Old Ladies is that they are everyone's personal mascot, and being able to spot how wonderful they are means we're a bit wonderful ourselves, too. This is why anyone who was anything less than entirely fulsome in publicly endorsing the Queen Mother as the Most Wonderful Old Lady in the World would bring down on himself a tidal wave of real anger from all those who have invested enormous amounts of themselves in the role they cast her for.

What must it be like to be told constantly that you are a Wonderful Old Lady? In the case of the Queen Mother (and in addition to having to carry round that particular title, which sounds as though she lives in a hive and is fed by bees) what an onus it must put on her, especially on mornings when she is not feeling specially wonderful. Now and again, instead of waving in her characteristically gracious fashion, she must have been tempted to stuff her fingers up the nose of the nearest photographer and tell him to try being wonderful and radiant all the time and see how he likes it.

Of course, no one knows what Wonderful Old Ladies are really like (though the late Philip Hope-Wallace did tell me he was once chatting to the Queen Mother and she said 'If you want to know what conversational rock-bottom is I doubt if you could beat the Guards' Club'), because part of succeeding as a Wonderful Old Lady involves staying at the right distance to preserve the illusion. Grandmas are Wonderful, because there's built-in distance in the relationship. They don't bear final responsibility and can always go home when they feel like it. This means they can devote themselves full-time to being Wonderful, which is what everyone wants.

Your mother can't be Wonderful, but other people's mothers can. Aunts and uncles can qualify, but sometimes people attempt to gate-crash the Wonderful category by trying to pass themselves off as aunts and uncles to the whole human race. This provokes creepy sensations all round, since any hint of self-appointment in the Wonderful category alarms everyone – what we are looking for in Wonderful Old Ladies is someone who can make us feel good by sheltering us under the magic umbrella of her own apparent self-sufficiency, not someone who is trying to invert this process.

On the other hand, of course, there are Dreadful Old Ladies. Dreadful Old Ladies pick quarrels in Post Offices and you develop an instinct for avoiding those queues in which they lurk, since you don't want to find yourself on the receiving end of a vengeful harangue on the subject of Jimmy Knapp or a monologue concerning the rudeness of the young, delivered in a querulous shout as though your own indecent advances were simultaneously being fended-off.

What a day out for the Queen Mother it would be if, suitably disguised in crimplene trousers, she could be chauffeured over to St Martins le Grand armed with a pension-book and left for a couple of hours to terrorize the counter-staff. To be a Dreadful Old Lady in a Post Office, once in a while, is the least anyone might hope for, after a lifetime of being Wonderful.

Why Horses Don't Buy People

'The beast is being sold with the greatest reluctance,' shouted the auctioneer, 'as this excellent horse is too keen for the owner's very young son.'

'Now that probably means he tried to eat him,' said a little bow-legged fellow out of Bela Lugosi by Mickey Mouse.

'He has a cunning piggy eye,' said his friend, a man almost certainly wearing someone else's raincoat, 'that'd make you want to lock up the spoons.'

'Can I say six hundred guineas? Six hundred? Five hundred then. I have a bid of five hundred. Five hundred and twenty. And forty. Five hundred and forty guineas?'

The people had big faces, if the horse sale had had to be called off they could have got up a Big Face Competition at a moment's notice.

'Quiet in every respect,' shouted the auctioneer, 'and will jump a gate in cold blood.'

But all the horses looked cold-blooded – cold-blooded and slightly sinister, making you think the only reason horses didn't go round buying people was that like Royalty they didn't carry money.

'Nice head and tail,' said the man in the stolen raincoat.

'Very polished – a horse like that'd stop and pick your hat up for you. But his feet are a bit boxy, a bit on the mulish side,' said Bela Lugosi, 'and he might turn out to be a flat-catcher after all.'

'He'll take a deal of cleaning,' said his friend, who could have taken a touch himself, 'with those white legs.'

'He has consistently hunted,' cried the auctioneer, 'and can show the way to go, being well-mannered and a great galloper. A wonderfully quiet ride in traffic, and without vice of any description.'

'Now I looked after a horse without vice of any description for a man once upon a time,' said Bela Lugosi, 'and all the horse ever did in the way of not being the bargain of the world was to swell himself out when you put the saddle on him and draw himself in when he'd got the master on his back. I wish I had a shilling for every time I saw that saddle slide slowly round underneath the nag's belly and the master, decent man, lying on his back waiting for the horse to laugh. You couldn't call that vicious, it was more satirical.'

In the paddock, under a stone white sky, other horses that were to be sold were being put through their paces for the benefit of onlookers whose impassivity would have done credit to a Melton Mowbray pie. Whatever feat the horses might have performed, say standing for Parliament or juggling with three oranges, you felt the onlookers wouldn't have thought of applauding. Sensing this, one horse kept knocking the pole over whenever the man who was selling him put him at the demonstration-jump. After all, what was in it for him?

But this horse was an exception (one of nature's dogs, really, he hankered after approval) because the rest of them went on doing their stuff quite unmoved by the lack of enthusiasm which when you came to think about it only meant they were in the presence of onlookers who weren't so impressed with horses being horses that (unlike the great television show-jumping audience) they had to pretend they were people.

Many of the beasts were still in their little stalls, being looked at. Bela Lugosi was trying to get his fingers into the mouth of one of the horses for the purposes of examining his teeth but the horse refused to open, tossing its head imperiously in a way which made the attempt seem impertinent.

'Perhaps he thinks you're going to make off with them,' suggested his friend.

'He has a hard-looking mouth, you'd need a whole blacksmith's shop in it. Is he nappy at all?' he asked the groom.

'Nappy? Amiable as a clergyman,' said the groom, brushing the horse down and hissing through his teeth as all grooms do. 'Did you hear of the duchess who married her coachman,' muttered the man in the stolen raincoat, 'she could never get used to the way he hissed when he carved the meat at table.' Bela Lugosi ran his hands over the horse's hindquarters. 'Nice back on him, neither hollow nor sharp. And a good height, sixteen three,' said the groom.

'Living out?' asked the raincoat man. The groom nodded. 'Had a lot of stone walls, has he?' asked Bela Lugosi. 'Yes, and he's a great man over timber too,' the groom said.

The dealers' nagsmen were running the horses up to the auctioneer's ring, holding the rein close up to the bit so that the horse's head shouldn't nod. Some of the horses sold for four hundred guineas, some for four thousand. The great mystery to the onlooker was how the buyers managed to conceal their apprehension that ten minutes after they'd bought the animals they might fall down dead, not through any undisclosed defect but simply because the purchase was flesh and blood.

'Is that horse as young as he looks?' asked the man in the stolen raincoat, for he and his friend were back at the ring. 'I couldn't say I'm sure,' said Bela Lugosi, 'but it's surprising what a little bit of shoe-blacking will do when it's applied in the right places.'

'Well known in the Cut-'Em-Downs and only in the market because the owner is going in for breeding canaries,' roared the auctioneer. This nag was so dejected it looked like the ghost of that famous horse well known in the Surrey 'Unt – 'a three-legged four-cornered hack, with one eye, a rat-tail and a head as large as a fiddle-case' whose rider had 'had him in the shay until eleven last night, and he came forty-three mile in our traveller the day before, else he's a good one to go. Do you remember the owdacious leap he took over the tinker's tent at Epping 'Unt, last Easter? How he astonished the natives within!'

'Doesn't look as if he got beyond his twice times table,' said the man in the stolen raincoat. The horse looked at him – the man in the raincoat had his hat pulled well down over his eyes and was eating an individual meat pie – and fetching a great sigh said thoughtfully, 'Houyhnhnm.'

Suburban Dream

I SUPPOSE the last thing anyone might expect would be to find his own ordinary brick and mortar part of someone else's dream. I thought it was something of a plain number coming up when John Bratby (who'd politely invited me to let him paint my picture) said he'd lived in the same suburb as I had lived in, when he was a boy. But the extra dimension was the novel he'd written about it, *Breakfast and Elevenses*, and before I left he told me the name of the road he'd lived in. This rang a bell, and I drove twenty-five miles to make sure it was where I thought it was. I was right. Bratby and I are of an age. It was therefore an actuarial impossibility that I wasn't romancing a girl over a gate in Amberwood Rise while ten paces across the road in Bramshaw Gardens Bratby was doing the same. But while I was just doing it, he was dreaming it as well. Odd to find your own avenues and crescents have a bard, that asphalt and pillarboxes and by-pass roads you had all but forgotten turn up in someone else's song.

Nostalgie de la Boot

I WASN'T a bit surprised to learn that a man had found a penguin in his boot, since one of the reasons I never open my boot is the fear of finding a penguin inside. I keep it closed because I think the boot of a motor car conceals the true character of the owner, and I keep the lid well down in case I find out more than I want. As when I once opened it and found a giant bar of Toblerone, bought in Shaftesbury six months before, crawling round the inside in a blue phosphorescence.

The boot is where decay begins, as the boot is so one day shall the whole car be, and the earth from potted plants, the small ineradicable pools of Belgian dripping, the corners crammed with the pine needles of Christmas trees past, the quartz-like crumbs of a thousand picnics, will eat their way forward, invading the part where the human beings sit, until the passengers lie buried fathoms deep in a Sargasso of old toffee papers and the true sloblike spirit of the driver is revealed for the world to see. The car becomes a boot with windows, you start throwing things into the car that once you would only have thrown into the boot, it becomes a privately-owned dustcart within which the actual travellers fight for precedence over broken screwdrivers and old bathroom cabinets.

The boot is a moveable burial ground, not least for corpses. How often we read of murderers driving round and round with chopped-up bits of the body in the boot. Yet no one really feels a murderer's boot is nastier than their own; no one would let anything they value come into contact with the floor of their boot. It would be easy to keep it clean, but nobody ever does. Indeed, if you came across a man with a virgin boot you would suspect him of folding his trousers before making love.

Who does not edge away from those car-parks which feature boot-sales, cars with their rear ends gaping open, so that you avert your eyes, fearful of intruding at the wrong moment. There's a sort of *pudeur* about looking into someone else's boot, but if anyone looked into mine they would find ample evidence of a man who never paints behind anything if it can't be seen.

Needs No Introduction From Me

A BOOK on public speaking tells you that when practising your ghastly speech you should balance telephone directories on your toes, smother your face in egg-white, and bounce a tennis ball throughout – presumably on the grounds that if you really are the sort of narcissist who volunteers for this sort of thing you will endure any humiliation in pursuit of a captive audience, a fish tea and your train fare home. The book perversely attempts to stop decent people being terrified of making speeches, when what we need is a book designed to make people more terrified of making speeches.

My own disinclination to make a speech is outweighed only by my disinclination to listen to one. Of all the speeches I've been unable to avoid I remember not a single word. The form is to be mistrusted: at best, an instrument of ingratiation, at worst a tool of deceit (a statement which very nicely hits off the fraudulent cadence that makes speeches stick in your craw).

There is some slight excuse if you do it for money –

> *Since merit but a dunghill is*
> *I mount the rostrum unafraid:*
> *Indeed, 'twere damnable to ask*
> *If I were overpaid –*

– but Auden knew public speaking condemned him to giving everlasting imitations of himself. He liked the cash, but he knew that putting yourself up before an audience, in bite-sized chunks, as a sort of second helping of dessert, is addictive. Those who come to depend on this sort of attention will have it on any terms, yea, though they are consumed by Rotarians —

Spirit is willing to repeat
Without a qualm the same old talk.

Debauched as a form of communication by amateurs longing for the acclaim which rewards the low comedian, public speaking is entirely discredited in the mouths of politicians. Are they present in their own persons or do they mouth what some hired hand churns out for them? Do they believe what they say, or do they simply want *you* to believe they believe it? Remember how chilling it was to learn, long after the event, that all those early speeches of Kennedy had been composed for him by a man called Sorensen. Refuse all substitutes — but when it comes to public speaking, how do you know?

Put to its proper uses, a speech is a ritual thing, best trundled out in commemoration or celebration. Nobody remembers a word of the funeral oration or the centennial address, it's simply an aid to remembering the occasion: the actual words wouldn't really be any good if they were memorable, it would be like someone dazzling you with a hand mirror. Talks and lectures are different again, because they are delivered as from one person to another, but speeches are tannoyed out to people in general, never to people in particular.

Public speaking is always done by someone the audience is expected to have heard of. When the Chairman says the speaker needs no introduction, he is simply putting it squarely to those who can't quite place the face that the committee, though unable to get the man they actually wanted, could never ever be accused of inviting someone who was — unimaginable! — anonymous. Most public speakers have something to do with television, and apart from a high tolerance to a nagging suspicion that the audience would have preferred Nureyev, they also have to face the fact that the speech they climb into is the equivalent of the costume worn by Jacko. That this does not deter them should surprise no one who was present one evening when a man who had been entertaining a bunch of dentists at a hotpot supper was paid his fee in ten-pence pieces counted out of a biscuit tin while he was still sitting on the platform.

Decent people will always be frightened of speaking in public, and from time to time their fears will be reinforced. The author James Lees-Milne recalls his father having been invited by the vicar to address the congregation, and speaking at inordinate length (all public speakers do this). At last Lees-Milne's mother who was sitting in the front row attempted to stop her husband by gesturing towards his trousers as though his flies were undone. Flustered, Lees-Milne's father came to an abrupt halt, and returned to his pew, surreptitiously checking his trousers. Whereupon his wife dug him in the ribs and chuckled 'April Fool!' Her husband looked at her. 'But it's August,' he said.

The abiding image of the inauthenticity of public speaking is provided by the man ranting on a podium in the street. As you walk past you feel two things: that he is avid for your attention, but has nothing whatever to tell you.

Philistine

WHEN Nicolas Ridley was Minister of the Environment someone accused him of going round the country 'like a Philistine'. I was torn between two images, one where Ridley is covered in walnut juice like Ernest Borgnine and carrying a slingshot, looking for someone small to have a fight with, and one where he's dressed up like an alderman played by Stanley Holloway and complaining the Henry Moore altar looks like a camembert.

Good word, philistine, some people actually claim it's what they are, as when the parents of a friend of mine decided to recoup the family fortunes by going to America as cook and butler. They were so well-bred they frightened the life out of their employers, and the first day they were shown round the mansion which included a private art gallery. My friend's mother politely admired all the pictures but ended by saying, 'But I'm afraid we're simply Philistine.' 'Oh that's all right,' said the lady of the house, 'we're Episcopalian, ourselves.'

But the real philistine aren't so entertaining. They're always people who've closed their minds to something, and it doesn't have to be art or opera or architecture, it can be football or gardens or cooking. They're philistine because they boast about what they don't like without telling you why. And claiming to be a philistine is claiming to be a bit of a character, and that's worse than being a philistine.

Of course, you musn't mind being *accused* of being a philistine just because your opinion goes against the prevailing trend. All sensible people must be willing to risk being mistaken for philistine when necessary, reminding themselves that just because they agree with Norman Tebbit for once it doesn't make them one. But a temptation that is to be avoided is *pretending* to be Norman Tebbit. It happens when you judge the man who's doing the talking is getting above himself and coming on fancy, and you are seized with a sudden rush of no-messing commonsenseness which out-pretends the pretender. If you feel an attack of salt-of-the-earth (*manie du sel du monde*) coming on, it doesn't necessarily mean the other man's over the top, it usually means you're feeling left out.

Some people don't sound like philistine until they get going. When the father of a friend of mine started his monologue about the Atlantic alliance, a flame (as he put it) he had promised General Eisenhower he would personally see was never extinguished, the opening staves were moderately interesting, but when ten or twelve minutes had elapsed and he'd instructed by-standers that in this faith he had never wavered, it had become clear that it wasn't so much the flame or the faith or even General Eisenhower (who by now had been relegated pretty much to the status of straight-man) which counted, it was the speaker's own claim to attention. This is the hallmark of the philistine; whatever the subject, they manage to block the view.

My friend's parents packed in the cook-and-butling in America, but her mother still kept her end up in the philistine stakes. When they went to the opera at Covent Garden, she would turn to the stranger next to her during the flatter stretches of recitative and invite him, *sotto voce*, to join her in a game of noughts-and-crosses.

Buying a Picture from Lowry

On 6 August 1962, about four o'clock in the afternoon, I bought a picture from L. S. Lowry. I was sitting in the back room of his house in Mottram-in-Longdendale and he was showing me what he'd been painting, setting them up on his easel and saying, 'Hey, hey, I keep on doing them, don't I?' There was one he'd shown me early on, a small single figure, a girl in a black dress and red shoes. I plucked up courage and asked him how much the little pictures fetched, and he said, 'Oh, they go very well, forty pounds or thereabouts.' I asked him if he'd let me have another look at the girl with the red shoes, and I told him it reminded me of my wife in old photographs, long before I knew her.

He swung it up again and studied it. 'Yes,' he said, 'I think I like her, I think I do. Poor little thing, poor little thing.' I was rather shy. I asked him when it might come on sale. 'Oh, it probably won't, it probably won't – why, do you like it? What do you want to give me for it?' I said (going a bit hot in the face) that it was up to him. 'Well, they fetch forty.' We looked at it again and he went on talking. 'Give me thirty for it if you like.' I said I didn't want to get it at cut rates. 'Wait a bit, then, forty with the frame, you'll have to get it framed yourself, forty minus the frame. Give me thirty-five then. Is that a fair price?'

Then he said, 'Shall I sign it for you?' He dodged about looking for a brush, dipped it into a rather dry bit of black on his palette. 'This is the hardest part,' he said. He painted the letters, then incised them with a penknife. 'I'll put the date on the other side, balance it up a bit, you know. I'll put 1960, it's easier to paint. I think I started it in 1956. Shall I wrap it up? I've got a bit of brown paper here.' He went out and got the paper, and as he was doing the wrapping he picked up a sketch he'd done in biro on a lined pad, a drawing of two people, and said, 'I'll *throw it in*. It's only a note, you know, I find I do these things in the street. I'll throw it in. I'm very pleased you like her. Can you see where I've painted over the –?' He broke off and it occurred to me he thought I might not like a painting that you could see had been altered. But he went on, 'I painted her dress red first but I didn't like it, so I painted it over black and left the red shoes, and the red underneath gives the black a very nice quality. There was a lot of work went into that. Oh yes, all out of my head, you know.'

I had to send him a cheque because I didn't have enough money with me at the time, and when he wrote back thanking me for what he called 'the enc.' he said, 'I'm glad the poor little thing has found a good home.' I wrote all this down the day afterwards, and stuck it on the back of the picture so that my children will know all about it. I wrote an article about Lowry, and it elicited the following letter from someone who read it:

I am a portrait painter, one of that tribe who hates parting with paint-ings, so I hoard them. My brother was the same – maybe a case of not much savvy.

Well, the thing is, I once felt I needed a Lowry painting. My brother was a friend of his. I gathered together my money, all of twenty-five pounds and a few shillings, and set off from Euston. I got there, a shabby enough young woman, and knocked at the door and Lowry opened it and looked at me. We looked at one another for a minute then I said, 'I've come to buy a painting. I paint too but I won't sell any. But I'm telling you this so you won't feel too badly at having to say I can't have one.' And I added I had brought my money.

He said to come on in and we had some tea. Then he brought a picture out and said, 'You can have this one,' so I emptied my purse and gave him the lot. It included my extra for a cup of tea and bus fares but who cared or thought – well, we didn't. He didn't count it, so didn't know what I'd poured out on the table. Then I left. We were alike really.

I walked to the station and got into the train neither happy nor unhappy and got out at Euston and started the walk home. It was when I reached the Park I suddenly realized I was walking without my painting. Back I went to the station but it was never found. It was a snow scene – with a loneliness I know about, having been brought up in Burnley not far off. It had black factories and three figures, black like the factories. The sky was dark and like a grim threat. Although I never saw it again, I know it in detail – having that sort of memory, I guess. I ask you, what a thing, eh? Oh well, he has gone, bless him. I'm glad you wrote that thing about him.

The letter makes me feel there is more than one way of owning a picture. It tells a real story, by which I mean that though it actually did happen, it need not have done, since it's true anyway.

Stop Press: America Discovered by Welshman

No one for a moment doubted the newspaper report that bow-ties were to be made compulsory for workers on the London Underground, and the additional information that scarves were to be permitted only if they matched somehow put the matter beyond question. The whole thing was inherently unlikely, but a hint of the surreal makes the truth more convincing.

As when you read that in Greece fat people weren't going to be allowed to drive. Anyone 70 per cent over normal weight was to lose his licence, and you visualized policemen carrying enormous portable scales in the squad car – 'Just hop on, sir – right, Andreas, let's have the weights' – and tail-backs building up while fat men stood naked on weighing-machines at crossroads. In the same Dadaist category was a report of the succouring of 10,000 widgeon in Suffolk: a local farmer supplied them with umpteen bushels of wheat gratis because they found it too cold to go on to Holland. 'Thank you, sir, just another bowlful with a little warm milk and I believe we'll thaw out sufficiently to make Amsterdam.'

But the stumer, the dud, the counterfeit, muddies the water. A picture of the wife of the Archbishop of Canterbury was captioned 'Mrs Rosalind Runcie, driving a double-decker bus – for a short distance.' Had Mrs Runcie seen the bus careering by, minus its driver, and jumped into the driving seat to arrest its progress as one might in earlier days have leapt to the saddle of a team of runaway horses, I should have had no trouble understanding why the report appeared in the paper. Had it been an illustration of a decision on her part to take up part-time work with London Transport, I could have seen the point. But the last four words of the caption are not only finely calculated to remove all possible interest, they make it perfectly clear that nothing in fact was happening.

This is street-theatre rather than news, which adulterates the currency and makes you suspicious of small innocent items that may be perfectly genuine. Did a burglar *really* steal someone's gramophone records and finding they featured Max Bygraves, send them back with a note saying 'Can't stand him!'? Or was this a plant by Max's PR man, well knowing the value of the comic 'knock'? Our consul in Shanghai was (according to the *Daily Telegraph*) 'the talk of the tea-houses of the Whang-Poo river' because he is bearded, wears pince-nez and sports a tweed hat and Inverness cape. But a hair-crack ran through this carefully assembled portrait, since the man was alleged to have had a London taxi shipped out for him by way of personal transport. *Real* characters never own taxis for fear of being confused with the late Nubar Gulbenkian. Was our man just such a work of fiction?

Infected by non-events, news begins to seem awfully iffy. Could you feel a hundred per cent sure about the man who stood upright in an open car at 90 mph and succeeded in releasing the jammed landing gear of a light aeroplane zooming overhead, using only his right hand? Well, yes, its the bit about the right hand that clinches it – he couldn't have used both. But once the agnostic mood sets in, even reports that the Sultan of Brunei has moved into a new palace with *two* gold domes, solid of course, and is not only Sultan but Prime Minister, Minister of Finance and Home Secretary as well, are viewed with reserve.

It's a pity the hocus pocus whose purpose is to sell you something ever gets mixed up with the real thing. So long as the ads are kept in the margin their ingratiatory prattle is no more than an irritant, and sometimes they score such a splendid own-goal the reader gets a bonus. One wonderful series of plugs for Jallop and Brimstone's noted rum featured Telly Savalas swigging the stuff on a desert island, in the company of a model in a grass skirt, and a caption which gurgled something about forbidden fruit. But what, delightfully, the devisers had overlooked was the message that the tableau was really delivering, *viz*, drink our rum and it will make you stupendously bald.

However, in the own-goal category Cathay Pacific won the coveted Order of the Golden Noodle. Powering the ball bang into the back of the net they announced 'Only Cathay Pacific fly to Hong Kong and back. Non-stop.' Hara-kiri, and as neat as you please. Though no connoisseur of the blindingly stupid will forget the Air Canada ad which proclaimed 'Our flights are so good you won't want to get off.' Whoever dreamed that one up was living in a world where people plead for a second spoonful of castor-oil and beg the dentist to fill just one more tooth.

But when this sort of thing is stage-managed into the news columns in the interests of promoting something or other you begin to think everything is paste. I spent some time with my jeweller's eyeglass studying a report that America had actually been discovered by a Welshman called Lloyd. But having passed it as genuine, I fell to wondering why, having discovered America, Lloyd hadn't thought it worth mentioning. Was this why the story didn't feel like a scoop? Or was it simply that it was open to anyone to say a man called Atkinson discovered Australia and a chap called Smithers got to the North Pole first?

On this occasion, the sceptical mood was compounded by an announcement in the anniversaries column of the *Guardian* that an ex-MP who had had enough of being plain Ted Short and had re-christened himself Lord Glenamara of Glenridding was that day celebrating his 763rd birthday. While this offered a hint as to why Ted's conversation often included vivid accounts of the Siege of Constantinople and the Battle of Agincourt, it did nothing for my lapsing faith in the pure milk of accurate reporting.

This was only restored by a paragraph noting that Islington Borough Council was to fund 'an elderly lesbians conference on women-only graveyards', and a subvention was also being made towards 'gym-mats for a lesbian self-defence course'. Since you couldn't put this in a work of fiction, I took it to be true.

The Bum's Rush

'WE retired down the stairs as quickly as possible and closed the front door behind us. That's how I put it in my report,' said the bailiff, 'those were my words. And seeing as how she was stark naked and throwing pailfuls of hot water on us prior to insinuating her legs between the banisters to impede progress down the stairs, well —'

'It was an understatement,' said his colleague.

'Well, yes,' said the bailiff.

'It's a continual drama,' said the third man, 'only the public doesn't know. Who but a bailiff gets a man dodge up from behind a sofa with a hacksaw in his hand? He'd have got me if he hadn't stubbed his toe on a cast-iron Alsatian.'

'Billy was with me,' said the first man, 'Billy tried to shroud her in a rug –'

'Preserving an element of –'

'She bit him,' said the first man.

After a silence in which the first man looked searchingly at his companions, one after the other, the third man said, 'She didn't dash out from behind any sort of venetian blinds, did she?'

'No, no, no, nothing like that,' said the first bailiff, whose ears lay close to his head.

'Only I had a ladder against the front of a house, went up it, shouted through the top window and was just going to climb in when a fist shot out through the venetian blinds and got me bang on the nose.'

'You summonsed him,' said the second bailiff.

'He got seven days. They marched him off. "No ill-feelings," he said.'

The second man, whose cheekbones looked as if they'd been polished said, 'No door can stand up to a well-placed boot.'

The first man said, 'Or then there's those who greet you very gaily. "What have you got for me?" As if you were Father Christmas.'

'Well you do advise them,' said the second man, nodding, 'you do your best. We all have hearts. We get a lot of life stories.'

'I don't believe life stories,' the third man said. 'When you've had a designerized lavatory seat hurled at you, followed by a bottle of blackcurrant cordial, you go off on your mo-ped very close to disillusioned.'

'What I don't like is when they say they'd sooner sweep the streets than do *your* job,' the second man said. 'It disturbs my mind when people say that. Only temporary, mind, but it does. It does me anyway.'

'She hurled it at me,' said the third man, 'as if I was a hoopla-stall. She shouted "Where would you lot be if it wasn't for people like me not paying their debts?" She was logical, in a way – even in the heat of it all.'

The three men wore long blue mackintoshes. Once every three years each was issued with a new one.

'Evenings and mornings are the only times to catch debtors. Otherwise they're always out. Even at five in the morning the wife says, "You've just missed him." But when she came to the door you heard her draw the bolt. Now if he'd already gone out, is it likely the wife would have got up and bolted the door a second time?'

The consciousness of shared expertise united the men, and they smiled.

'We've seen a lot of early mornings,' said the first bailiff. The third man agreed and added, 'Sometimes so early that when you get your client to the prison you knock on the door and they say "We don't open till seven." It happens oftener than you'd think.'

'I wonder if we get sufficient credit for the general awkwardness?' queried their colleague. 'Like say seizing a hen-house.'

'I had to distrain two cows,' the first speaker said, 'and it was Billy seized the black Arab stallion that went for a couple of thousand quid.'

'It's not easy,' the second man said. 'Every warrant tells a story.'

'I don't mind when they get obstropalous, you know where you are then,' said the first speaker, 'it's the smooth-tongued ones that lead you up the garden.'

'Like the one who asked me in as nice as pie and when he'd got me into the hall *he* nipped out and locked the front door on me. He wasn't what you might call an experienced man in having bailiffs about.'

'The venetian blind mentality,' the third man said.

The Little Holthausen

MOST of the time our behaviour is a controlled account of the way we are and the way we want to appear, but when we are in the grip of our habits, such as never walking on the joins between paving-stones and tapping every railing in three, we are not so much admitting something about ourselves as being unable not to admit something. This puts me in mind of C. L. Wrenn, one of the giants of my youth.

He was Rawlinson and Bosworth professor of Anglo-Saxon at Oxford when I was an undergraduate. He would never, ever, begin to lecture without turning round three times in front of the lectern, entirely without explanation. He was also given to stopping half way down the aisle on his way to the podium to dig a member of his audience in the ribs and whisper 'Who's lecturing here?' And when the startled undergraduate would blurt 'You are, sir!' he'd whisper again, rather more piercingly, 'Do you think he's any good?'

When he got up on the dais, he'd go through the text of *Beowulf* or *The Wanderer* and come across some tremendously difficult crux, something that had baffled Mullenhof and Klaeber, even Krapp and Bugge, and he'd parse it like an acrobat somersaulting through a hoop while spinning plates on sticks, and then he'd say, looking solemnly at the room, 'But your guess is as good – or almost as good – as mine.'

When Wrenn was going through his repertoire of habits I always felt I was catching him unawares; that this was the real Wrenn, the irreducible essence of the man, the inexplicable fragment of which all the rest was merely the rationale. There was no possibility of pretence, the man was in the grip of compulsions that came from his innermost being, and the adjective 'eccentric': so often attached to those who merely court the description by calculating the effects of their behaviour – could properly be applied.

Of that genus, Wrenn was the only example I ever had first-hand experience of, and with the spread of mass communications eccentricity seems to have died out: a cloistered environment was essential to the unconstrained expression of private humours, and the universities when they were more removed from the world than now they are, supplied it.

So that Dr Buckland of Corpus Christi College, Oxford, a student of the antique and the curious who liked to eat his specimens, was perfectly at home. He was once in an Italian church where a certain statue was understood to bleed, and lying down on the floor Buckland licked the stains, before rising and saying 'Bats' urine!' Once, he went on his bicycle to Nuneham outside Oxford where there was a holy relic that was supposed to be the heart of a French king. They brought him the box so that he could have a look, and opening it he stared inside and said 'Well, I've eaten some strange things in my time, but never the heart of a king,' and before they realized what he was going to do, he picked up the relic and swallowed it. He also had a weakness for mice in batter.

Ruskin was lecturing in the Schools and drawing some birds' wings on a blackboard to illustrate a point in aesthetics, when a band struck up outside the window. He threw down the chalk, gathered up his gown, and fell to marching back and forth across the room, crying 'Gentlemen, I cannot resist martial music!' Frowde of Corpus was irritated if the grass beneath his window was trampled. One day he set a man-trap, heard a scream, and found he'd caught the Professor of Moral Philosophy. As penance, he condemned himself to attending the man's lectures for the rest of the term. Frowde exercised on wet days by jumping over chairs placed round the room, until a man in the rooms below, madder even than he was, fired a pistol through the ceiling. Frowde rushed down crying 'Would you, bloody minded man, would you!'

These tales are well attested, but further first-hand news of Wrenn reached me from Mr David McLintock, once Wrenn's pupil and later his colleague. Wrenn had his own way with the personal pronoun, apparently, and would address McLintock as 'They'. He would vary this with 'We' and sometimes, if truly mortified by an error, as 'It'. A portrait of Wrenn's old master, Joseph Wright, author of *The English Dialect Dictionary*, hung on the wall, and if McLintock made a cock-up of some more than ordinarily interesting matter in Gothic morphology, Wrenn would stare wildly at the picture and cry 'It shouldn't do it, It shouldn't do it! It's offended Old Joe!' And if McLintock might enquire about the etymology of an Old English word, Wrenn would ask 'They've consulted the little Holthausen, haven't They?' (Holthausen being a sort of handbook). 'No, I'm afraid I haven't, sir.' 'Oh dear, dear,' Wrenn would say, much perturbed, 'they don't *despise* the little Holthausen, do They?' If McLintock mispronounced a vowel in Old High German, and then corrected himself, Wrenn would comment mildly 'I'm so glad They've come round to the Orthodox view.'

McLintock says that Wrenn looked on his *Beowulf* lectures as designed for 'the mob', rather as though he were giving the equivalent of a pop concert. And one thinks of a group called The Little Holthausen and their new single 'Grendel's Mother'. But such a facetious gambit misses by a million miles Wrenn's true singularity. When he died, it was as though a species died with him.

The Higher Tiredness, Or Heroic Fatigue

I KNEW a man who had a wife called Muriel and you'd say, 'How's Muriel?' and he'd say 'Oh fine – apart from the fatigue.' He never said why Muriel was fatigued, because he felt he didn't have to. Muriel did a lot of voluntary work, and the way he said the word fatigue – as though it scarcely needed saying, as though it were axiomatic – suggested he spoke of someone whose sensitive temperament the rest of us could only guess at; indeed, he seemed to imply he found it difficult enough himself to give it the full measure of understanding it deserved, even though he lived in such proximity to the source and a little of Muriel's heroic fatigue may well have rubbed off on him.

I was reminded of this chap by the title of a book called *Farewell to Fatigue*, and noted that the word 'fatigue' canonizes the idea of feeling tired by giving it the sort of name that tells everyone it's their duty to stand to attention; the author would never have considered calling it *'Farewell To Feeling Knackered'*. 'Fatigue' is for people who want to advertise something about themselves and while I'm not against people feeling tired I'm absolutely against their telling me.

Once someone admits to tiredness they invite a further enquiry, and this will elicit the reluctant admission that they have been 'overdoing it'. Not of course overdoing it in the way of drink or sex or anything that might remotely be supposed to be enjoyable, but overdoing it in some arduous or distinguished way: finishing the novel, perhaps, shouldering rather a heavy burden of committee work since, well, the others did tend to depend on one, taking on additional commitments because one simply hadn't the heart to say No. People wearing the badge of fatigue often use a certain phrase: they say they have been working 'a nine-day week'.

Such a person is telling you that his style of life elevates his tiredness into a coronet or halo, and the litany sometimes ends with the man saying, 'Pam's persuaded me at last. I'm just going to let them get on with it for a few weeks, and we're off to Barbados where I shall do *absolutely nothing.*' The murmurs of sympathy from his hearers often seem to be fighting their way through rather tight little smiles.

None of this should be confused with 'lack of vitality' which was one of the famous chronic conditions in the twilight days of patent medicine advertising. It was offered as a sop to the overlooked and undervalued, who could feel that the makers of Bile Beans and Parish's Chemical Food and a white powder called Sanatogen were rushing forward with the support that life itself was denying them. But lack of vitality went out with constipation and 'superfluous hair' (a wonderful concept, as though Nature had got the accelerator stuck when it came to hair and if you didn't smother yourself in Dulcamara's Hair Vanisher you'd be covered in the stuff) one Wednesday round about 1956.

This was because being tired was a concept that had to be re-designed for the aspiring classes who were now seen to be the market. Instead of the wage-slave being reassured by his all-smiling consumerist wife that his natural inclination to fall asleep in his employer's time was nothing to do with revolutionary tendencies, it was 'just one of those Tiredness Peaks, dear' and Lucozade was the answer, fatigue as a selling point was moved from the passive to the active. Being tired was transformed into something you suffered from if you were an Achiever. This word was devised by the creative staff at Volapuk Wagstaff Nicely, the advertis-ing agency which converted the dozy fathead in the carpet-slippers into Action Man, a robot clad in chain-store suits who carries a brief-case as though it were a Field-Marshal's baton. Fatigue wasn't a word that fitted the new commercial strategy, so it was changed to Stress.

Whatever word it goes by, being tired continues to be popular. It's hoist not as a flag of distress but more as a plea for special consideration, the grounds for which are never made quite clear. Sometimes the chosen word is Exhausted, though whenever I hear it in ordinary discourse I see black smoke coming from the tail end of a car that is conking out, and begin to wonder whether the speaker would pass his MOT.

Now Hear This

A correspondent from Kidderminster sent me an anthropological curio. Enclosing the specimen, he wondered if I had ever seen such a thing before, and admitted he passed it to me out of sensations of ungovernable rage. 'Indeed,' he wrote, 'in quieter moments I am appalled at the strength and spontaneity of my reaction.' He went on to say that in making the object available to me he had no feelings of guilt that perhaps he was breaching any unwritten law of politeness or confidentiality, since the writer evidently wished it to have the widest possible circulation.

It was a letter – or more properly, a circular – issued by a family, and crammed with information about themselves. But as my correspondent savagely notes (he receives a number of these duplicated news-sheets at Christmas time), 'the bulletins only include success stories. Whereas George's promotion and Caroline's A-levels are prominently featured, no mention is made of George losing his licence, or Caroline helping the police with their inquiries.' In short, it is an advertisement, and the example I was given went as follows:

Dear All – Sending this out in a bit of a rush since Eric and I are preparing for our trip to China. Shanghai, Peking and the Wall are all on the itinerary, and we're taking no chances, clothing-wise (our wonderful month in North Dakota – did I tell you? – taught us a thing or two about dressing for the occasion). How different from Madeira it's all going to seem – we had a gorgeous time there in the spring, and Deirdre's Spanish improved wonderfully. It was a much needed *break*, as Eric had been working non-stop since his appointment as sales director of the Loamshire Fodder Mills, and what with moving to a new house (ravishing views, but landscaping six acres can be a headache!) we felt ready for a little pampering.

Deirdre has turned into quite a little gymnast and has represented the school on the parallel bars, while Douglas's nose is still in his books – the headmaster feels he's scholarship material, and he's now grappling with the sort of physics that even Eric, with his B.Sc., finds testing. It's a wee bit isolated here, and Eric's chauffeur has been a pet, ferrying the children to and from school, in between carrying the lord and master to board meetings.

Jinny, the tortoiseshell, had six kittens, and Rug, our darling Old English Sheepdog, stands guard over them just like Nanna in *Peter Pan*. All in all, life's very hectic, but *very* satisfying, and we wish all our friends as happy and successful a year as we've just enjoyed ourselves . . .

'It's just possible,' adds my Kidderminster correspondent, 'that my distress arises from the fact that neither I nor any member of my family seems to have done anything remotely worth bringing to public attention in this way. But if we ever did do anything spectacular – perhaps going to Clacton for the day, or winning a toffee-apple at a fair – I hope we would resist this kind of indecent exposure.

'Oh, just before I finish,' he concludes, 'the only nice thing about the round robin I sent you is the information that Deirdre's Spanish improved wonderfully during their holiday in Madeira. Since they all speak Portuguese on that island, she must have worked like a beaver.'

How To Butter Rusks

MY friend from East Molesey had trouble with his ball-cock, and round about midnight after a second glass of brandy, decided to fix it. At three in the morning he was straddling the beams in the loft with the ball-cock under his arm, and all the water in the pipes had somehow turned into steam coming down his nose. By four-thirty am he had bled the system three times, got the hot water to work but not the cold, and was making little whimpering noises.

The experience must have turned his brain, for later in the day when I presented him with a newly-minted copy of *The Household Encyclopedia – 4000 Things You Really Ought To Know* he said thank you, placed it carefully on the floor and started to jump up and down on it. The four thousand and *oneth* thing you really ought to know is if you have been drinking brandy avoid all contact with ball-cocks as the mixture is inflammable.

As for a book that *is* called 4000 *Things You Really Ought To Know*, the title does tend to make you argumentative, and on reading that before clearing snow I should spray the shovel with furniture polish, and that I could always renovate soft toys by rubbing cornflour into them, I became seriously doubtful that I needed to know this. Later, when I read that you can clear the air of a room where people are smoking by distributing small containers of vinegar, I thought it was a good way of clearing the room of people at the same time, though an easier method would be to put your hat on sideways and pretend to be Napoleon.

Much of the text sounds like instructions for doing conjuring-tricks, and when you get advice on how to butter rusks without breaking them – 'stack them in a pile, butter the top one and put it at the bottom of the pile. Repeat until they are all buttered – they will not break' – you expect the entry to conclude, 'I have been performing this trick successfully in church halls all round the country for many years.'

Sometimes the information is seasoned with a delightful ambiguity, as in 'your spectacle frames will not get stained round the ears when you dye your hair if you wrap these parts with foil'. This evokes a vision of people preparing to dye their hair by carefully wrapping their ears in foil and donning their spectacles. And the advice often rests on wildly unquestioned assumptions, as in the entry which starts 'When re-covering a deckchair –' or 'When stuffing a cushion –', as though such activities were seasonal rituals that were never overlooked, and men on Spring evenings tapped out their pipes, saying 'Well, mother, deck-chair time again, I suppose – see you get plenty of sage-and-onion into those cushions.'

You also begin to study the advice with a very beady eye, as though looking for logical errors in Heidegger. For instance 'Always start washing a wall at the bottom. If you start at the top, water will run down on to the dirty area, leaving streaks that are very difficult to wash away.' BUT – if you start at the bottom won't streaks run down on to the *clean* area once you get to the bit above it? And won't they be (a) as difficult to remove and (b) won't this entail cleaning CLEAN areas more than once? To find the number of times the clean band at the bottom of the wall will need to be *re* -cleaned, count the number of bands you wash before reaching the top of the wall, and multiply. Alternatively, leave the wall dirty.

And then some of the entries are very eliptical. 'To find out the exact amount of wrapping paper you need to cut for your gift, first go round the present with string.' But what if the present is a-symmetrical, say an ear-trumpet for an aged aunt? How many times, and from how many angles, will you need to go round it with string? And where do you find the string?

You can clean a settee by rubbing warm bran over it, and there is a useful footnote – 'For how to warm branch, see page 319'. Reading a book like this you get a curious picture of a country filled with people brushing their shiny suits with black coffee, cramming their dusty sea-shells into the dishwasher, freshening their hands with shaving foam, and cleaning delicate oriental rugs by turning them upside down on clean snow and trampling on them. Compulsive mania is endemic to all such manuals, and this one seems to suffer from a particularly virulent strain. 'Half bury an old suitcase in the garden,' it feverishly insists, 'and place your seed-trays inside. When bad weather and frost are predicted, you simply close the lid.' Always remembering not to climb in yourself.

Sleep Doth Murder Macbeth

FALLING asleep in public is somehow shocking. I don't so much mean the way in which you fall asleep in a railway train and wake up dribbling and then try to assume a preternaturally intelligent expression, as though you'd been brooding on an alternative to the higher calculus; nor even the way you fall asleep at concerts, and try to turn the tell-tale jerk of the chin into a sort of natural, even masterful, twitch symptomatic of the true connoisseur. I'm thinking of those times when to fall asleep looks like an unforgivable comment on everyone else.

I was discussing this with the author Leslie Thomas, and he said he'd been at a dinner party the night before and the man opposite had gone to sleep actually at the table, halfway through the meal. What troubled Thomas was the fact that the man had only one arm, and Thomas couldn't get it out of his head that the arm had been eaten by the lady next to him, and the man hadn't noticed because he'd been asleep.

At the Greenwich Theatre once, I was more slept against than sleeping. The lady on my left dropped off the instant the play (*Oedipus at Colonus*) began, and just as instantly dropped her head on my shoulder. Since she was a perfect stranger, politeness enjoined that I should not disturb her, but this was achieved at some cost, since we were sitting in the front row, it was an apron stage, and all the actors were going round thumping the stage with bits of stick, and it seemed to me thumping ever harder as they tried unsuccessfully to get what they obviously supposed was my wife to wake up. Miss Siobhan McKenna in particular, who was playing Jocasta, approached the very lip of the apron, eyes blazing with fury, and roared 'Ho, *Thebes*' in a voice like thunder, but it was no good. The lady woke up refreshed at the interval and simply said to me, with real pleasure, 'That was lovely.' Later, Paul Eddington, who had been in the audience and awake, said he was surprised 'Ho, Thebes' hadn't done the trick, because Ellen Terry had once been slumbering peacefully at a performance of the same play, and when Jocasta shouted 'Ho, Thebes' Ellen Terry woke with a start and cried in piercing tones, 'Edie, quick – there's someone in the house.'

But nobody uses sleep as a weapon to more deadly effect than my friend Philip Purser, the novelist. On being forced by some friends to view their home movies, Purser not only drowsed as soon as the lights went down, but the sofa on which he was sitting being a low one, he rolled quietly off it, and when the lights were switched on again he was discovered in the foetal position on the hearthrug, fast asleep. But Purser's greatest coup, unequalled in every way, but above all in his choice of victim, was to fall asleep when interviewing Noel Coward. Coward pretended he thought he'd fainted, but only because he couldn't bring himself to face the truth. People said Coward's legendary poise received a blow on that occasion from which it never completely recovered.

Junk Songs

THE gormless strains of 'Roll Out the Barrel' coming from the open window of the car next to me made me feel I was sitting the wrong side of an extractor-fan, and I thought if we could actually win a war while breathing the stale air of dreadful songs like that, we were indeed a nation inspired.

I was only ten in 1938 but I felt in my bones war was on the way as soon as I heard Bud Flanagan singing the one about the 'Umbrella Man'. There was something so wheedling in the way he put it over I knew there was castor-oil in it somewhere. And when I heard another comedian sign off with 'Blue Skies Around the Corner, Everything's Going to be Right', I crawled straight under the dining-room table and waited for the first bombs.

Intimations of doom echoed from the nation's Philcos: the doleful cadences of 'The White Cliffs of Dover' and 'Bless 'Em All', the pinchbeck bravado of 'We'll Hang Out the washing on the Siegfried Line', the strange wooden jerkiness of 'Run, Rabbit, Run, Rabbit, Run, Run, Run', like fingers drumming in expectation of the worst – how did we survive these junk songs? That morose anthem, 'We'll Meet Again', sounded like a doctor at the bedside of a patient telling him spontaneous cures were not unknown, even in hopeless cases: I always imagined it being sung by John the Baptist's head, the eyes rolled well back.

What might account for the fundamental glumness of these ditties is the way it wasn't just soldiers who were going to be killed in this war, it was everyone. Where the first time round a junk song writer could feel jaunty enough to tell soldiers to 'Pack Up Your Troubles in Your Old Kit Bag and Smile, Smile, Smile', this could have had something to do with his feeling that he wasn't himself going to Die, Die, Die. But now that lyric-writers had as good a chance of a bomb dropping on them as anyone else, their sense of the possibility may have seeped into their compositions like rising-damp.

But it's funny that the songs were ghastly, when other parts of the propaganda business actually displayed wit and humour: I'm thinking of those Ministry of Information films, with the fat man doing all the sneezing, or the Fougasse cartoons warning against careless talk, with Hitler peeping out of the bus queue or sitting next to you in Lyons. And the man who might have been most unpopular of all, the Minister of Food, was turned into an eccentric old buffer out of a fairytale who tended to cry if people left anything on their plates.

I suppose these days the closest thing to the lousy junk songs of wartime would be the spiritless chanting at football matches: 'You'll never walk alone', 'We are the greatest', those mournful invocations to victory that sound like predictions of defeat. I never hear them but I wonder how we won.

Preserving Monday For the Nation

MAN wrote to *The Times* saying he wanted to abolish Monday. It had never been popular, he said, and it would be a great improvement if we had sixty-one six-day weeks instead of fifty-two of the seven-day sort. You could chop each week in half, three days for work, three for the weekend.

Apart from the unbearable prospect of an extended weekend – is the man a sadist? – how can days which have been used to identify the passage of one lot of twenty-four hours suddenly be given the job of naming a different stretch of twenty-four hours? How impossible for Thursday to take on the vibrations of Friday.

Friday (and think of it as you thought of it in your schooldays, when your view of the days was the clearest it would ever be) Friday was crackling with possibility – FRY-day, it positively sizzled in the frying pan of expectation, because the *next* day you got parole. Now Thursday was all right, I don't say Thursday was other than amiable; after all, the faint scent of freedom had begun to drift in through the open windows. But nobody could ask Thursday to be Friday, any more than you would think of asking Little John to be Robin Hood.

And before I get round to making a case for Monday, there's this

to be thought about: as an addition to the weekend, is the new Friday
treated as another Saturday or another Sunday? It might still be called
Friday, but it can't go on *being* Friday, since it would have become an
integral part of what Friday used to exist to prepare you for.

I can't see anyone voting for it to be a second Sunday, because if
you turn life off at the mains twice in the week you may never get it
turned on again. So Friday becomes a duplicate of Saturday, which means
an extra day's uncertainty about whether the parking-meters finish at
one o'clock or go on till six-thirty, another day in which to be sure
that if you suddenly want to go to the theatre all the tickets will be
sold, and an extra opportunity to turn up at the butcher's at four o'clock
in the afternoon to find them already swabbing down the slabs.

And in passing, all this stuff about an extended weekend is based on
a sort of ukase that we've all got to get used to more leisure. Leisure
isn't something anyone wants, except in due proportion, and 'preparing
for leisure' sounds like a euphemism for dying; you only hear the horta-
tory note when someone's trying to sell you something unpleasant, if
leisure were nice, people would go round telling you to stop doing it.

And the leisure myth is itself founded on the erroneous assumption
that the world contains a fixed amount of work which electronic chips
mop up more and more of. In fact, there is an unlimited supply of *undiscovered* work which you find when the chips force you over the border
into territory you couldn't imagine existing before (note how men
covered in woad in the forest sauvage said the wheel was the end of
full employment, only to find they had to do something called building
roads, a dimension hitherto unknowable).

But let's hear it for Monday, don't let Monday go by default, we need
the day and I'll tell you why. Monday is the day that requires all of
us to, as it were, jump about twelve feet into the air from a standing
start. To go from the inertia of Sunday to the fully-engaged necessities
of Monday takes such enormous energy that there is this to be said for
the day: you are so busy snorting through your gumshield with the
effort of getting the fly-wheel of Monday to turn over, that you don't
notice its awfulness.

This means that on Tuesday you can sit back and let the fly-wheel
which is now on the move take you forward. But by Wednesday the
true state of affairs has to be faced. Wednesday is the most spiteful day
of the week: too far away from the last day of liberation for it to be
remembered, too far from the next for it to be looked forward to, Wednesday was the day (you'll remember) when even the mild-mannered chaps
who hadn't quite got the hang of the detention system handed out a

full two hours for the least infringement, and the beaters and the caners prowled the corridors smelling blood. Wednesday brings the worst out in everybody, Wednesday is the day the pools coupon which is to make you a millionaire slips down behind the radiator, and Wednesday was the day Grendel nipped into Heorot and tore off the arms of the warriors.

No consolation on Wednesday. Do you remember that none of your favourite comics were published on a Wednesday? And little wonder Wednesday is early-closing; the shop-keepers at once trying to cut down by half on the bad luck which is endemic to the day, and at the same time inflicting the ultimate inconvenience on all those who turn up at showrooms hoping to collect their renovated vacuum-cleaners.

Thursday, you start noticing how nice people are: they brought the good news from Aix to Ghent on a Thursday, new bikes were always delivered on Thursday, and if by chance no homework was set, that was Thursday too. Friday always proved that anticipation is the better part of pleasure, because the sunshine and blue sky you planned in your head on Friday for Saturday was always belied when Saturday dawned raining; but while Friday lasted, the possibility of Saturday was perfect and intact, nothing could be ruined on Friday, because it had yet to happen. If there is an eternity, it will be an eternal Friday, a day of eternal anticipation.

So hands off the seven-day week. If it was good enough for God, it should be good enough for the rest of us.

Auditioning With Mr Coward

THE theatre smelt of old fag-ends at that time in the morning, but there was a whiff of something else in the air, blood perhaps, something gladiatorial. A solitary musician filed into the pit, 'Good morning.' The potted palms at the side of the stage looked threatening. Early arrivals limbered up. A young man in red knee-breeches and calves wandered on to the stage and might have been going to go seventy rounds with the Suffolk Bantam, except that he went la, la, la, and practised his steps.

'Keep them out of the wings because it terrifies the others, they're terrified of having to sing if they're dancers,' said a man in a green shorty raincoat who had appeared in the auditorium speaking to a sombre individual who had manifested himself in the prompt corner. 'Maaarvellous, maaarvellous,' said the man in the green raincoat, pronouncing the word as actors do. All the red opera glasses in the empty seats looked malicious, as if they didn't care who they were used to stare at.

A grey-haired lady or two came in, carrying cardigans, then a man in a camel-hair coat, square specs. 'Listen, dear, I've completely lost the list.' Another man said to another man, 'I think you'd better be Joan.' (Joan had left.) 'I'll be Joan,' 'You be Joan.' 'I'd better be Joan and take the notes.'

The Master came in whistling, wearing a blue coat with a fur collar. He met a grey-haired lady and put his hands delicately together and sang, 'K-K-K-Katie, K-K-K-Katie.' He sat down behind a drawing-board that had been balanced across the stall seats in front of him and the house lights dimmed. A nice girl walked on to the stage and said, 'Do you want me to sing?' 'Yes, dear,' said Coward. 'What shall I sing?' 'Whatever you feel comfortable with, dear.' So she sang.

When she finished. Coward said, 'How are your high kicks?' 'Fine.' 'Let's see some of them, dear.' She really was very good. 'That's very good, Indeed, yes. Come and see my choreographer in a month's time. I'm sure he'll like you. Thank you so much for coming.' The pleasure in the girl's face would have moved a stone.

The man in red knee-breeches came on and sang about the simple life, and in the absence of the Suffolk Bantam went a few rounds on his own. 'Thank you so much.' A man in khaki trousers, very square, possibly on leave from an agricultural college, sang in a slow inoffensive baritone suitable for tea-time. Then a small green bandy boy tipped a stave. Coward didn't interrupt him. He interrupted nobody. His courtesy was iron-clad.

Two men sang the same song, danced the same dance, to the same tape-recorder, one after the other. A girl danced in black tights with seams down the front. One man with a face like a chapel-window and confident ears sang 'The Floral Dance'. A girl, very vivid and wearing the smart equivalent of a gym-slip, kicked her shoes off and had holes over each large toe.

The sombre individual who had been instructed to keep the wings clear announced each gladiator in a gloomy voice reminiscent of the Veneering's butler (you remember him, the Analytical Chemist, who offered people Chablis with the air of saying 'You wouldn't, if you knew what it was made of').

An older lady came on to be 'seen'. She looked like my mother. How I would have hated it if my mother had come on to be 'seen'. Another mature lady came on. Recognition! 'It isn't, it can't be,' said Coward. 'It is, dear, in the flesh,' said the lady. 'Am I to sing?' 'Well, I'm broad-minded, dear.' 'Ha, ha, ha.' 'I don't *think* there is anything for you in this one dear.' 'Not even an old walk-on, dear?' 'I won't promise darling, but if there is I'll let you know like *anything*.' It was unbearably sad.

More songs, more dancing. You could tell the good ones, they annihi-lated the space around them. Among the others a short young man, slow in the legs, a man in black who laid the song he sang, like a foundation-stone. A schoolboy three feet high roared a song about girls in a voice like Jehovah. Another, two foot six, did the same. The Analytical stepped out and said, 'That's all, sir.' 'The nicest words I've ever heard,' said Coward. 'It turns you a bit brown at the edges. Still, we didn't get "Phil the Fluter's Ball".'

The gladiators, the corpses, went home by bus, and the house lights came up.

High Life

I HAD to hire a suit of tails for the Lord Mayor's Midsummer Banquet. Tails are OK for tall thin snooty people, but all they do for the rest of us is exaggerate our deficiencies. Putting on a suit of tails, I feel that I am already wearing a surgical boot which I am carefully whitewashing so that it will show up better. By the time the man who was kitting me out had said, 'Don't pay any attention to the label, sir,' and I'd looked at the tab inside the collar and saw that it read 'Portly', I realized the evening was already ruined. On the actual night I was so disappointed with the figure I cut in the bathroom mirror – I looked like an ill-conditioned bouncer – I started to shout with rage, and I worked up such a lather that all the starch ran out of the collar of the shirt before we left the house. I sailed steaming into the Mansion House, and somehow I hadn't done up those little tabs on the bottom of the shirt and the white waistcoat that keep the whole lot anchored to the trousers, so it was all riding up, and I was shaking hands with the Lord Mayor with one hand while holding the other elegantly across my middle as though us swells always walked around like that.

I was so angry I was ready to explode, and it's funny when you're disappointed with yourself you somehow contrive your own downfall, which is literally what I did. As I stormed off to collar a couple of glasses of champagne, teeth chattering with self-hatred, I managed to get my foot into one of those big copper fish-kettles they put on the floor as ashtrays, and I thundered to the floor. My wife, who was talking to some people, said she saw my big maddened red face and then suddenly it disappeared and she heard this terrible rumble as I hit the parquet, and a waiter came over, I thought to give me a hand, but as I looked up at him from the floor through the starred lenses of my broken glasses, he said, 'Would you be kind enough to give me your autograph for my small daughter?'

Eggs

THERE are three great topics of conversation, one is the weather, one is class and the third is eggs. You can't open your mouth on any of these subjects without falling into a bottomless lake of feeling, and the minute you make a point about any one of them (as for instance that an egg is unacceptable to a man at any meal other than breakfast) the atmosphere is suddenly bursting with affect, and nobody is neutral.

I wish I could rely on an egg being fried properly. I've had many properly fried eggs but have never once felt that a properly fried egg was what I was certain of getting. I do not refer to eggs so improperly fried that they cannot be said to have been fried at all, eggs whose suspiciously glistening yolks float in a transparent sea of albumen (the sort you get in France if you are unwise enough to order *oeufs sur le plat*); I mean the far more sinister version, the egg which arrives *disguised* as fried, the white apparently solid but seen by the sad experienced eye to be a mere skin beneath which fathoms of uncooked mucilage still quake. It is an irony that you are more likely to be presented with this when you have tried to insure against it by asking for the egg fried 'over': early-morning cooks in hotels (that is, the youngest waiter at dinner the night before) take the skinning-over of the top of the egg to be a sign that it is cooked, and what you get is raw egg swathed in a fried-egg bandage.

There is only one way to fry eggs: baste them. Not with a knife because the fat will go over your shoes (especially if they are suede), what you must use is a tea-spoon. You will have to do this for yourself, since no one who is frying an egg for you can ever be bothered to take the trouble.

Of course, the hazards increase when the egg is boiled, since you can't look inside and see if it's done. Once upon a time there was a category of polite novel written by calm, undemanding women, and stocked by Boots when it was also a Lending Library. The books featured middle-class people about their smiling domestic affairs, and breakfast was a meal much frequented. For some reason, one of the authors (in those days they were called authoresses) in making her inventory of the breakfast-table (spotless napery, steaming coffee, crisp rolls, fresh butter – the adjectives were unchanging) included a three-and-a-half minute egg, and all the other practitioners began to include it too.

Of course, it was an aberration, but by repetition rose from being a mere item from the property-box of light fiction to the status of myth. Ever since, people have been eating uncooked three-and-a-half-minute boiled eggs, and the fact that they are doing it for no better reason than that's what the people in Mazo de la Roche told the maid they'd like, has been long forgotten.

Reform it altogether, and put the egg in while the water is cool. Start your stopwatch (indispensable to the operation, since the buzzer on the cooker works to far cruder tolerances) as the bubbles begin to rise, and remove the egg after four minutes and twelve seconds. The white will be solid, the centre of the yolk will be liquid and its outer layer will have begun to congeal. Sometimes the totality will be a little softer, sometimes a little harder, according to the age of the egg. But the *second* boiled egg of the same batch can have its perfection guaranteed.

This is an immense subject. For the millionth time I say to a member of my family How on earth can you eat a boiled egg without salt, and for the millionth time they say Couldn't possibly have salt – too exciting. And there is the mystery of why women will eat eggs for lunch and men won't. Is this because eggs are the one food you can't drink a glass of wine with (the title of Elizabeth David's cookery book *An Omelette and a Glass of Wine* is surely an error)? And why are big-endians prose-lytes, and little-endians not? If I ever were to volunteer the little-endian case, I should point out that it seems more satisfying to start in a small way and dig your way into a larger broader seam. But I do not seek converts.

We are somewhat in the realm of the irrational with eggs. Taking them back from the country is a ritual act, as though by doing it you incorporated the fields and the farmyards. And though by any scientific test the colour of the shell does not modify the flavour, it is certain that an egg that is your favourite shade of brown tastes better. Nor has anyone ever explained the greed that overcomes even the purest in the presence of egg sandwiches. Men who had dined on roast sucking pig, walking into a room which featured a plate of egg sandwiches, would eat the lot.

Lower Pleasures

WHEN the last election was being fought, the coverage was so comprehensive it seemed to destroy everything else, and I found I was terribly grateful for small instances of individuality. My friend Bridges wrote and told me that the two little girls next door were having a bath with a visiting small boy. As the various mothers were soaping and lathering the trio, one of the little girls, contemplating what was evidently her first sight of the male anatomy, said in a small appalled voice to the other, 'It's a good job it doesn't grow on his face.' When I read this from Bridges, I recognized with relief that we aren't just voters after all.

P.W.J. Oldroyd of Acton, for no better reason perhaps than that he, too, wanted to remind himself of the peculiarity rather than the predictability of the way we all are, drew my attention to a notice in a local Bournemouth park that announces 'NO CARPET BEATING BEFORE 6 A.M.' I rejoice. Not that I believe getting up early to beat carpets in public stunts your growth, but the prohibition hints at something more magical than any election promise or the opinions of three experts weighed for balance by a visiting apothecary.

He also told me that, in Bournemouth again, cast-iron plaques inscribed 'UPPER PLEASURE GARDENS' have had the word 'Pleasure' deleted, a natural consequence, Oldroyd believes, of the earlier decision to erase the word 'Pleasure' from the other plaques which read 'LOWER PLEASURE GARDENS.' You probably remember yourselves how the thunder of feet disturbed your childhood slumbers, as *le tout Bournemouth* raced at nightfall to the gardens where the lower pleasures were to be had, and how the noise didn't compare with the thin tread of the righteous, plodding to the Upper Pleasure Gardens in the early dawn, all carrying their carpets to the ritual beating, prompt at six.

The rather awful thing about the election coverage was the way it actually did a lot of covering: it was drawn up like a winding-sheet over the whole world. The news I got from Bridges and Oldroyd poked up through it like primroses.

The Spirit of Constipation

DELIGHTED to learn that the Ideal Home Exhibition had been re-consecrated as the Cathedral of St Andy Warhol, patron saint of consumers, and there in a side chapel I lit a candle of monosodium glutamate to commemorate the man who went shopping twice a day and never unpacked his purchases. The spirit of constipation, of which Andy was the perfected incarnation, slowly exerted its old magic, and in less than five minutes I felt I had swallowed several fitted kitchens, a family-sized carton of self-adhesive wallpaper, a generous portion of double-glazing, and a side order of wardrobes.

Nonetheless, with a savagery I usually reserve for switching off the signature tune of *The Archers*, I ate a Jersey ice-cream, followed it strangely with a slice of pizza, half a pint of stout, and finished with an angry doughnut that spread sugar over my chops. I don't pretend fully to understand my impulses, but I seemed to be responding to a massed choir of three-piece suites singing a hallelujah chorus in praise of getting, spending, having and consuming.

A man darted out of a booth and said 'You probably live in a bungalow', then cried, 'People only have to *breathe* to cause black spots on the walls of bedrooms!' I heard myself saying 'There's no alternative.' He smiled, as one whose work has been made easy – 'You mean – to black spots?' 'No,' I said, as it was foretold I would, 'to breathing.' How effortlessly he saw me off by forcing the explanation. When he asked if I had ever considered insulating my walls, in a wild despairing way I knew what was coming but still warbled 'Never!', and of course he went on 'May I ask why?'

For the same reason, I cried, that I had never thought of barbecueing a goat, but he smiled again. I was living on my capital, and he knew it. 'Would it surprise you to learn that from next April it's *mandatory* to insulate your walls?' It wasn't even going to be a draw. 'We're moving to Dewsbury,' I said, 'so we shan't bother', and turning on my heel, twiddled my tie like Oliver Hardy when he's been rumbled yet again.

Fancy footwork won't dent the evangelical solemnity, the wonderful

presumption, with which the grafter saddles you with the obligation.
'Who likes chips? Anyone got a freezer? Ever been into a hamburger
joint?' Whether its the chap with the miracle pastry-cutter or the device
which turns a cucumber into a Mobius strip, he forges the spurious
bond. 'For all your kitchen preparations, your vegetables, your omelettes,
your pot roasts.' Ah, the colonizing power of the possessive – to resist
it, how cold the eye must be, how unswerving the infidel. 'Now,' said
a stallholder, busy shaving with a carving knife, 'you do believe me when
I say this knife has not been specially sharpened –' 'No I don't,' said
a woman flatly, and he seemed to vanish in a puff of smoke.

Under the soaring roof-beam, brand names hung, the heraldic banners
of Round Tables that met every Thursday. An electronic pianola supplied
a selection from the Muzak Hymnal, its keys moving under the pressure
of invisible fingers created by the computer. Small Eiffel Towers left
over from Christmases when the world was young were still having gyro-
scopes balanced on them; two-pronged twist-and-wriggle corkscrews
waited to be bought so they could be abandoned in obscure unused
drawers. But children's faces registered disappointment: it was almost
like a fair, but when you looked again it was only stuff borrowed from
shop-windows. Red-nosed foreigners in electric-blue suits urged those
who passed by to enter their booths and taste their sweet white wine,
prior to signing forms which committed them to the purchase of hogs-
heads.

At the oil-painting stand snow-clad landscapes, woodland scenes with
ponds, heaving seascapes, were slightly flushed, as though the physical
effort of doing pictures quickly had transferred its symptoms from the
artist to the canvas. Not one man, but two, explained the stallholder.
One wouldn't touch anything but trees and hills, the other stuck to marine
subjects. How was it done? 'They paint six canvases simultaneously,'
said the stallholder, 'like chess champions playing six games all at once.
In the time you or I might have written a two-page letter of thanks,
they've painted a picture.' I said I'd been wondering if they sprayed it
on. 'No, no,' said the stallholder, 'it wouldn't be possible.'

I bought a ticket for an instant lottery and felt gloomy when I won;
cashed the prize in for further tickets, and was more at peace when they
turned out to be losers. Blissful oldsters, surrounded by millions of arm-
chairs they didn't mind not being allowed to sit in, stretched out on
the concrete floor in a trance of wellbeing, having come through their
passive obedience heats ; others, still hoping to qualify, were throwing
their loose change into the Warhol Memorial Pool.

The muezzin sounded. 'All those who have not yet purchased a copy of the catalogue are advised to do so *now*.' I had a vision of the true faith on my way out: passing through the galleries of fast food, a phantom emptiness assailed me – curry, tacos, spring rolls, hamburgers, which would I have? And lo, I could not decide, for to pick one was to forego the rest. The very perfection of greed! The Bags of St Andy would have remained unpacked to eternity, for to unpack is to choose, and to choose is to relinquish.

When I left, the senna pods of apostasy were stirring.

Good Morning

I WALKED into the dentist's waiting-room and saw there was only one other chap there, so – question – do I say good morning? Easier to say than not to say, because once the acknowledgement's made you can both forget about each other. So OK – 'Good morning.' There was a sort of rumbling noise from the other chap, as of a drawbridge rusty with disuse being reluctantly let down, and he said, 'Good morning,' only he stretched the words out resentfully, as though they were someone's collected works I'd forced him to read, as though I'd really given him an awful lot of trouble, as though I'd presumed on the fact of us both being in the same room to invite him to a Tupperware party.

So I thought right, that'll teach me. And the next week I had to go again, but this time I was the first in the waiting-room, and another chap came in, about eight feel tall and wearing an anorak that curiously seemed to come down to his ankles, and I thought, Right, mate, *you* can say good morning to *me*. But he didn't. He scrabbled about among the mags on the table, and then did the unforgivable thing. There were lots of comfortable chairs and perches in the room and I'd sat modestly on a small settle at one end, and behold, instead of choosing one of the other seats, this geezer picked up his copy of *Horse and Hound* and without saying a word sat plump next to me on the same sofa, crowding me over to one side. One thing to give the time of day (it sets the limit of the relationship) but to sit next to a chap when you might have sat anywhere else is either to pretend he isn't there at all, or to assume an intimacy that doesn't exist. I was thinking of wrong-footing him by asking whether the vet only doctored cats on a Friday or (and then I was going to fumble in my pocket) whether it was all right to bring in a stoat, when the nurse called him out, possibly to have his anorak removed under anaesthetic.

I don't like stand-offishness, but on the other hand there are women of sixty-five touring the West Country cathedrals, travelling always in pairs and driving Triumph Sodomite motorcars, who insist on saying good morning to everyone at breakfast-time in hotels: one total stranger in a twin-set once asked me how I'd slept. Good morning is often a preliminary to a life-story, and I sometimes think that what makes the idea of a cruise so hideous is that it is good morning elevated into a way of life.

Chestnuts

A FRIEND of a friend of mine is a bishop, and when he took over from the outgoing bishop he thought the decent thing to do would be to invite the old chap back to dinner, especially since the way they arrange these things in the Church of England you not only get the superannuated bishop's job, you get his palace as well. So the old bishop returned to what had been his house, and he and his wife were entertained by his successor. They went into dinner and after the meal had ended, and the new bishop was thinking things had gone off very well, the old bishop turned to his wife and said, 'You know, my dear, we really are going to have to dismiss that cook.'

This sort of chestnut comes like a folksong from deep within the collective unconscious. It creates such a vivid picture that you can hardly believe you weren't present when it happened. But it didn't happen at all, it is part of an endless dream that we are all jointly dreaming. The dream has many mansions, in one of which there is a famous actor who (you remember) was very fond of drink, and came reeling on in *Richard III*, declaiming:

> Now is the wister of our dincontest
> Made glorious Yorkshire by the summer sun
> And all the cloused that loused upon our housed –

The audience starts to mutter, and a voice shouts 'You're drunk,' whereat the Duke of Gloucester (for it is he) sways down to the footlights and cries, 'You're right – but just wait till you see the Duke of Buckingham.'

Perhaps it was *The Last of Mrs Cheyney* in which that great lady of the theatre Jean Forbes Robertson had some difficulty finding the right entrance, and the backcloth could be seen ballooning as she made her way uncertainly across, trying to fight her way through it on to the stage. At last she emerged, smiling rather glazedly. The other actors who had been waiting for her were sitting in frozen silence round a dining-room table, centre. Miss Forbes Robertson teetered up to them and with the same smile still on her face inquired, 'Why the fuck doesn't someone say something?' Stung, one of the other actors cried, 'Because it's your line, dear.' The curtain was rung down, and the manager appeared in front of it to explain that Miss Forbes Robertson was suffering from fish-poisoning.

This seems to have something in common with the occasion when Lady Ottoline Morrell (or Lady Sybil Colefax or Nancy Cunard, it scarcely matters which) saw in the course of one of her grand dinner-parties that the butler was drunk. Hastily, she scribbled a note and passed it to him. Unfolding it, he read the words, 'Your are in a disgusting condition. Leave the room,' and swaying slightly he re-folded the paper and placed it in front of Sir John Simon.

These are poems, small and bright. As when an affectionate wife, seeing her husband's legs poking out from beneath the kitchen sink he appeared to be mending, bent down and tickled him privily. At which he jumped up, knocked himself unconscious against the sink and it turned out to be the plumber. When the ambulance men were called to carry him out on a stretcher, they were manoeuvring it down the stairs when someone explained how the accident had happened, and they laughed so heartily they let go of the handles and the plumber crashed down the stairs and broke his leg.

I wonder if it was the same lady who put a batch of scones in the oven, then went upstairs to her bath. Dipping her toe in the water, she decided it would be better if she turned the oven off, tripped downstairs, *toute nue*, and went back into the kitchen. Hearing footsteps outside, she realized this must be the baker, a friendly soul whose habit was to walk straight in and put the bread on the table. Quick as a flash, she nipped into the broom-cupboard and closed the door. The footsteps walked in and across the kitchen floor, and the owner of the feet threw open the broom-cupboard door. It was the man to read the electricity meter: as he stared at the lady in the cupboard with no clothes on, she said – very reasonably, when you come to think about it – 'I was expecting the baker.'

These tales have a curious virtue. When you think about them days afterwards in a quiet moment, you burst out laughing.

Genuine Old Wimbledon Cucumber

MELTON Mowbray pies sound different from any other sort of pie, but because I know they aren't I haven't tried one for years – couldn't face the disappointment of that pink rubber stuff surrounded by vaseline and encased in cardboard. But I wouldn't mind a slice of the *words* 'Melton Mowbray pie'; momentarily they still have flavour.

Like Cumberland sausages. I never see the words, but just for a second I wonder where exactly in Cumberland the Cumberland sausagemakers pursue their centuries-old craft. This is a fleeting aberration, savagely corrected by the ensuing image, that of Cumberland Marketing Men dancing round Scafell Pike, clad in smocks. There is no such thing as a Melton Mowbray pie, a Cumberland sausage – no such recognizable entity – for they are products of the anonymous process which markets everything, from handmade Bedfordshire roller-skates to Old Mother Eczema's Damson Preserve. Only the names are individual, stolen from signposts and smuggled onto labels by the Resurrection Men.

Those of us old enough to remember should have been innoculated against the fraudulent lure of the regional name by the Vienna Steak, a wartime rissole which lingered on into the early Fifties. This pleistocine-burger was so entirely anonymous in substance that some restaurants hadn't the face to bill it as from Vienna, and it was downgraded to

Cambridge Steak. Anyone still responsive to the fairy gold of local nomenclature after a course of Vienna Steaks really shouldn't expect sympathy, especially not if they'd been given a booster of Hungarian Goulash.

This was a non-specific stew served under chandeliers and accompanied by a band, and though it appeared in the immediate post-war days it's still chalked up on blackboards in pubs. Actual Hungarians may know what proportion of paprika to cowheel you need to make the real thing, but the only common factor in the various English versions will be the angry shade of orange they never miss. I can't see the colour without thinking of light-tan shoe-polish, and sometimes I look at light-tan shoe-polish and wonder if it tastes of Hungarian goulash: is light-tan shoe-polish the condensed form you smear on your hard tack when you go on expeditions to the North Pole?

And who does not feel foolishly rhetorical when asking in the baker's for French bread? *French*, as though you'd travelled in far places. They produce the stuff from the same steam ovens they use for the ordinary English flab, but the amateur sophistication inherent in the regional adjective surfaces in the waiter's lofty enquiry, 'French bread, sah?'

Grade One disappointment is stored up for all who set out to find the locally-named product on its native heath. At Whitstable they looked vague when I asked for oysters and said 'Never heard of them, mate'. After canvassing eatery after eatery I had a faintly delirious feeling that Whitstable would have had Bath Olivers, Eccles cakes and Dorset Knobs, but you would have to go to Devonshire to find a Whitstable oyster, though you wouldn't be able to have a cream tea.

Roast Aylsbury duckling, roast Surrey capon – when I was a lad, Kettner's restaurant advertised such items as being 'served every day'. Now all you get is that professional hayseed on the telly telling you his Norfolk turkeys are born with lumps of butter stuck up their backsides. Counties are interchangeable in the strategy of marketing, though so far Middlesex has been shied away from. No one's tried to sell you a Middlesex pie or a Middlesex bap, and if there are old saws such as 'A Middlesex man'll do ye if he can' or 'A Middlesex parsty is a narsty parsty', I haven't heard them. You couldn't take a place in Middlesex and use it as brewers do when they advertise beer – a pint of Burton, yes, but you couldn't have a pint of Hounslow, could you? And so far we haven't had the heavy-metal version of 'The Way of a Middlesex Man wi' a Maid' or 'The Brentford and Hanwell Horn Dance'.

Such chimeras are no more fanciful than Lymeswold or Mr Kipling. And yet, once upon a time there must have been the individual, the singular thing, made by the particular hand in the particular place, or why would salesmen work so hard to reproduce the label? Of course, the original thing might not have been very good. Did Cumberland sausagemakers make sausages full of gristle, did Chelsea buns bear the imprint of black thumbs from the Chelsea milk-maids who kneaded the dough?

Pre-lapsarian Merrie England might not have been as merry as the pictures on the boxes in Waitrose's deep freeze. But in the olden days the article produced the name. Now the name produces the article.

Kidnapped

IN a town in the south of France I was lunching with a French professor who had written a bestseller, and these days in France he is rather a star and people tend to recognize him. We were there to do some filming with him, and the director and the professor and I were sitting at a table on the terrace of the restaurant, and some way away at another table there sat a French woman with a face like a hand-made boot. Suddenly, she recognized the Prof, sailed across and cried, 'Oh you must all come and have a drink at my house.'

We murmured our regrets, how nice it would have been, but alas, there just wouldn't be time. 'Quite so,' the lady said, 'it is arranged. My house for drinks.' We stepped up our demurrers: it would have been fun, but time pressed, we had to fettle the camera, take the cosies off the microphones. 'We are just round the corner,' she declared, 'it will not take five minutes.' Ah, alas no. 'My house,' she said. 'I'll lead the way.' I raised my voice very slightly and said No. At this point the lady's son-in-law (one of those fat French not-so-young men, who look like capons) smoothly interposed – 'What is half an hour?' 'Well,' I said, and I was still struggling to keep an agreeable smile on my mush, though my whole face was beginning to feel like as windscreen that was shortly going to have to be replaced, 'that does rather depend which half-hour it is, really.' The son-in-law replied, 'No, it doesn't.' 'Oh, yes, it does,' I said, nodding gravely, which is quite hard to do when your voice seems to have gone awfully high. '*Le monsieur est si obstiné*,' hissed the Medusa, and she meant me, not her son-in-law, who to my by no means unjaundiced eye was looking more and more like a piece of fennel that had gone cold in brown sauce.

Well (*bref*, as the Froggies say), the monstrous woman won: she suborned the Prof, and then our director, and of course I had to go with them. 'She only wants to show us a little Gallic courtesy,' our director muttered, his natural innocence not uncut with malice, it seemed to me, on this occasion. 'Oh no, she doesn't,' I shouted, 'she wants to show us her furniture!' And I was right. I think there were eighteen rooms in her house and she spared us none, pricing every object in each. 'Why don't you make her an offer for the lot?' I said to our director, grinding my teeth, and the ancient besom, whose ear for imagined slights was as acute as her manners were grotesque, cried 'Nothing reproduction here – all authentic!'

When she struck the manacles off and we were out in the street at last, I stood in the sunshine and the steam coming out of my head obscured a distant view of Mont Blanc. Back in England, I said to a friend, Living as you do in East Molesey, could you imagine dashing out into the street and entangling three perfect strangers in your butterfly net and forcing them to come in and admire your G-Plan? Funny you should say that, said my chum, I know some people who've just moved to East Molesey from Isleworth, and the last time I met them they said, 'We've got so many nice things in our house these days we don't invite people any more, it only makes them jealous.'

No Escape From Gormenghast

EVERYONE uses language without thinking, but on those odd occasions when you find yourself trying to visualize the instrument you're using you feel like someone hoping to include the camera in the picture it is taking. It can't be done, though you could always include it in another picture by simply using a second camera. But how do you get hold of a second language that would give you a picture of the one you are using? Since language is part of what it puts you in touch with, in what universe would you have to be, on what other dimension of thought would you have to be perched (as on some handy but uninvocable filing-cabinet, some inconceivable pair of step-ladders) to see the process whole?

Well, whereof we may not speak, thereof we must be silent. Since the walls of language are themselves the limit of experience, we must live within the mystery and be content from time to time to be shown round the echoing mansions of the exotic prison into which we are born, our guide on the present occasion being the diligent editor of *The Oxford English Dictionary*. His conducted tour * of what is in essence limitless (a labyrinth running out to the edges of the universe, as inescapable as any in the fairytales of Borges) must necessarily be concerned with the more amenable of the fixtures and fittings, leaving the edifice itself, a sort of Gormenghast, to testify to its own strangeness by its mere existence.

But the candles in the sconces flicker. Is the substance of the structure we are to be ushered through what it seems? 'The general use of Speech, is to transfer our Mental Discourse, into Verbal ; or the Trayne of our Thoughts, into a Trayne of Words,' says Hobbes, quoted by Dr Burchfield. But where was the thought before it was transferred? Is thought available in any other form than words; aren't the words themselves the thought, as it thinks itself into existence? Our guide with some asperity calls us to attention – 'The origin of language is unknown,' he tells us, 'the faculty of speech precedes recorded history'; and he counts us

* *The English Language* by Robert Burchfield (Oxford University Press)

briskly through the turnstile as though, like the objects in the glass cases in the Natural History Museum at Kensington, the English language were a succession of moments that could be inspected.

Yet even as we walk out of the darkness of the Delivery Room, (the cloud of unknowing) and find ourselves inside the Main Hall, brightly lit in the daylight of Dr Burchfield's historian's common sense, still the ambiguities surrounding the unknown premises on which his exhibits find themselves on show continue to distract: as though the dimensions of the room were not quite fixed, as though the specimens, if once you took your eye off them, might move.

Everything is clearly labelled, succinctly named. We follow behind the author as he gives a special nod to the *futhorc* (splendidly stuffed) and leads us out into the *runes*, through the *eths* and the *thorns*, pausing momentarily for *The Great Vowel Shift*, then rejoining the main party as it moves through the Colonnades of the Dictionaries, and out through the distorting mirrors of Spelling and Pronunciation. Yet all the time, just beyond the range of your vision, there seem to be movements you don't quite catch; something elusive that you never swing round fast enough to spot, some ripple or spasm of the linguistic dimension which makes you wonder again about language being simply an arrangement for pointing things out, when, in being inseparable from what it indicates, it must at the same time be what it refers to.

It would be hard indeed to conceive of a brief tour of the English language that combined expedition with illumination in proportions more attractive than we find in Dr Burchfield's book. Its excellence, however, reminds us that the central mystery of language remains: not what it is, but that it is.

Henry the Third vs George the Fifth

WHEN George Bush was campaigning to be President of the United States he said he was a relative of Henry the Third. Distant, of course, but Henry the Third seemed to be someone he thought it was worth his while laying claim to. Perhaps Bush had said everything else about himself that was worth saying, and maybe one of his aides suggested he play the Henry the Third card. A moment's thought would have alerted everyone to the downside risk: at that time a lot of people were saying 'Who is George Bush?' and this gave the same people the chance of saying 'Who is Henry the Third?'

I know little about the kings of England but if there's one king I know less about than any other, it's Henry the Third. It may be the number – Third is only just in the frame, and if he was known to have invented the orrery or gone barefoot to Rome it would at least give one a toehold. The first Henry is distinguishable because he *was* the first and the second is actually remembered because of his carelessness in the matter of Thomas à Becket.

But I only start to feel easy among the Henries with Henry the Fifth, who was far more intimately related to Laurence Olivier than ever Henry the Third was to George Bush, and Henry the Sixth sticks in my mind because he was the one Henry who came in three parts. I go off the boil with Henry the Seventh, and start simmering again with Henry the Eight who was a murderous tyrant seems to get marks because he was once played by Charles Laughton.

I'm not surprised Bush fell to daydreaming about monarchs: as a candidate in a democratic election he was having to suck up to everybody, dancing attendance on people whose hands he shook, whereas monarchs never do anything but please themselves. Even the faintest sense that their convenience is not going to be met is unbearable to monarchs, as when a visiting plenipotentiary had an audience of Louis the Fourteenth. The ambassador arrived bang on time. 'I was within an ace of being *kept waiting*,' said Louis, sharply. So monarchs don't have to bother about presenting themselves: unlike ordinary mortals, they don't have to charm an audience. Bush may have been thinking wistfully of this as he delivered the obligatory pleasantries devised for him by his front men, envying Henry the Third for not having to be 'on' all the time. Well, Henry didn't have to be a crowd-pleaser, but as far as dullness goes, in a fair fight, weight for weight, I don't see him lasting the distance with George the Fifth.

George the Fifth has my money because of an unmatched ability to state the obvious without ever making any attempt to season it; he never behaved as though he was trying to beguile. The message he sent to the conductor of the Grenadier Guards who had been playing extracts from Richard Strauss's *Elektra* read simply, 'His Majesty does not know what the band has just played, but it must NEVER be played again.' And refusing to go to Holland, he cried, 'Amsterdam, Rotterdam and all the other dams! I'm damned if I'll do it.' Adding, 'Abroad is bloody.'

During the First World War, he took rationing very seriously. One of his guests was detained by a telephone call at breakfast time, and when he finally came into the dining-room there was nothing left to eat. So the man rang a bell and asked for a boiled egg. George the Fifth said, 'I see you are a slave to your own stomach and do not realize that this sort of gluttony could lose us the war.' His style was wonderfully leaden. When he was being shown round the Tate Gallery and he came on the Impressionists, he turned to his wife and said, 'Here's something to make you laugh, May.'

Even the fabrications which involve George the Fifth would never have been fathered on Henry the Third. Can you imagine a bottle of Scotch whisky made in Japan bearing a label which announced 'This whisky is produced from pure Scottish grapes, trodden by His Majesty King Henry the Third in the cellars of Buckingham Palace?' But substitute George the Fifth and the label assumes total credibility.

Only such a man could have sent a telegram congratulating Hardy on his seventieth birthday under the misapprehension that it was the Hardy who made his fishing-rods. This story and others will be found in Peter Vansittart's anthology called *Happy and Glorious*, a treat for all who, like George Bush, hanker after the absolute licence a monarch is given to be just as dull as nature intended. But though Vansittart quotes Robert Graves and Alan Hodge on the king's funeral, he makes no reference to the curious etiquette attendant on the king's actual dying.

Tucked away in someone's diary, and recently brought to light, was a report that the king's doctor speeded up his death to spare him the appalling solecism of having the news appear first in the *Evening Standard* rather than the *Times*! George the Fifth was ushered into eternity an hour or so early, via a syringeful of morphine and cocaine, in the interests of protocol and precedence, and to catch the morning editions. One rather hopes God wasn't put out by his distinguished guest arriving so much before time – 'No, no, not at all, let me get you a drink, I perfectly understand, where the devil's the woman with the harp, she'll give you a tune while I get back to the kitchen for a minute.'

Dying peacefully is one thing, but dying politely is a novel concept. I hear George the Fifth descanting on the trend to the Almighty with the sort of disapproval he reserved for the Prince of Wales's turn-ups.

No Sign of Tiptoes

THE racecourse was filling up with the usual crowd of elderly orphans and superannuated sheep-stealers. A police car threaded its way out of a street full of houses which looked as if they'd been put up for the purpose of being rained on. 'I think Tiptoes is doing time,' said the Superintendent. 'Aye, and Dark Solly,' said the Chief Inspector.

The car edged on to the course and the two policemen, together with a citizen who was furthering his education in their company, got out and leaned against the bonnet.

'But there's plenty left to work the spinning-jenny with the magnets under the board,' said the Superintendent. 'It must be as old as time, but the world's full of mugs.'

'Especially on a racecourse,' said the Chief Inspector, and added, explanatorily, 'The pointer always stops where the magnet is and the magnet's never where your money is –'

'So you never win,' said the Superintendent.

They both looked reposeful, as policemen always do.

'I have to admit,' said the Chief Inspector, 'that the mouse had me fooled. You know the stall – the one where you back the mouse to run through a certain hole. It was a long time before I tumbled that the holes with the long odds were always too small for the mouse to get through anyway.'

The Superintendent laughed. He wore a tweed suit and looked like the Bursar of an Oxford College. 'They'd do anything sooner than work,' he said. 'What about loaded darts? Filled with lead down one side so they throw crooked and you never stick the packet with the fiver in it.'

'Or the fellow with the balloons. He's got a balloon about six feet long floating over the top of the stall but when you try and blow up the one he's sold *you* it's about the size of your little finger.'

'Well, I'll tell you this,' said the Superintendent, 'there was a fellow selling deaf-aids for fifty pence at one course. Deaf lad comes up, buys one, walks away a bit shy then opens the packet. Inside there's a bit of string about five inches long with a knot in the end. Well he goes back but the fellow's gone. Later that afternoon he catches up with him. 'What about this then?" "What about what?" says the grafter. "This bit of string with the knot in. That's no deaf-aid." "It is," says the grafter. "You stick that knot in your ear and everyone who talks to you will have to shout so bloody loud you'll hear every word."'

'They'll sell you stockings with no feet and shirts with no backs to them,' said the Chief Inspector.

A man in a trilby hat, blue blazer, and what appeared to be a false moustache was selling tips at the top of his voice. The policeman studied the crowd as peaceably as two archbishops who had long ago reconciled themselves to the fact that the whole human race had larceny in its heart.

'Hello,' said the Chief Inspector, recognizing a mutual acquaintance. 'He was done for immoral earnings in Salford.'

'I didn't think that was illegal in Salford,' said the Superintendent, winking heavily.

'It runs in families, like wooden legs,' said the Chief Inspector, ritually amused.

The citizen said: 'The three-card trick went out with Nat Gould, didn't it?'

'It did not,' said the Chief Inspector, who was a dark and nimble man. 'They still play it in big lavatories with a look-out at each door. They lay out the cards on an open umbrella so they can shut it up quick if anyone comes. You know how it's played, do you? You guess which of the three cards is the Queen. Well, the mugs are just going to put their money on — two to one chance, not a bad gamble — and all of a sudden someone calls out from the back of the crowd and the fellow running the college looks round. Another accomplice nips forward while the first fellow's pretending to keep his back turned, turns up the Queen, shows it to the crowd and bends up one corner. Naturally, everyone backs the bent-up card. But when the fellow's finished talking to his mate at the back he turns round again, shuffles the three cards, and though there's still a bent-up card and everyone backs it, believe me it's never the Queen.'

'Oh yes,' the Chief Inspector went on, 'I've watched Blackpool Jack's progress in that trade. He started as look-out man, graduated to pusher – edging the crowd forward – and now he's the boss. Mind you, he's gone very, very bald.'

'Thin cadaverous man,' nodded the Superintendent. 'I think he lost his way. If he'd put all that talent to legal use he'd have owned half Lancashire by this.'

Three bookies walked by.
'Notice the way their trouser-legs are wider than anyone else's?' said the Superintendent idly. 'That's because they've got special long pockets in 'em for banknotes.'

'What about pickpockets?' asked the citizen.
'We know most of them, said the Chief Inspector. 'We're shown videos of them when we're cadets.'

The Superintendent burst out laughing. 'We send plain-clothes men round taking films of them at race meetings and you wouldn't believe the way they all nod and smile at the camera – they think it's the telly. Oh, we get all the *à la mode* cons here.'

The Chief Inspector said, 'You even get actors and film-stars and well-known people asking for the loan of police cars to get them home. Well, in an emergency, yes, but otherwise they can go and tickle their fat aunts, or words to that effect, depending who's in earshot.'

The man in the blazer who had been selling tips walked across.
'Good afternoon, Superintendent, is there anything you can give me? I haven't got a damn thing.'

The Superintendent brought out a marked race card and said, 'I don't guarantee them, mind.'

The Chief Inspector said, 'We get them off the trainers, but personally I'm cynical.'

Opening Remarks

BREVITY'S the thing, when it comes to introductions. Hold out your hand and say what your name is. The French do it this way, and I rather admire Englishmen in France who abruptly announce they are Cart-air or Vilkeens. I once tried Rob-an-son, only everyone fell about laughing because there was a film on at the time with Fernandel, and he was playing a fathead who wrote to agony columns calling himself *Robinson d'Amour*.

Better than the American method. You wait, nodding and smiling, while the host recites two lengthy biographies, then you and the other fellow stand there covered with information like a couple of billboards – you know so much about each other without knowing anything at all that all you can do is conduct an interview.

Being presented with a stranger and a sheet of instructions like this makes you wonder when he turns round whether he won't have a clockwork key sticking out of his back. I prefer the English style where the names are rattled off in a hurry as though they were faintly discreditable and best forgotten, which of course they instantly are. And then all you do is cry with sudden gusto, 'How do you do!' and the other party barks the same words back (might just as well shout 'Mesopotamia!', to which the correct response would be 'Mesopotamia!').

But this meaningless exchange of conventional signs spares all concerned the wrong sort of effort. When my neighbour Harrison Boysenberry the American commodity broker met me in the street, instead of just saying Hello he'd intone 'And how are YOU today, Robert?' and under the pressure of this horribly *interesting* form of address it was all I could do not to tell him, in some detail. Still, I preferred it to the variation he used on alternate mornings – 'And what's the GOOD WORD today, Robert?' I should say that Harrison, crisply bearded, spent lots of time making himself orange under a sun-lamp, wore a jacket with fronds, and had a bust of himself looking like Jesus, made out of melted-down stair-rods.

Rather surprisingly, I never heard him use Long Time No See. This palid opener owes a lot to Hemingway, who held the patent. On the phone to Dietrich in the Plaza Hotel, with Lilian Ross of the *New Yorker* interviewing him and a bus-boy carrying in a fresh pitcher of dry martinis, he still had the gall to look out of the window at the Big Apple and boom 'Big Treat for Country Boy'. An even purer instance of this cigar-store Indian stuff came when Hemingway and his wife, on safari in Africa, escaped unharmed from all manner of threatening situations such as crocodiles and hostile tribesmen. Finally their light aircraft crashed, but they survived with only cuts and bruises. Staggering out of the wreckage, Hemingway instructed his wife on what she should say when they got back to base. To the waiting reporters her first words were to be, 'Our Luck, She is Running Very Good.'

Such an example should put you off fancy openings for life, but I've heard grown men cry. 'How's Every Little Thing?' and clap each other on the back to shouts of 'Kiddo!' and 'Many Moons!' And once – just once – I shook hands with a man who yodelled 'Step right up and call me Speedy!' This won't do at all. Restraint is the watchword, and here you might expect Prince Charles to give a lead. Alas, when he was introduced to Tina Turner, he opened up with, 'I say, what marvellous legs you have! They are the best I have ever seen,' which made him sound like an antiques dealer appraising an unrestored piece of furniture.

Of course, desperate situations call for desperate measures, and we shall none of us forget the advice of Stephen Potter on what you say upon entering a railway carriage occupied by an attractive girl you don't know, who is reading the *Daily Telegraph*. A simple 'How Do You Do' would have her pulling the communication-cord, so instead you bound in and cry, 'I say, are they still publishing that paper?' But such breezy ad libs, as Potter was careful to point out, are only for advanced students. Among whom must be numbered the actor Seymour Hicks. Walking into the bar of the Garrick one evening he saw there was only one other member present. After a bit, he went over to him and said, 'Dreadfully dull in here this evening. Shall we exchange false teeth?'

But for the rest of us, an avoidance of the colourful in opening exchanges will protect us from any suspicion that we are hoping to *entertain*. Above all, never refer to the legs of the person you're introduced to in case they turn out to be riddled with wood-worm.

The Play's the Thing – But Which?

THERE was a touch of the peculiar about all the shows I had a hand in at Oxford, an unscheduled ingredient which lingers on in my memory like garlic which refuses to metabolize. For instance, when I was Mephistopheles in a modern dress production of *Dr Faustus* I had to sit in the audience until it was time for me to jump up and speak my first line.

Quite dramatic in its way, but the trouble was it meant I was acting in two plays at once: I knew the lines for the one on the stage, but what part was I playing while I was sitting doing nothing in the audience? Did I tell the people next to me I was only pretending to be a member of the audience, or did I keep it dark until I sprang up as Mephistopheles?

The lights went down and the play started and just as the elderly lady on my right offered me a chocolate I heard my cue, jumped up and yelled 'This is Hell –', and pausing slightly to allow the audience and the other actors to register my presence before I sauntered down the aisle towards the stage while delivering the other half of the line, '–nor am I out of it!', I heard the old lady say – slightly muffled as she scrabbled about under the seat for the chocs I'd knocked out of her hand – 'Oh, come on, its not *that* bad'.

Of course, I only imagined this tableau in the few minutes I was sitting there in the audience, an invisible actor in an invisible one-man play. The fact that no one else could see this abstract drama made it curiously alarming and I was immensely relieved when the play we'd sold the tickets for took over.

But sometimes the play on the stage was overpowered by these other possibilities. When Othello came on at the Oxford Playhouse in a long gown down to his ankles I realized as I sat in the stalls I was never going to find out for certain that he had broomsticks stuck up a pair of trousers he was wearing underneath. On the evidence of the way he walked there seemed little doubt, but my feeling that the whole audience was preoccupied with this question raised the curtain on a new version of *Othello* in which a perceptive director had spotted stiff legs as the key to the character –

This ghostly *other* play threaded its way through the entire five acts, but mostly the retro-viruses of Oxford drama erupted in short, intense deliriums that were complete in themselves. As when a chap playing a sailor in *The Tempest* spoke his lines while tottering sideways, left and right, to evoke the heaving deck of a ship about to founder. This drew such a wondrous hilarity out of a situation nobody would have guessed had a laugh in it that for a moment *The Tempest* was something else.

And then there was a great black-pudding of a Jacobean horror comic which perked up no end when the plywood arch the heroine was standing under decided to fall over. It did this as a spontaneous demonstration of its ability to move through an angle of ninety degrees without, geometrically speaking, altering the relationship. A promising initiative on the part of a piece of scenery, but it was instantly overtaken when the heroine sneezed. Draped in the sort of winding-sheet that passed as day-wear for seventeenth-century juvenile leads, she might as well have gone on to hook it up and pull a hanky from her knicker-leg. Sneezing is unassimilable, and you felt the arch in all its horizontal smugness, together with the heroine's incestuous brother who was by now passionately impaling himself on a rubber sword, both knew they had been up-staged.

Among such tangential dramas, the two-handed play that preceded all the ones you saw on the stage deserves a mention. I mean, the audition. You'd walk through the lodge of someone else's College just as the lights came on at dusk, and climb up the alien staircase with the fatuous expectation of a punter entering a casino : wondering if you'd be given the part was far more exciting than getting it. What made the encounter between producer and aspirant so pleasing was the nice balance between the candidate's sense of being judged, and his examiner's awareness that they both knew *he* was self-appointed.

Seldom did the relationship bear such pear-shaped fruit as when a chap, listening to me read, criticized my impure vowels but still offered me the lead in the play he was putting on. Not until he was showing me to the door did I realize that one of the walking wounded had recognized another – 'Don't worry about those vowers of your's,' he said, 'I'm sure they'll come along sprendidry.'

It wasn't often that the whole play was hijacked by the mysterious forces that kept on bursting through the fabric, but it did happen. Naked save for a pair of shiny knickers, and covered in green scales, I once found myself being poled across the Isis in a punt strewn with fairy-lights.

As River God in a masque written by a girl poet for the birthday of one of her chums, I was being ferried over to where the audience clustered on one of the College barges, to open the proceedings.

This proved more difficult than anyone had allowed for since the current was running strongly and the oarsmen were drunk. Three times we bore down upon the barge and three times were swept past it. By the time the punt was sullenly twisting on its axis in front of the barge, the audience lining the rails was crying with laughter as I began to deliver the poet's lines. Well-turned they may have been but not as well-turned as I was, since the punt revolving in one direction, it obliged me to revolve in the other. At this point the first penny landed at my feet, one of the oarsmen tipped over into the briny, and both poet and friend were in floods of tears.

The play disintegrated, and the action transferred itself to the barge where the strange and powerful forces which had subverted the masque set up a drama of their own, involving cast and audience in an orgy of fisticuffs and South African sherry, with a tucket (off) heralding the arrival of the Proctors.

But the most effective of all the plays I didn't know I was in until the trap was sprung must be the one that began while I was standing about on the stage as the Duke of Burgundy in *King Lear*. Nothing has ever been able to shake my conviction that the relationship between Lear and Cordelia cannot compare in intensity with those moments lived through by a man who has stuck his toy crown together with elastoplast and in full view of an audience feels it creeping millimetre by millimetre down his skull.

In this brief space of time it seemed to me that the whole apparatus of *King Lear* had been brought into being simply so that, a short while after the play began, a fifteen-second micro-drama could develop, in which once again I was the single performer. Lear grabbed me by the shoulder, we waltzed into the wings, but not before the crown had spun round my neck like a well-thrown horse-shoe. No audition, no rehearsal, had been available. The play, of which mere *plays* are but the insubstantial shadow, had once more claimed its own.

I Know the Face

WHEN the man in the commissionaire's uniform who sits at the desk behind the window just opposite the stamp-shop in the Strand re-appeared that week, I walked in and said 'Lucky for some – you missed all the rain. Cruise OK? What did Doris think of Naples?' And *he* said (his agreeable nutcracker face, as ever, smiling) 'Sorry – have we met?'

Or that's what he *would* have said. It was a close call. I'd actually pulled up short when I saw him through the window in the arcade and as I caught his eye I had to pretend I'd got a stone in my shoe. What I shook out of it was the dialogue above, which for a split second I couldn't believe we hadn't uttered. What is it about this man's face that puts me in the position of having to *remind* myself I don't know him?

But you can't parse the thing, there's no grammar when it comes to physiognomy; some faces seem second-hand, some are incomplete without a custard-pie, some arrive through the post, unsolicited, from an old-established firm of Borneo head-hunters, and each one a code without a key. I heard a woman say to another, 'Your face is worrying me', as though overwhelmed by the thought that the face she was addressing included all its predecessors, that this particular face was not only the latest in an endless series but was the sum of them all.

And sometimes the earlier faces peep out. The commentator was saying how Steffi Graf had the will and the skill and temperament, and I thought Yes, and the face as well – the face of one of the tax-collectors in the great picture by Cranach, whacking the ball back across the net in revenge for some immemorial slight, while an elderly woodcutter from Transylvania seemed for the moment to be wearing Martina's spectacles, and inheriting her strength.

Spot the face is often better fun than the actual game: cricket teams, for instance, share a face that belongs to a prefect's father who has entertained loads of clients, footballers have the faces of punters who are going to come off badly in some deal involving double-glazing (this was particularly so in the Nobby Styles, Bobby Charlton era), rugby men's faces suggest they have manorial rights over the pitch itself –

hands on hips, steam blowing from their nostrils on November days, they might be saying to the whole world, 'Get orf my land!' Some faces seem never to be in their rightful places, so that snooker-players are waiters from a sea-side hotel who've slipped out for half an hour between first and second sitting, and darts champions notch up the final one hoondred and eighty before going back to Wandsworth to bang up the inmates of D block.

Nice to come across a face that belongs to itself, though. I went to *Don Pasquale* at the Metropolitan and from the dress-circle saw an old fellow sitting in the orchestra-pit with his trumpet upside-down on his knee. There was a younger man sitting next to him, also with a trumpet, and now and again the old chap would lean over smilingly and pass him a word. They were both seated a little way away from the other instrumentalists, and the opera was giving them a very quiet time. But there *is* a trumpet solo, a romantic and melancholy thing, and which of them was to play it? Both were fiddling with the mouthpieces of their instruments, flexing the stops, alerting themselves for the moment. Once again the old chap smiled across at the other player, leaned over to him, and when the conductor nodded, it was the young man who raised the trumpet to his lips and played. At the end of the piece the older man reached out his hand and patted the young man's knee, on his face an expression of transcendental contentment.

Perhaps it was a season for such epiphanies. The next night I went to a party at the home of Bernard Malamud, writer or possibly magician. Books were the subject of passionate conversation. A popular novelist of the moment was suspected of anti-semitism, not least by the handsome woman who was arraigning his latest story on that account. But her argument, though fierce, overlooked the condition of fictions – even the least of them is separate from its maker, the umbilicus has been cut, the fiction lives in its own universe, is itself; all writers seek to make something that is other, something that is wholly not themselves. As I said this, Malamud reached out and squeezed my cheek gently between his finger and his thumb, smiling, and his face was the face of the senior trumpeter.

In the Strand a day or so later the nutcracker commissionaire was walking towards me along the pavement, with a friend. I pretended to look into a shop window (avoiding a man I don't know!) and saw them reflected in the glass. 'Seen him before somewhere,' said Nutcracker as he looked across at me, 'no idea who he is, but I'd give him six months on his face alone, then hear the evidence.'

Daydreaming

We'd like to change, but we'd like to change without hazarding the security inherent in not changing. Is the feeling we'd like to change *promoted* by this security? Is a desire to change dependent on the state it would destroy? Is change a fantasy indulged in because you have a permanent base from which to do it?

What you have always done must be what you have always wanted to do, and its single disadvantage is (or might seem to be) that you *have* always done it. The manifest advantages of what you have always done allow you to consider this single disadvantage. But should you swap all the pluses for the single minus?

Fear of not having been someone else, fear of it suddenly all being over, is a powerful stirrer-up of fantasies about change. Can a man by leaving home take up residence in some other part of himself, and become another creature? Or when he leaves Sheffield does the man he was go with him to Isfahan where a crowd of sightseers scrambling off a bus see him in his burnous with a falcon on his wrist, and one of them cries 'Charley, you don't alter!'

Stopping isn't changing. Stopping squeezing the toothpaste tube in the middle won't start you squeezing it from the end. If you stop doing what you've always done because you think this will change *you*, the first entity you recognize when you start doing something else is that same self. Change is doomed when change is used as a magic spell. But a salesman for a paint firm who all his life has also been interested in the life-cycle of the butterfly, if he finally takes himself off to a formal course of study in the subject of which he's always been an amateur, isn't he truly changing? He's not interested in 'change', he is interested in the lepidoptera, he is becoming a lepidopterist. If you were to say to him 'You've changed' he would reply 'No, no, whoever I was, I am.'

You get the millionaire who says it was leaving his job as a clerk in local government that gave him the opportunity of making money in army surplus. He forgets he was fired for being late three times in a row, omits the accidental element, and finds it was his buccaneering spirit in embracing change which allows him to preach the virtues of 'taking a chance'. But taking a chance is just that, and is best confined to the game of roulette, where the odds are only thirty-five to one.

When you daydream about changing it's as though you're in pursuit of something. Through a sequence of endless changes you see yourself arriving at – the opposite of change. You pursue permanence restlessly, drumming your fingers. But perfect content is a chimera, and it's only connection to permanence would be the endlessness of the chase. Yet fantasies about change must be universal. One imagines urging change on someone else, egging him on to submit to an experiment one wouldn't care to risk oneself. And he says My life is the only one I have – it is far from ideal, but further yet from being intolerable. By a stroke of good fortune I found a wife I like, a house I could live in, a job I could do. If I had not had the luck to find all this at the first time of trying, would it not now be the life I would be forced to change *to*? And where could I hope to find it?